CRITICAL PRAISE FOR 'MURDER HOUSES OF LONDON'

Jan Bondeson conducts us on a masterly mystery tour of London's 'black plaque' houses, where murder has left a bloodstained visiting card ... Wherever Dr Bondeson shines his torch into dark places, he sheds new light with the application of his powerful logic.
Richard Whittington-Egan.

I cannot recommend this book highly enough. It is a definite must-have.
Stewart P. Evans.

Jan Bondeson can be guaranteed to tell bizarre and quirky real-life tales and to find stories that were thought to be unfindable.
Paul Begg.

Jan Bondeson delves into the clandestine corners of city life to tell stories that would probably have preferred to have been left undiscovered. You'll never look at the closed doors of London the same way again. A catalogue of crime covering more than two centuries. Murder Houses of London combined relentless research with splendid story-telling to provide a book of unrivalled interestingness.
James Harkin, Head Researcher at *QI*.

A gripping tour of London's bloodiest buildings, the particulars of which have been meticulously researched and entertainingly presented.
Adam Wood, editor of *Ripperologist*.

Houses of Death: Chilling tales from behind the doors of homes that were the scene of gruesome murders over the last 200 years. *Daily Mail*.

In London, you are never far from a murder house: from restaurants where homicide was on the menu to Soho flats in which serial killers strangled their victims ... *Fortean Times*.

This magnificent volume is a treasure-house of information on the murders and murderers of London. *Books Monthly*.

The chilling details are revealed in a new book identifying London's so-called 'murder houses' – homes which have witnessed terrible crimes and still stand today – and telling their grisly stories. Crime history writer Jan Bondeson – a consultant doctor in his day job – spent 15 years writing and researching his book, *Murder Houses of London*. *Hampshire and Highgate Gazette*.

If you were choosing a city to star as a crime story character, London would be front and centre. Bondeson delves into the many dark corners of the city's history to catalogue the crimes that have occurred everywhere from the narrowest and the darkest streets to the stateliest mansions, providing a peek behind its bloodiest closed doors for over two centuries. *All About History*.

Everyone is acquainted with the grisly facts of Jack the Ripper ... but there are so many other stories to tell of murder and mystery in London. Jan Bondeson delves into these chilling tales, illustrating that you can never really know what goes on behind closed doors. *Discover Your History*.

Every house has a history of some kind but few are as bloodthirsty as these dwellings where behind the fresh paint, clean windows and grand entrances lie grisly tales of murder.
True Detective.

There is more, much more, and although the East End can lay its claim to be a starting point for lurid Victorian murders, Bondeson exhaustively details the grisly history of the rest of London too. So grab the book, grab an A-Z (or actually just tap Googlemaps into your smartphone) and go hunting for London's gruesome past.
East End Life.

Jan Bondeson is a curious author and I must confess that I approached this book with a mix of apprehension and excitement … there is a fascinating discussion to be had here about murders and 'dark tourism'.
London Journal.

I once said that Jan Bondeson is incapable of writing a bad book. *Murder Houses of London* once again proves that statement correct … it packs a lot of information into 350 densely printed and liberally illustrated pages. It only walls could talk, what tales they would have to tell. Fortunately we have Jan Bondeson to tell the tales for them. An excellent book, highly readable.
Ripperologist.

The work contains compelling details not only of famous crimes, but also of homicides ranging from the obscure to the long-forgotten.
Ripperana.

CRITICAL PRAISE FOR JAN BONDESON'S
'PHILLIMORE'S EDINBURGH'

Phillimore produced nearly 100 postcards based on the city, providing an unique snapshot of Edwardian Edinburgh in all its pomp ... brought together for the first time in a new book.
Scotland on Sunday.

Many of Phillimore's drawings are extremely rare, making this collection immeasureably valuable. The exquisitely detailed illustrations are enhanced through Bondeson's well-written and informative prose. A lovely read.
Scottish Field.

Reginald Phillimore (1855-1941) was one of Britain's leading postcard artists. This book contains all 95 of his Edinburgh postcards, plus descriptions of each scene.
Scots Magazine.

The end result is a book that gives a lovely insight into aspects of Edinburgh considered to be attractive to tourists in the early years of the last century, and a book that will also be of huge interest to postcard collectors.
Undiscovered Scotland.

Oil and watercolour artist Reginald Phillimore was typical of the publisher who rode the wave of the Edwardian postcard boom – and suffered from its decline after World War One.
Picture Postcard Monthly.

Snapshot of a bygone era – Dunbar author turns county artist's historic postcards into new book.
East Lothian Courier.

Phillimore's Edinburgh brings together in one volume the artist's delightful and often anachronistic drawings and paintings. The book will be of interest to all who wish to see how an Edwardian artist saw Edinburgh through his own eyes and through those of an earlier generation on whose works he used as a basis for some of his cards.
Book of the Old Edinburgh Club.

Between 1904 and 1914, [Phillimore] was one of Britain's postcard kingpins, admired and collected by many, and easily able to make a living for himself.
Shropshire Star.

Postcard king who drew on local roots ... He had ridden the wave of postcard popularity in the early 20th century but, when they began to go out of fashion, times were less good, although kept his Bridgnorth property.
Bridgnorth Journal.

The chapter titles give clues as to the location of some murder houses: the Stockbridge Baby-Farmer, the Demon Frenchman of George Street and the Triple Killer of Falcon Avenue being just three.
EEN Online

Gruesome murders in the Capital detailed in a gripping new book.
East Lothian Courier

Jan Bondeson has always had 'bit of fantasy for the macabre and odd' and now the physician and author has shed new light on Edinburgh's famously criminal history.
Edinburgh Live

Jan Bondeson looks for traces of Edinburgh's most infamous serial killers in the modern city.
Fortean Times

Jan Bondeson's books are guaranteed to contain illustrations and photographs conjuring up the atmosphere of the particular period when the ghastly crimes were carried out.
Bobby's Blog

This is fantastic, lots of information that I didn't know about so many areas.
Amazon.co.uk

Interesting read if you're local or know Edinburgh, I remember a few of the murders from less than 30 years ago.
Goodreads.com

MURDER
HOUSES
OF
EDINBURGH

Jan Bondeson

Matador
9 Priory Business Park,
Wistow Road, Kibworth Beauchamp,
Leicestershire. LE8 0RX
Tel: 0116 279 2299
Email: books@troubador.co.uk
Web: www.troubador.co.uk/matador
Twitter: @matadorbooks

ISBN 978 1800460 676

British Library Cataloguing in Publication Data.
A catalogue record for this book is available from the British Library.

Printed and bound in the UK by TJ Books Limited, Padstow, Cornwall
Typeset in 10.5pt Aldine by Troubador Publishing Ltd, Leicester, UK

Matador is an imprint of Troubador Publishing Ltd

Contents

INTRODUCTION

But Echo never mock'd the human tongue;
Some weighty crime, that Heaven could not pardon,
A secret curse on that old Building hung,
And its deserted Garden.

The beds were all untouch'd by hand or tool;
No footstep mark'd the damp and mossy gravel,
Each walk as green as is the mantled pool,
For want of human travel.

Which of Edinburgh's most gruesome murders has happened in your street? And were they committed by Burke and Hare, by the Stockbridge Baby-Farmer, by the Demon Frenchman of George Street, by the Triple Killer of Falcon Avenue, or perhaps by one of the Capital's many faceless, spectral slayers, whose name and misdeeds has long since disappeared from the public eye?

In that tall Royal Mile tenement, a woman fell from a top-floor window in 1912 – but was she thrown out by a sinister male presence inside the house, as many witnesses thought at the time? In that old house in Candlemaker Row, not far from Greyfriars Bobby, a woman was brutally murdered by a man without arms in 1919. In that flat in Rose Street South Lane, a horrible triple murder in 1917 wiped out an entire family. That peaceful little bungalow in busy Glasgow Road is home to one of the Capital's most impenetrable murder mysteries, which has baffled the police for 54 years. In that stairway in South Clerk

Street, a woman was found battered to death in 1995, and her killer has never been brought to justice.

Research on this book was begun in 2009, as a spin-off project from my trilogy on London's murder houses: it gathered momentum after I had retired in 2017 and moved to the outskirts of the Capital. With the help of court records from the Register House, newspaper databases from the National Library of Scotland, and the 'murder ledgers' of the Central Library's Edinburgh Room, I have been able to write, for the first time ever, a comprehensive account of Edinburgh's architecture of capital crime: houses inside which once celebrated murders have been committed.[1]

For a crime to qualify as murder in this book, it has to have been classified as such during some stage of its investigation and/or prosecution. Thus it remains a 'murder' even if the prisoner is ultimately freed or sentenced to prison on some lesser charge, as long as he or she was originally on trial for murder. Women dying after botched abortions were not uncommon in Edinburgh, but although the clumsy abortionists were formally charged with murder, only one of these cases, from the heart of the New Town, has been included to represent all the others. Insane or desperate women murdering their children was (and still is) a not uncommon phenomenon, but just a few cases have been included in this book. Drunken husbands murdering their wives were common in old Edinburgh, but only a some of them are represented in this book, to allow space for the more spirited murderers. The older the murder the better, and more central locations have been preferred to obscure suburbs; thus an interesting historic unsolved murder in the heart of the New Town has a high chance of making it into this book, some mindless thug murdering another hoodlum in a suburban high-rise block a very low chance indeed.

Armed with this book and a good Edinburgh map, you will be able to do some murder house detective work of your own.

Sometimes, peaceful little terraced houses can hide terrible secrets from the past: read about the forgotten murders of Edinburgh, where only the murder house remains to tell a tale. Unsolved murder mysteries abound in these pages: read about the Dean Path Tragedy, the Yeaman Place Mystery, and the spectral killers of Wester Coates Terrace and Kingsknowe Road North. Unlike the chimaeric phantasms of the Capital's fraudulent ghost tours, I will show you fear in a handful of dust: follow, if you dare, the Spectre of Murder as it stalks, still as Death and unseen by the multitude, the silent shadows and hidden houses of horror in the Edinburgh streets …

> The BLOODY HAND significant of crime,
> That glaring on the old heraldic banner,
> Had kept its crimson unimpaired by time,
> In such a wondrous manner!
>
> O'er all there hung the shadow of a fear,
> A sense of mystery the spirit daunted,
> And said, as plain as whisper in the ear,
> The place is Haunted!

I.

THE OLD TOWN

As late as the 1700s, Edinburgh was a small and overpopulated city, mainly concentrated along the Royal Mile from the Castle to Holyrood, consisting of Castlehill, Lawnmarket, High Street, Canongate and the Abbey Strand, with a myriad of pends and closes going either north or south from the main thoroughfare. In addition, there was the West Bow leading from the Lawnmarket down to the Grassmarket. A number of streets and wynds led from the Royal Mile to the Cowgate, the second main street of the Old Town. Between 1829 and 1832, George IV Bridge was constructed, an elevated avenue leading from Bank Street to Candlemaker Row and Chambers Street in the south.[1]

In Victorian times, large parts of the Old Town consisted of slum tenements. This meant that murder was rife in the teeming closes off the Royal Mile and the Cowgate, although the houses of murder have often perished in slum clearances or rebuilding schemes. Big Jock's Close off the Canongate, where James Craig murdered his wife Helen in 1877, does not exist today; Thomson's Pend off the northern side of the Grassmarket, where Robert Kennedy was murdered by the Robertson brothers in 1874, no longer frowns upon the passer-by.

The Cowgate has been particularly hard struck by Decay and the Developer; known for its ancient and picturesque houses in Victorian times, it today looks like some drab thoroughfare in Burnley or Scunthorpe rather than a dignified Edinburgh street.

1

1. A postcard from an old photograph by J.G. Tunny,
showing houses in the Cowgate.

No. 8 Cowgate, where Neil Quinn murdered his wife in 1920, no longer frowns upon the passer-by; nor does 27 Cowgate, where James Kelly murdered his wife in 1888. No. 115 Cowgate, where Andrew Douglas stabbed John Mulvey to death in 1896, no longer stands; nor does 264 Cowgate, where the bricklayer James Ison attempted to murder his workmate Edwin Dolan in 1874, before murdering his own child and committing suicide. No. 9 Alison's Close, Cowgate, where William M'Ewan murdered Catherine McLachlan in 1894, no longer stands; nor does 1 Kitchen Close, where Hugh Mooney murdered Helen Lobban in 1902.

From High Riggs, one of the city's worst slums, comes an extraordinary murder story from late Victorian times. In the crowded tenement at 69 High Riggs lived the Farmer family: the workman Robert Farmer, his wife Isabella, and their little son Robert Jr, just 13 months old in early 1892. Isabella had taken to drink after her marriage, and one day she cut her little son's throat in a fit of desperation and then attempted suicide. More squeamish with her own throat than that of her flesh and blood, she survived without any permanent injury. On trial for murder before the High Court of Edinburgh, she pleaded guilty to culpable homicide and was sentenced to eight years in prison. She was released in September 1899, returning to the family home at 69 High Riggs. Just a few months later, Robert Farmer struck his mother a mighty blow on the head with a pair of tongs during a quarrel, killing her. Aghast at what he had done, he ran out of the house and plunged into a canal in a feeble attempt to destroy himself, but paddled ashore without misadventure and gave himself up to a police constable. On trial for murder at the High Court, he pleaded guilty to culpable homicide and was sentenced to just six months in prison. I hope that this amazing account of two members of the same family being done to death in the same building, with an interval of more than seven years, is unique in Britain, if not in the world. High Riggs today consists of modern buildings, and all traces of its notorious murder house are gone.

But although many of the historic murder houses of the Old Town have gone, a healthy population of them remain standing: read about the wife-slayer of Blackfriars Street, murder by an armless man in Candlemaker Row, and the Tron Square Bloodbath of 1954 ...

BRITAIN'S MOST ANCIENT MURDER HOUSE, 1566

London's oldest standing murder house is the Black Lion pub at what is today 123 Bayswater Road, where the soldier James Hartley stabbed his colleague George Scott to death in 1800, and was found guilty of murder and executed for his crime. This 300-year-old murder pub, a coaching inn back in 1800, was recently in the news when it was sold to an investor for a cool sum of £27 million, to be 'developed' into luxury flats. The oldest standing murder house in England is likely to be the Mary Blandy house in Henley-upon-Thames, where she murdered her father back in 1751.[2] But in Edinburgh lurks an even more ancient murder house, or rather murder palace, inside which blood was shed as far ago as 1566 …

Mary Queen of Scots was born in 1542, the only surviving legitimate child of James V of Scotland and his wife Mary of Guise. When King James died from a fever after the defeat against the English at the Battle of Solway Moss, Mary ascended the throne when aged just six days. At the age of five, she was taken to the French court to escape attention from the old English enemy; she grew up there with her mother's family and was educated as a French princess. At an early age, she was betrothed to François, the Dauphin of France and the son of King Henri II, and they married in 1558. Whereas Mary was tall, vivacious and good-looking, her husband was far from a prepossessing specimen of humanity: abnormally short, feeble and sickly, and afflicted with a nasty stutter. When Henri II died in July 1559, from injuries sustained in a tournament, François ascended the throne, although the country was largely run by Mary's two powerful uncles, the Duke of Guise and the Cardinal of Lorraine. Poor François II was not destined for a long and happy reign, however: he died already in 1560, from complications to an ear infection. Mary was tempted to return to Scotland, where the political situation had become somewhat less turbulent: a party of Protestants, led by her illegitimate half-brother James Earl of Moray, had taken control of state affairs, and they formally invited her to come back home. When Mary landed at Leith on August 19 1561, many were pleased to see her: the Royalists and the remaining Catholics in particular. The scheming and ambitious Moray, who continued to act as regent, thought he could use Mary as a pawn in his various political

2. *Two cabinet cards showing Mary Queen of Scots and David Rizzio.*

intrigues. But Mary also had an indomitable enemy: the rabble-rousing preacher John Knox, who had risen to an influential position due to his near-maniacal energy, uncompromising language, and fanatical Protestantism. Urging that Scotland was to be swept free of Catholics, for good, he was outraged to hear that Mary desired to celebrate Mass in private. A misogynist even by the standards of the time, he considered that although women had their uses in the kitchen and in bed, their feeble intellects did not qualify them for taking part in matters of state, or in religious debate for that matter.

David Rizzio was born about 1533 in the village of Pancatieri, some twenty miles south of Turin, in the Duchy of Savoy. When, in 1561, the Marquis di Moretto was selected to lead a diplomatic mission to the court of Mary Queen of Scots, Rizzio was selected to join the entourage in a menial capacity. The personable young Rizzio, who spoke fluent Italian, French and Latin, had been able to learn English with alacrity during his stay in Scotland: he decided to remain in Edinburgh, where he was employed as a chamber valet at Mary's large court. Mary liked to have foreigners in her service and she could appreciate Rizzio's good bass voice, which enabled him to join a quartet of singers employed at the musical entertainments arranged by the carefree young queen. By all accounts, David Rizzio was far from a handsome man: short, hunched and swarthy. Yet there must have been something about him, since Mary liked his company, admired his musical prowess, and appreciated his loyalty. When her secretary for French correspondence, Augustine Raullet, fell from favour in December 1564, she appointed Rizzio his successor. This was an important post, since Mary had many dealings with her French relatives: Rizzio was constantly in the Queen's company, and soon became her acknowledged court favourite. A scheming, unpopular man, he was known as 'Seigneur Davie' as he swaggered about the court in his elegant attire.

Mary had many offers of marriage over the years, from the Earl of Leicester, from various foreign princelings, and even from King Erik of Sweden, but she turned them all down. She realized that to get rid of irksome Regent Moray, she needed to marry one of the great Scottish nobles. Her choice fell on Henry, Lord Darnley, a son of the Earl of Lennox. He was a handsome and personable swain, and Mary thought she would be able to dominate him since he was not particularly bright. Realizing that as Mary's husband, Darnley would be a person of considerable influence at court, Rizzio tried to ingratiate himself with the vain and foolish youth, initially with some success. Since Moray was unwilling to give up his position of power, Mary and Darnley raised troops and drove him south of the border after a short civil war. In this enterprise, they were helped by two influential loyalist Scottish nobles, the Earls of Bothwell and Huntly. As Mary took over the reign of Scotland, Rizzio was more powerful than ever. He was virtually her prime minister, meddling in all matters of state. Fearful of a Catholic backlash led by Mary and Rizzio, John Knox spoke of the 'monstrous regiment of women' and likened himself to Paul who had to endure the tyranny of Nero.

3. The Conspirator's Doorway.

Scotland was home to a considerable population of angry, dissatisfied noblemen, who were normally occupied with infighting and local quarrels. When they joined forces against a mutual enemy, they were a force to be reckoned with, however. There were rumours that Rizzio was a foreign agent in the employ of the Pope, or that he was a necromancer who had put a spell on Mary to take over the government of Scotland; a troop of 200 Italian mercenaries had been recruited by Mary, it was falsely bruited, 50 of whom were to serve as Rizzio's personal guard. When it was said that Mary intended to give Rizzio a Scottish Earldom and officially make him chief secretary of state, the Protestant lords had had enough. They joined forces to conspire against Rizzio, since they found it an abomination that this foreign upstart gained prominence at court. They decided that Rizzio must die, and cunningly swore the weak and foolish Darnley into the conspiracy, persuading him that the Italian was Mary's favourite in more ways than one, and that he had perhaps fathered her unborn child. The foppish 'Seigneur Davie' was entirely unaware that the Protestant nobles hated and despised him: when warned that he was in danger by the priest John Damiot, he unwisely said that the Scots were given more to brag than to fight.

On March 9 1566, the conspirators forced their way into Holyrood, with a force of 500 men. They subdued the palace guards, snatched the keys from the porters and secured the gate. Patrick Lord Ruthven then led a force of 80 henchmen up to the royal apartments. The feeble, elderly Holyrood servants ran for their lives as the heavily armed desperadoes rummaged around the state rooms looking for Rizzio. But since Lord Ruthven rightly presumed that the hated Italian was in the second-floor suite of rooms occupied by the Queen, he led his men up the spiral staircase to Mary's apartments. The Queen was having a meal in her supper-room, attended by Lord Robert Stewart and Lady Argyll, her equerry Arthur Erskine and the ubiquitous David Rizzio, when the conspirators burst in upon them. Lord Ruthven was the first to speak out: "Let it please your Majesty that yonder man David come forth of your privy-chamber where he hath been overlong!" Indignant when she saw the familiar figure of Darnley among the intruders, Mary angrily asked him what knowledge he had of this treacherous enterprise, something that he cravenly denied. Mary was able to hold the conspirators at bay for a while, the terrified Rizzio cowering behind her, but the murderous throng had little respect for her, holding her at gunpoint and waving their daggers in her face. All of a sudden, a number of noblemen rushed forward and

4. Queen Mary's supper room.

grabbed Rizzio with a hearty goodwill, wrenching his fingers away from the Queen's skirts. The wretched Italian could only scream "Giustizia! Giustizia! Sauvez-moi, Madame!" as the conspirators dragged him through the bedroom into the outer chamber, where they finished him off with 56 stab wounds. With his final breath, he yelled out "Madama, io son morto!" [Madame, I am dead!] in a terrible voice. The Queen wept bitterly when she heard his desperate outcry, and exclaimed "Ah, poor David, my good and faithful servant, may the Lord have mercy on your soul."

The conspirators also wanted to settle the score with the loyalists Bothwell and Huntly, but these two leapt out through a window and escaped. In the meantime, Lord Ruthven did his best to browbeat Mary, but she would not be having any of that, angrily swearing revenge against the murderers of Rizzio, her faithful servant for many years. Ruthven retorted that Rizzio had been a mean and base character, an enemy to the Scottish nobility, a shame to herself, and destruction to her country, but Mary still threatened revenge, saying that she would see the dear blood of the conspirators for what they had just accomplished. The conspirators had not thought through what to do with Mary and Darnley, who were virtually their captives at Holyrood. Even the bold Ruthven had second thoughts about keeping the reigning Queen as his prisoner, under armed guard, so in the end Mary and her craven consort were just left in the murder room. Mary managed to put some steel into the cow-hearted Darnley, urging him that they must escape Holyrood at all costs. She suspected that the conspirators had invited the exiled Moray

5. The murder of Rizzio, a postcard stamped and posted in 1905.

to return, and that this ambitious individual would have less than agreeable plans for his half-sister, who had once defeated and outlawed him, and forced him to take refuge in England. Mary and Darnley were fortunate that Bothwell and Huntly managed to sneak back into Holyrood after the conspirators had left. They all managed to escape and take refuge at Bothwell's castle in Dunbar. Here they regrouped and gathered soldiers and support, before returning to Edinburgh in triumph, driving Moray south for a second time, and taking charge of the government. But the coward Darnley would not have long to exult after settling his score with Rizzio in such a definitive manner. Although Mary made use of her feminine wiles to keep her vacillating husband under control, her love for him was long gone, and she conspired with Bothwell and the other loyalist nobles to get rid of him. Although her active participation in the events that were to follow remain a mystery today, she must have implied to Bothwell that he could win her favour if something was done to end Darnley's career, for good.

Mary invited Darnley to stay with her at Craigmillar Castle, but fearful that the loyalist nobles were planning some lethal 'accident' for him there, he preferred to stay at his house at Kirk o'Field near the Cowgate, where he believed himself to be secure. But on February 9 1567, some evildoers had loaded the vaults underneath the house with gunpowder; after a tremendous explosion, Darnley's dead body was found in the garden. It appears likely that a servant saw or heard the dynamitards at work and warned Darnley in time: the conspirators had made sure that some loyal men were standing by to supervise the plot, however, and these desperadoes discovered Darnley making his escape, and strangled both him and his servant to death. Bothwell, who was widely suspected of being responsible for the murder, walked off scot-free, and later became Mary's third husband. But by this time, many people, the adherents of John Knox in particular, had had enough of Mary and her violent and immoral court: she would face imprisonment, and subsequent execution, among her enemies south of the border. As for the adventurer Bothwell, he would end his days as a state prisoner in the hands of the King of Denmark, under miserable circumstances. David Rizzio was the typical court favourite: cunning, self-seeking and promoted above his capacity. He learnt it the hard way that the old Scots were no friends of foreign upstarts, and that they had a strong penchant for mob violence. He had overestimated the strength of his position at court, and misinterpreted the respect shown for his influential position to imagine that he was tolerated, or even liked, in his adopted country. Mary was the only person who mourned Rizzio, and many people were happy that he was gone, since he had symbolized corruption, foreign influence and Catholicism. With his usual bloodthirsty attitude, John Knox disregarded the Sixth Commandment and openly gloated that the hated Rizzio was dead.

The apartments of Mary Queen of Scots at Holyrood were left unchanged for many years. The rooms were regularly visited by the curious, and in 1760, the future Duchess of Northumberland came to call: "I went also to see Mary Queen of Scots' Bedchamber (a very small one it is) from whence David Rizzio was drag'd out and stab'd in the ante room where there is some of his Blood which they can't get wash'd out." Throughout Victorian times, a regular stream of tourists came to see these rooms, some of them exclaiming 'Cor blimey!' when they saw the bloodstain that could not be washed out. During Queen Victoria's visit to Edinburgh in 1876, a group of courtiers are depicted admiring the room where Rizzio had been murdered, with its tell-tale stain on the floor. No bloodstain remains to be seen today, however, and it must be suspected that the Holyrood tourist guides had used to 'improve on' it with some fresh cow's blood.[3]

6. A plaster relief depicting the murder of Rizzio.

TOPOGRAPHICAL ASPECTS OF BURKE AND HARE, 1828

Much has been written about those fiends of the Old Town, Burke and Hare, Edinburgh's most celebrated serial killers, who murdered a number of people for the purpose of selling their bodies for dissection at the anatomy school of Dr Robert Knox. William Burke was born in 1792 in Urney, County Tyrone, as one of two sons to middle-class parents. In 1818, he deserted his wife and family, moving to Scotland, where he became a navvy helping to construct the Union Canal, settling down near Falkirk with his common-law wife Helen M'Dougal. Moving to Edinburgh, he became a hawker selling old clothes to impoverished people, before trying his luck as a cobbler. About the mystery man William Hare, little is known except he was an illiterate Irish lad who turned up in Edinburgh in the mid-1820s, living in a small lodging-house off Tanner's Close, West Port, run by a man named Logue. When this individual died, Hare moved in with Logue's Irish-born wife Margaret. In 1827, Burke and Hare both worked as agricultural labourers in Penicuik; they became friends and it has been suggested that Burke and Helen M'Dougal moved into the Tanner's Close lodging-house as well, drinking and carousing, and leading a riotous life.

In late November 1827, an old army veteran named Donald died at Hare's lodging-house, owing £4's worth of back rent. Thinking that the old man would be worth more dead than he had been alive, Burke and Hare sold his body to the celebrated Edinburgh anatomist Robert Knox, at his anatomy school in Surgeon's Square, for £7 10s. This princely sum paid up, without any awkward questions asked, for the cadaver of the old soldier, set the two ruffians thinking. What if they murdered various down-and-out characters in the slums of Edinburgh, in a way that made it difficult to tell that they

WILLIAM BURKE.
(From a Sketch taken in Court)

WILLIAM HARE,
(From a Sketch taken in Court)

7. Burke and Hare, drawings from G. MacGregor,
The History of Burke and Hare (Glasgow 1884).

had been deliberately done to death, and then sold the corpses to Knox? There is reason to believe that their first victim was a miller named Joseph who lodged in Hare's house: after he had been sedated with some liberal tots of whisky, Burke pinned him down by laying across his upper torso, as Hare suffocated him to death with a pillow. In total they claimed sixteen victims, all killed in the same manner, among them the young prostitute Mary Paterson and the invalid lad James Wilson, a street character known as Daft Jamie. Their final victim was an Irishwoman named Margaret Docherty, whose body was discovered by some other lodgers who called in the police. Burke and Hare made haste to sell the cadaver to Dr Knox, but a public-spirited lodger identified it in his dissection-room and the two ruffians were arrested.[4]

15

8. The execution of Burke, from The West Port Murders (Edinburgh 1829).

9. *Replica death masks of Burke and Hare, with a desinformationist inscription, purchased on eBay for £15. They are very heavy and their origin is obscure.*

At the trial of William Burke, which opened on Christmas Eve 1828 before the High Court of Justiciary in the Parliament House, the slimy Hare turned King's evidence, blaming Burke for everything. Burke was found guilty of murder and was sentenced to be hanged and publicly dissected. Awaiting execution, Burke made a partial confession, putting much of the blame on Hare. He was hanged on January 28 1829 in front of an enormous crowd and publicly dissected by Professor Munro a few days later: his mounted skeleton stands at the Anatomical Museum of the University of Edinburgh, whereas Surgeon's Hall has his death mask and a book bound in his skin. Helen M'Dougal escaped Edinburgh in a hurry, pursued by an angry mob. Although Daft Jamie's family urged that Hare should also be prosecuted, this was not possible according to the legislation of the time. Hare also left Edinburgh in a hurry, probably for his native Ireland, although no historian has been able to track him down. A cutting from the

Newry Commercial Telegraph of March 31 1829 claims that Hare turned up at a public house in Scarva, County of Armagh, with his wife and child, but he was recognized by the mob and run out of town.[5] According to an article in *Lloyd's Weekly Newspaper* of December 22 1861, the Canadian correspondent of the *Scotsman* had heard a story that Hare had died in that country. The *Weekly Scotsman* of August 26 1916 prefers a more sanguinary tale: Hare got employment at a lime kiln, but the other workers found out about his true identity and threw him into the lime so that he was blinded; he ended his days as a blind beggar in London's Oxford Street. In an article marking the centenary of the murders, the *Nottingham Evening Post* of November 26 1927 prefers the version that Hare ended up as a blind beggar selling matches in London's Burlington Arcade for forty years.

There has been a good deal of gibbering, from various ill-informed 'internet monkeys', that Burke and Hare lived on the southern side of what is today the West Port, but a map in the 1884 book *The History of Burke and Hare* by George MacGregor, and perusal of the 1852 Ordnance Survey map of Edinburgh, clearly demonstrates that the two villains lived on the north side of this thoroughfare, roughly where the large modern tenement called Webster's Land is today. The MacGregor map may well be somewhat over-simplified: on the Ordnance Survey map it looks like if there is another tenement between Burke's house and Grindlay's Close, whereas Hare's humble dwelling is situated behind another, taller house in the West Port, and accessed through Tanner's Close. The 1893 Ordnance Survey map shows Tanner's Close and Hare's house still intact, although the building situated at the site of Burke's house now has a different shape. In July 1902, the Edinburgh newspapers could announce that Hare's house was to be demolished as part of a slum clearance; Burke's house had been pulled down some time ago, it was stated.[6] Thus nothing remains today of two of Edinburgh's most celebrated murder houses; both Tanner's Close and Grindlay's Close have

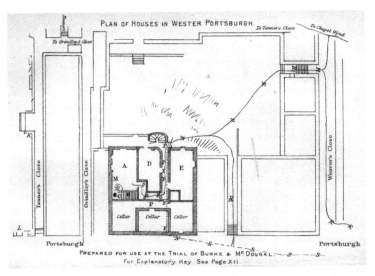

10. *A map of the West Port neighbourhood, from G. MacGregor, The History of Burke and Hare (Glasgow 1884).*

disappeared from the Edinburgh map, for good.

Many Edinburgh people were outraged that Robert Knox, who was widely thought to share the moral responsibility for the murders, had escaped entirely without punishment. On February 12 1829, a large mob congregated on Calton Hill, before setting out for Knox's house at 4 Newington Place, carrying with them a life-sized effigy of the anatomist, clad in a gaudy waistcoat and bearing the label 'Knox, the associate of the infamous Hare'. They hung the effigy from the branch of a tree and tried to set it alight; when it failed to catch fire, they instead tore it into little pieces. Knox's house was stoned and many windows broken, the railings destroyed and the front garden trampled. The fearful anatomist sneaked out through the back door and took refuge in the house of a friend. Knox remained in Edinburgh until 1842, but his career never recovered. He then moved to London and died there in obscurity in 1862.[7]

11. *Hare's house in Tanner's Close, where most of the murders took place, from the Weekly Scotsman of July 19 1902. Hugh Douglas, Burke & Hare (London 1974) reproduces what is alleged to be an 'old photograph' of the entrance to the house.*

BURKE'S HOUSE FROM THE BACK COURT.

A. Burke's Window.

B. Back entrance, where the Bodies were brought out.

12. *Burke's house, from The West Port Murders (Edinburgh 1829).*

13. A sketch of the interior of Burke's house, from G. MacGregor, The History of Burke and Hare (Glasgow 1884).

14. Burke and Hare at Madame Tussaud's in London.

15. A caricature of Robert Knox.

It is not generally known that Robert Knox's house at 4 Newington Place, from which he had such a narrow escape from the Edinburgh mob back in 1829, is still standing today. In 1885, the terrace of Newington Place was incorporated into Newington Road, and the houses renumbered; in Victorian times, a shop was constructed in its front garden. This shop is today Euroclean Dry Cleaners, and behind it, Dr Knox's house at what is today 17 Newington Road, is daily passed by throngs of people oblivious of this curious relic from the days of Burke and Hare.[8]

16. Knox's house at what is today 17 Newington Road.

A LETHAL 'GOOSE' IN SOUTH BRIDGE, 1878

Andrew Heggie and John Dale were two tailors employed in the workshop of Messrs J. Middlemass & Co. at 18 South Bridge. On April 24 1878, the two tailors quarrelled about a window, which Dale wanted open and Heggie wanted closed. John Dale, who was deaf and dumb, somehow managed to make his opinions known, as the two angry tailors threatened each other with violence. All of a sudden, Heggie waved his 'goose' [tailor's heavy iron] about in Dale's face and screamed 'I'll do it, if you provoke me any longer!', but Dale gave him a push to the chest. Furious, Heggie then struck Dale on the head with the 'goose', sending him bleeding to the ground. Dale went down for the count but at first seemed little the worse for his experience: he had his head bandaged by a doctor, worked the remainder of the day, and was then taken home to 5 Thistle Place, Viewforth, where he was staying with his family. On April 25, he was clearly unwell, however, and at

17. A postcard showing South Bridge, stamped and posted in 1916.

18. The murder house at 18 South Bridge.

the Royal Infirmary, a severe fracture of the skull was diagnosed. Andrew Heggie was taken into police custody and charged with assault to the danger of life. When Dale expired on April 30, the charge became one of murder. Being 64 years old, and a steady and sober character, Heggie was liberated on bail, but on June 3, he was examined before Bailie Anderson at the City Chambers and committed to Calton Prison on a charge of murder.

Andrew Heggie stood trial for murder at the High Court on June 24, having spent three weeks in jail. Several of the other tailors employed on the premises described him as a morose, difficult character, who wanted everything his own way. They had seen the fight and agreed that although Dale had pushed Heggie in the chest, he had not struck him. Andrew Heggie pleaded guilty to culpable homicide, and this plea was accepted by the Crown. Mr Maitland, advocate for the defence, said that the lethal assault arose from a stupid dispute between the two tailors about the opening of a window. The medical gentleman who had attended Dale concurred that if his skull had been of normal thickness, the blow from the 'goose' would not have had a fatal result. In the end, Heggie was sentenced to imprisonment for eight months.[9]

MURDER IN MILNE'S COURT, 1892

In the 1890s, the mason's labourer David Kane lived in the third flat at 5 Milne's Court off the Lawnmarket, with his wife Elizabeth and their 16-month-old son David. 'Wee Davey', as the little lad was called by his doting mother, was the only one remaining of a brood of four sickly children. The Kanes had married in 1884, when David was 20 years old and Elizabeth just 18; they had lived in various slum lodgings, before being allowed to live in the Milne's Court flat by Elizabeth's mother Ann Brady, who herself lived in the flat above with her son and two other daughters. David Kane seems to have been a tolerably industrious labourer, and capable of keeping dire poverty from the door, but he was very fond of drinking whisky and often beat and kicked poor Elizabeth, who was fond of the bottle herself. In 1889, he had served seven days in prison for beating her up severely.

On October 15 1892, David Kane was reprimanded by his brother-in-law, the butcher's assistant John Brady, for his foul and blasphemous language. When the burly Kane got angry and challenged a fight, Brady ran away. When Brady eventually returned to Milne's Court, the two drunks rekindled their friendship and Brady was sent for a gill of whisky and a pint of beer. In the evening of October 15, the police were called to 5 Milne's Court because

MILNE'S COURT, EDINBURGH

Built by Robert Mylne in 1690. Mylne built many of the most
beautiful bits of the Old Town, and was the last of a long
line of Royal Master Masons, descending from father to son,
from the reign of James III.

19. A postcard showing Milne's Court in olden times.

David Kane had again been beating his wife. He managed to get
rid of them, before giving the next-door neighbour Alison Hume a
hard knock in the face for her 'interfering', and kicking her into her
own flat. At about 2 am, Alison Hume heard a terrible squealing
sound from next door, but after the treatment she had received, she
did not dare to go and investigate.

On the morning of October 16, David Kane came up to
Ann Brady's flat, saying 'Lizzie's dead!' John Brady accompanied

him downstairs, where they saw Elizabeth lying on the bed in a pool of blood, her face very much bruised. When John Brady went for the police, Kane quickly absconded from the murder house, but he was caught on the George IV Bridge. Constable James Mathieson came to see the blood-stained little flat with the murder victim still lying on the bed; it had only one window, to the north facing the New Town. Dr Littlejohn also came to the murder flat, accompanied by two detectives; the cause of death was extensive bruising to the face and front of the neck, a shattered jaw, and three broken ribs. The murdered woman, who had never been strong and who was afflicted with a cough, turned out to have quite advanced pulmonary tuberculosis.

20. Milne's Court today.

On trial for murder at the High Court of Edinburgh, the odds were not in David Kane's favour. Ann and John Brady gave their evidence about finding the body without contradictions, and a number of neighbours in the crowded old house had heard outcries of 'Murder!' from the third flat, although they had been too fearful of David Kane's fists to interfere. In the end, David Kane was found guilty of culpable manslaughter and was sentenced to 15 years of penal servitude.[10] It is sad but true that motherless Wee Davie, who was taken care of by his grandmother Ann Brady in her crowded flat, died from measles on Boxing Day 1892. David Kane served his time, resumed his humble career as a labouring man, married the widow Mary Agnes Goodall and had a daughter named Catherine. He lived on until December 1939, when he expired in his flat at 30 Lady Lawson Street, from what was supposed to be heart disease.

MURDER IN BLACKFRIARS STREET, 1905

In Victorian and Edwardian times, Blackfriars Street, leading steeply from the Royal Mile to the Cowgate, had a distinctly seedy reputation, with many slum dwellings. In 1897, the drunk John Leslie murdered his sister at 36 Blackfriars Street, but the house no longer remains. But in 1905, the spectre of Murder again came calling, this time visiting the run-down old house at 56 Blackfriars Street, situated right at the junction with the Cowgate.

Thomas Anderson Farrell was born in 1873; the son of a telegraph linesman, he adopted the same profession himself. In 1897, when he was 24 years-old, he married the 26-year-old domestic servant Annie McAdam, the daughter of a horse dealer, who could only sign the marriage certificate with a cross since she was quite illiterate. By some stratagem or other, she brought a

21. The murder house at 56 Blackfriars Street.

good deal of money into the marriage, and her husband enjoyed a six-month holiday after that event. They lived in Murrayfield for a while, before going to Manchester. Both drank more than was good for them and there were no children of the marriage. Farrell, a hulking brute of a man, regularly disciplined his short, thin wife with his fists. In 1905, he was working as a casual labourer and living in a single third-floor room at 56 Blackfriars Street, with poor patient Annie, the recipient of much domestic abuse. The room was very dirty and badly furnished, even by Edwardian Old Town standards.

At 4 am on Sunday June 18, Thomas Anderson Farrell turned up at 16 Roxburgh Place, where his wife's married sister Mrs

Susan Murray was living with her husband, saying 'Annie's dead!' When he got an incredulous reply, he said 'Well, she is on the floor now, and I have been roaring to her, and I can get no answer!' Since it turned out to be nothing but the truth that Annie Farrell was lying dead in the hovel at 56 Blackfriars Street, her body was removed for a thorough post-mortem and her husband was arrested for her murder. On trial for murdering his wife at the High Court of Edinburgh on August 30, Thomas Anderson Farrell could not deny that he had been alone with Annie in their room when she had been murdered. The cause of death was haemorrhage from a rupture of the spleen, caused by direct violence, alongside severe injuries to the chest with six broken ribs, and cuts and bruises to the face. The neighbours had heard the sound of quarrelling from the room occupied by the Farrells, with Annie screaming 'Oh, Tam, don't and I will make your dinner!' Several witnesses living in or near Hall's Court, which overlooked the back windows of 56 Blackfriars Street, had heard poor Annie scream 'Murder! Police!' and moaning as if some person was beating her. The cad Thomas Anderson Farrell had always been a morose, taciturn fellow, and his wife had been drunk almost around the clock, drinking whisky thirstily with her breakfast every day.

In the end, Thomas Anderson Farrell was found guilty of culpable homicide and sentenced to imprisonment for ten years.[11] He served his time, became a works stoker and remarried the widow Sarah Hart Buchanan in 1922; the marriage was blessed with at least one child, a son born at 112 Nicolson Street. Sarah predeceased him, and he eventually died from senile myocardial degeneration in 1951, aged 78 and still living in his Nicolson Street flat. The murder house at 56 Blackfriars Street still stands, although it is looking quite dilapidated, with neither of the ground floor shops in operation.

MURDER IN NORTH GRAY'S CLOSE, 1911

William and Grace Newell were a middle-aged Edinburgh couple, living in an attic room at 2 North Gray's Close, 125 High Street. He worked as a painter on and off, but they were both very much given to drunkenness. On October 14 1911, the couple had both been drinking thirstily. William lurched into his room, helped by his stepson Patrick Horne and his sister Christina Glancy, who lived next door. Grace went to the 'Clachan' public house in the High Street to have a few more drinks. A fellow drinker eventually helped her up the stairs to the attic flat, where she rejoined her husband. At 10 pm, there was an outcry in the High Street: 'There's a woman over a window'. And indeed, Grace Newell was clinging to the attic window as well as she could, screaming 'They're flinging me over the window! Murder! Police! Help!' A silent and sinister male figure could be seen moving inside the room. The next moment, Grace Newell came crashing down into the unyielding cobbles of the High Street and died instantly. Since there had been no other person in the room than her husband William Newell, he was taken into police custody, charged with murder and tried at the High Court of Edinburgh on January 15 1912.

The first witness was Christina Glaney, sister of the prisoner, who had heard the outcry in the High Street and rushed into her brother's room. William Newell had said 'Well, Tina, I never done it. I don't know what was wrong.' A week previously, Grace Newell had threatened suicide. Patrick Horne, son of the murdered woman, had gone into Stewart's Waxworks at 10 pm, but he had seen the crowd in the High Street when he emerged from the exhibition. Jane Polombo, who lived in the flat below that of the Newells, had heard them jumping and dancing about while getting drunk. Just after 10 pm, she had heard the sound of a body being dragged along the floor above, and an outcry of 'Murder!' Her daughter had also heard something heavy dragged

22. North Gray's Close today.

along the floor. In the High Street, a number of witnesses had seen Grace Newell fall to her death. Annie Sullivan had seen her hanging on to the window for dear life for about a minute, before falling down with a terrible scream; she got the impression that she had been forcibly ejected from the room. Several other witnesses had seen Grace Newell fall, and they agreed that there had been a man in the room, one of them also seeing the arm that pushed the woman out of the window. Annie McVean had heard Grace scream 'Murder! Police! Help!' before she fell; then a man had appeared at the window, shouting 'Fetch all your policemen now!' The 19-year-old Annie Oldershaw had also seen this man, although she had interpreted his outcry as 'Bring up all your bloody policemen now!'; she confidently identified the person she had seen as the prisoner in the dock.

The miner Robert Raeburn had also seen Grace Newell fall; since he got the impression that she had been pushed, he and some other witnesses ran up the stairs to take William Newell into custody. He was the only person in the room and seemed dazed with drink. Barbara Aitchison, sister of the murdered woman, said that she had been 38 years old and her husband a year older; they had been married for 17 years but had no children. William regularly beat up Grace when they had been drinking. Three former neighbours of William and Grace Newell testified that not only had William been beating Grace severely, he had also brought home strange men and left them with his wife for an immoral purpose. Police Constable Robert Tough had made sure that Grace Newell had been taken to the Royal Infirmary in the Ambulance Wagon, but there, she had been declared dead. Inspector John Bell had found William Newell fully dressed. He had been drinking but knew what he was doing. He said that after they had been quarrelling about some money, Grace had threatened to jump out of the window; he had told her to get on with it, and in a moment she was gone. The Solicitor-General, prosecuting, must have caused some consternation when he said he was prepared to accept a plea of assault. William Newell pleaded guilty and Lord Guthrie, who said he had considered the case very carefully, sentenced him to imprisonment for twelve months.[12] This was an anticlimactic ending to an exciting old Edinburgh murder trial; I must confess that I wholly expected a verdict of guilty to murder when I read the legal documents, but something must have convinced the Solicitor-General that there were flaws in the case against William Newell, and that it was important not to allow him to get off scot-free.

MURDER IN CANDLEMAKER ROW, 1919

The head of Candlemaker Row is adorned, if that is the word, with the monument to that extraordinary dog, Greyfriars Bobby, erected in 1872 with money provided by the Baroness Burdett-Coutts. It is widely admired by the mawkish and the credulous, who weep and moan when they hear the pathetic story of Bobby's 12-year vigil on his master's tomb, shivering with the cold. The truth is, however, that although Bobby definitely existed, he was a jolly and independent stray dog who decided to take up residence at Greyfriars, where he was fed and taken care of by people who thought he was keeping vigil at his master's grave, according to the sentimental notions of the time. After being lionized by the *Scotsman* and other newspapers, Bobby awoke one day in 1867 to find himself famous; people came from London to see him, tipping the verger and purchasing a cabinet card photograph of Scotland's most famous dog. When the original Bobby died, having spent the latter part of his life in complete independence and security, a replacement dog was procured to continue the charade of Edinburgh's faithful dog; it is the bronze effigy of this animal, looking quite different to the original Bobby photographed back in 1867, that adorns the Candlemaker Row dog monument.

But if we turn our backs to the much-exploited Greyfriars Bobby monument, as we should, and descend down Candlemaker Row, we are treading the cobbles of a venerable Old Town street: it is visible already on Gordon's town plan of 1647. The magistrates wanted the candlemakers away from the High Streets, due to the noxious odours emanating from the boiling of tallow, and the considerable risk of fire. In the 18th century, the candlemakers flourished, since there was no alternative to candles for lighting a house, but the introduction of lamps, and the later invention of electric light, led to them becoming an extinct species. At the very foot of Candlemaker Row, near the junction with the Cowgatehead, is a 19th century tenement that is likely to have been a pub at some

23. Greyfriars Bobby and the head of Candlemaker Row.

stage of its existence; its cellars may well be from an earlier building on the same site. In 1919, it was a cheap doss-house for the poor of the Old Town, and the site of a murder so truly bizarre that its like has never been recorded, in Edinburgh or elsewhere.

William Lamb was born in Glasgow in or around 1864. He lived there for 27 years before moving to Inverness to become a chimney sweep. He was a steady and sober workman, married and started a family of three children, one of whom became a wartime soldier. He won the Humane Society's bronze and silver medals after saving several people from drowning. In 1908, he was knocked down and run over by a motor lorry in the Coatbridge Road near Glasgow, losing both his arms; the right one by the shoulder and the left one with only a short stump remaining.

24. Old houses in Candlemaker Row, a postcard stamped and posted in 1926.

Since William Lamb had been reasonably popular in Inverness, there was a public subscription to purchase him a treadle barrel organ so that he would be able to make his living without seeking poor relief. He stayed there until 1919, when he left his wife and family and moved to Edinburgh, where he lived in the cheap lodging-house at 88 Candlemaker Row with a 41-year-old woman named Agnes White, who had left her husband. She was of very drunken habits, and William Lamb also took to drink during his stay in the Scottish capital. During daytime, William Lamb sat treading the barrel-organ with his feet; during the evenings and night-time, he stayed with Agnes in Room 11 on the first floor of the house at 88 Candlemaker Row, drinking and carousing. Since both of them were quarrelsome while in their cups, they were a cross to bear for the housekeeper Margaret Ross, who had her hands full keeping the rowdy lodgers in check. Agnes had more than once complained to one of the neighbours that they often quarrelled, and that he sometimes used to kick her cruelly.

On July 23 1919, William Lamb sat playing his organ with his feet all day, dressed in a jacket and a kilt, before returning home to 88 Candlemaker Row, where he and Alice both drank deeply. In the night, the neighbours heard him cry out "Get up and give me my pipe!", and then a sound like a rhythmical stamping on the floor and a woman squealing with pain. The following morning, William Lamb walked down to the detective office in the High Street, telling the officer on duty, Detective Sergeant Francis Horace Berry, that Agnes White was dead. Police Constable James Mathieson walked back to Candlemaker Row with him; since there was blood on Agnes' face and on the wall, and since William Lamb's clothes were liberally sprinkled with blood, he was taken into custody and charged with murdering her. The autopsy showed that Agnes White had been brutally trampled to death.

On trial for murder at the High Court of Edinburgh in October 1919, the first witness was the husband of the murdered Agnes White: the workman Andrew Stirling, who testified that they had three children who were all dead, and that he had left her due to her incessant whisky drinking. Bridget Lamb, sister of the prisoner, described his unhappy life after the accident with the motor lorry, adding that he had a wife and three living children, all of whom he had left behind in Inverness. The landlady Margaret Ross described the conditions in the crowded lodging-house at 88 Candlemaker Row, followed by a number of lodgers who had heard shouting from the murder room, or the sound of stamping feet. Mary Ann Kerr, who lived in Room 13 opposite Room 11, testified that Agnes White had twice sought protection from William Lamb inside her room. Once he had seen him kicking her, only to be told to mind her own business when she tried to intervene. The pedlar William Wilson, who inhabited Room 8 with his wife, had seen William Lamb the morning after the murder; after telling him that his 'wife' was dead, Lamb had started crying. When asked by Mrs Wilson how she had come to expire, Lamb had just said 'I know nothing at all about it.' A number of police witnesses outlined how the murder had been investigated, before the medical witnesses described the prisoner's maimed condition and the injuries to the murdered woman.

The jury returned an unanimous verdict of guilty to murder, although with a recommendation to mercy, and Lord Anderson sentenced William Lamb to death. This extraordinary case arose a good deal of newspaper publicity in Britain and Ireland: after all, it was not every day that an armless man was sentenced to death for murder. William Lamb's solicitor Lindsay Crawford Steele wrote a petition to the Secretary of State for Scotland, pointing out that William Lamb had reported the death himself, and that he had experienced great sorrow and distress. Agnes White had led him astray with her drunken habits, he added. The real Mrs Lamb, who was still living at 86 Castle Street, Inverness, also took an interest in the case and did what she could to save her husband's life, although he had treated her and the family so very basely. But the authorities were not immediately willing to respite William Lamb, pointing out that his crime had been a sordid and brutal one: he must have known very well what he was doing when kicking and trampling the life out of poor Agnes. It was presumed that the cause of the murderous attack was that she had been too drunk to bring Lamb his tobacco pipe. The execution of an armless man might well be a painful and repellent spectacle, but this argument should not be used to save a murderer's life. In the end, a respite was decided upon, presumably by a narrow margin, and William Lamb now had to face imprisonment for life.

The convict William Lamb arrived at Peterhead Prison on April 23 1920. He soon became known as a truculent, foul-

Peterhead Prison | R.H. 2940
23.4.20 | William Lamb

25. A mug-shot of William Lamb in Peterhead Prison.

mouthed prisoner who was disobedient and destroyed prison property, even when punished with gruel diet and separate confinement. He was forced to work carrying tools on his back from the blacksmith's shop at the quarry. Lamb was entirely edentulous and used no false teeth. He could not feed or dress himself, and since it was trying for the prison officers to wait on him, an artificial left arm equipped with a spoon holder was purchased, but Lamb refused to use it. Although suffering from dyspepsia and an enlarged prostate, Lamb lived on throughout the 1920s. In 1931, when he was 67 years old, there was a debate as to whether he should be released. None of Lamb's children was willing to take him in, and although attempts were made to find him a home with his nephew Peter Keenan, a jobbing gardener in Glasgow, this individual had only one single room to house his entire family. In June 1931, William Lamb was handed over to the care of the Governor of Barnhill Poorhouse in Glasgow, where he soon made himself unpopular through his general truculence and fondness for smoking in bed. In March 1934, he escaped from Barnhill Poorhouse and tramped all the way to Edinburgh, where he asked a police official to return him to prison, which he liked better than this wretched poorhouse. The Governor of Barnhill Poorhouse was not particularly keen to have Lamb back, so another attempt was made to find room for him with a relative, but again without success. William Lamb died from bronchopneumonia at the Hospital Ward of Barnhill Poorhouse in April 1934.[13]

25. The murder house at 88 Candlemaker Row.

As for the murder house at 88 Candlemaker Row, it was the Greyfriars Kirkhouse for a while, but it is today home to the Grassmarket Community Project, run by Greyfriars Kirk and Grassmarket Mission to provide for homeless and disadvantaged local people. It is today 86 Candlemaker Row, although there is no doubt that it is identical to the 1919 murder house. It is identified as such by its Canmore record in the database of Historic Environment Scotland, although the assertion that the upper floors had been demolished after the murder is a misapprehension: the court records speak of a 'first flat' [on the ground floor] and a 'second flat' [on the first floor, where William Lamb and Agnes White lived]. Thus the murder house never had more than two inhabitable stories. Its present-day use may well seem innocent enough, as a much-needed centre for various Old Town unfortunates; but imagine a dark and foggy autumnal evening, with the inhabitants of the Grassmarket Community Project singing some rousing hymns.

The ghost of Greyfriars Bobby comes trotting down Candlemaker Row to listen to the singing, and the Angels of the Lord hover above the tombstones at Greyfriars nearby. But all of a sudden, there is an outcry of 'Get up and give me my pipe!' followed by an indescribable sound of kicking and stamping, and a woman giving a shrill wail as she departs this life. A dark and forbidding wraith appears at the door of 88 Candlemaker Row, mutilated and without arms, wild-eyed and foaming at the mouth: fly away angels, hide underneath the table-stones Greyfriars Bobby, escape Grassmarket unfortunates, for this fell spectre is Murder, bred by Pandemonium, and the legacy it leaves behind is Death!

THE CURSE ON TRON SQUARE, 1954

In early 1954, the 39-year-old Elizabeth McGarry was a Catholic single mother of two, unemployed and with few prospects in life, living in the slums of Edinburgh's old town at 57 Tron Square, in a flat consisting of just one room and a tiny kitchen. Her first husband, George Alexander Robertson, a veteran of the Spanish Civil War, was violent, abusive and intensely jealous; her second husband had left her after just a few months. Her 18-year-old son George Jr worked as a coal porter and would soon be called up for his national service; her 16-year-old daughter Jean had a job at a paper mill. For a while, Elizabeth McGarry allowed George Alexander Robertson back into the house, but he turned out to be as mean-spirited and vindictive as ever, so she showed him the door in February 1954. Since the family was fearful that the vicious George Alexander would return to beat them up, they kept the door locked at all times, with a chair wedged against the handle for extra protection.

On February 28 1954, Jean Robertson came home from a dance, to find that her mother had invited a few friends to 57

Tron Square for a sing-song. They had a jolly time, and George Jr later came home to join them. For once, they forgot to wedge the chair against the door handle when they went to bed. In the middle of the night, Jean Robertson awoke with a start when she could hear her father's voice inside the flat. George Jr also woke up and got out of bed, but only to be stabbed in the head by his father. George Alexander then attacked Jean and stabbed her in the stomach and arms with two large knives. When he heard his ex-wife try to escape through the door, he ran after her, stabbing her hard several times. He dragged her inside the flat, where the terrified children saw that her hands were tied together and that she had a white handkerchief stuffed into her mouth; her body was drenched with blood, and there was a gaping hole in her stomach.

As the murderous George Alexander threw the lifeless body of his wife onto the kitchen floor, George Jr made a desperate bid for freedom, running out of the flat and along the first-floor balcony until he reached the quadrangle outside. Throwing himself headlong through a neighbour's kitchen window at 42 Tron Square, he screamed 'Help me! Please will someone help!' This neighbour was Mrs Catherine Hay, who got the shock of her life when the badly bleeding George Jr came lurching into the bedroom that she shared with her husband and two children. George Alexander, who had also leapt in through the window, viciously attacked his son, stabbing him hard in the face and chest with two large knives. In front of the terrified Hay family, he murdered his son, promising them the same treatment if they tried to intervene, before reeling back to 57 Tron Square, carrying George Jr's mangled corpse in his arms. Here, he surveyed the bodies of his daughter and ex-wife, before turning on the gas and putting his head inside the oven.

The terrified Hays ran to the Central Police Station, saying that there had just been a murder inside their own flat. Since they were almost hysterical, Sergeant Walter Middlemist at first thought they were delirious, but when he and two constables accompanied them back to 42 Tron Square, a grisly trail of bloody footprints led up the stairs to 57 Tron Square, where the policemen pulled the unconscious George Alexander's head out of the oven. Elizabeth McGarry was dead from a number of deep stab wounds, and so was the badly mangled George Jr, but Jean was still alive in spite of her appalling injuries; she was swiftly taken to the Royal Infirmary, where an emergency operation saved her life. 'Tragedy in Royal Mile!' exclaimed the headline of the *Edinburgh Evening News*, whose photographer took some helpful snapshots of the murder flat, the second one from the right along the first floor balcony, and the bloody footprints leading to it.

On trial for murder at the High Court of Edinburgh in early June 1954, George Alexander Robertson looked defiant, like if he was proud of nearly exterminating his entire family. He had left a note with his old mother saying that Liz had provoked him for the last time, and that he would take action against her. Jean Robertson, who had recovered from her injuries, gave a blow-by-blow account of the Tron Square bloodbath together with Catherine Hay. Sir David Kennedy Henderson, professor of psychiatry at Edinburgh University, testified that he had interviewed the prisoner and found no sign of mental unsoundness. Mr Sloan, for the defence, suggested that there might have been an acute brainstorm, so that he had not been responsible for his actions, but the polite expert witness replied that although he would have liked to come to that opinion, he was sorry that he was unable to do so.

The Solicitor-General Mr Milligan, for the prosecution, pointed out that the attack had clearly been premeditated, since George Alexander Robertson had brought two large knives with him on his nocturnal visit to 57 Tron Square. Two doctors had found no signs of psychiatric disease. The extraordinary horror of the attack did not imply mental abnormality. Lord Thomson

27. Tron Square today.

pointed out that if the prisoner had been mentally sound at the time, this was a case of murder, whereas if there was diminished responsibility, this was culpable homicide. The jury found Robertson guilty of murder and Lord Thomson sentenced him to death; he was executed, as the last person ever, at Saughton Prison on June 23 1954.[14] In 1999, the *Edinburgh Evening News* had an interview with Margaret Hay, who had been 12 years old when George Jr had been butchered by his own father inside the Hay family's bedroom at 42 Tron Square.[15]

Tron Square remained murder free until 1973, when Margaret Bain strangled her violent and unsatisfactory husband Andrew McLaren Bain to death at 15 Tron Square. In 1969, a woman named Mary Henderson had attempted to murder her husband

Robert at 7 Tron Square, but he appears to have survived and recovered. Between 2001 and 2003, Tron Square was tidied up and 60 modern flats constructed; the houses were renumbered during this operation, but it is still possible to follow George Jr's final run from one murder flat to another, due to the helpful *Edinburgh Evening News* photographs. Nothing is mentioned about any ongoing haunting at Tron Square, something that is extraordinary to a close student of the works of Elliott O'Donnell: surely, there must be an unworldly nocturnal outcry, stains of blood appearing in the murder flats, and the hissing of a gas oven, to mark one of Edinburgh's worst ever cataclysms of murder, enacted in a quiet square just off the Cowgate.

THE MURDER OF EDWARD LINTON, 1977

The 57-year-old Edward Linton had once been one of Scotland's leading exhibition ballroom dancers. He then became a baker and confectioner with St Cuthbert's Co-operative Association Ltd, retiring in 1970 after 29 years of service. After becoming a widower, Edward Linton developed into something of a recluse: he eked out a gloomy and solitary existence and lived in an unmodernised attic flat at 27 South Bridge, right in the middle of Edinburgh.

Early on May 26 1971, Edward Linton was found dead in his flat by a police constable performing a routine check. He had quite horrific injuries from a brutal beating with a blunt instrument like a hammer: six broken ribs, two broken arms and a broken leg, and a multitude of cuts and bruises. His hands had been tied up with electrical flex. He might well have lived for several days after his murderer or murderers had left him behind in the silent flat, tied up and gagged with a tie, but he had been dead for 3-7 days when found. The police initially took an interest in two men seen with Linton a few days, prior to the murder, drinking in various

28. The top-floor murder flat at 27 South Bridge.

Grassmarket and Cowgate pubs, but they came forward to be eliminated from the murder inquiry. Edward Linton's attic flat was the only residential property in the large house at 27 South Bridge, which mainly consisted of shops and storage rooms. The winding tenement stair was full of litter and rubbish, which was sifted through by the police looking for clues.

On May 31, five days after Edward Linton's body had been found, the police had an anonymous call, incriminating the two young thugs Alan McCartney and Frank Gallagher as the murderers. Although the 19-year-old McCartney and the 18-year-old Gallagher were known burglars, they lacked convictions for more serious crimes. When arrested and questioned by the police, young Gallagher admitted that he and McCartney had done the 'job' in South Bridge; it had been his cohort who had beaten up the old man. The reason for the burglary was that they had wanted to go to Wembley to see the England vs Scotland decider in the British Home Championship. McCartney, a nasty piece of work who described himself as an unemployed whisky bond worker, blamed Gallagher for beating the old man up with a hammer; he himself had come to the rescue, he claimed, to take the hammer away and drag Gallagher out of the flat.

On trial for murder at the High Court, the two young thugs once more blamed each other for the murder. Michael McCartney, the twin brother of Alan, testified that after coming home late in the evening, Alan had admitted breaking into a flat, although he said it was Frank Gallagher who had beaten the householder up. Later, when Michael and Alan went to drink with Gallagher in a pub, Michael asked him what the truth was about the burglary and assault, but Frank had been evasive. When Michael suggested that they should return to 27 South Bridge to see if the householder was alive, Frank sullenly refused, and Alan said he would not be going there alone. Another day, after Michael and Alan had been drinking in a pub at lunchtime, they had seen a police van parked outside 27 South Bridge; Alan had bought a newspaper and exclaimed 'The man's dead! The man's dead!' It also turned out that Frank had told his brother Alexander that he and McCartney had 'screwed a hoose' in the Bridges; when disturbed by a man, Frank had run away, leaving his fellow burglar alone in the flat with the householder. As for technical evidence, a fingerprint from McCartney had been found in the murder flat.

After the jury had found both thugs guilty of murder, they were sentenced to imprisonment for life.[16] The identity of the anonymous caller, who had been instrumental in solving the South Bridge murder, was never divulged; it may well have been a bystander in a pub who had heard the two murderers talking about their burglarious exploits, and the man left behind in the flat, and realized what had happened when the newspapers announced the death of Edward Linton. The reason for the excessive violence used may well have been torture, to force the wretched householder to divulge the whereabouts of his valuables, but there is nothing to suggest that solitary old Edward Linton possessed any great riches to begin with. As for the Wembley football match the two thugs had vainly hoped to attend, it ended England 1 – Scotland 2; there were ecstatic scenes afterwards, with kilted Scots invading the pitch, playing the bagpipes and waving their Saltires about. The murder house at 27 South Bridge still stands, and there is still a rather grim-looking attic flat. It is the fourth and latest murder house in this busy Edinburgh thoroughfare; the first of them was 82 South Bridge [the house has been pulled down], where the brothel madam Mary McKinnon murdered a customer in 1823, the second a South Bridge brothel where Christian Paterson struck down Margaret Baird in December 1823, and then we have the still extant 18 South Bridge, where the tailor Andrew Heggie swung his 'goose' with lethal effect in 1878.

MURDER IN HERIOT PLACE, 1977

On May 28 1977, the Edinburgh police telephone operator received a very strange call. If the police went to 8 Heriot Place, off the Grassmarket, they would find an 'IRA girl' who would probably be dead. And indeed, the body of the 20-year-old Mrs Yvonne Butler was found in the common stair at this address; she had been strangled to death with her own brassiere. It turned out that Yvonne Butler had nothing whatsoever to do with the IRA: she was a divorced mother of two who lived with her parents in a flat in Oxgangs Avenue. Her mother and sister agreed that after receiving a telephone call from a man, Yvonne Butler had gone

29. The murder house at 8 Heriot Place.

out in the evening of May 28. She did not know any person in Heriot Place, and they had no suggestion to explain why she had ended up there.

But the police received information that on May 28, Yvonne Butler had been seen with the 33-year-old Glaswegian Albert Joseph Anderson, and he was taken into custody and charged with her murder. He was also charged with attempting to murder another young woman in Glasgow, again by strangulation. On trial at the High Court in September 1977, Anderson changed his plea to guilty, and admitted murdering Yvonne Butler. They had been kissing in the stair at 8 Heriot Place, when she had begun laughing at his lack of sexual prowess; in a furious rage, he had strangled her to death. He was sentenced to imprisonment for life.[17]

DRUGS AND MURDER IN
CORNWALL STREET, 1984

The 18-year-old schoolgirl Ann Douglas was a very disturbed young woman. In the end of 1980, she took an overdose of paracetamol, and in the following years, she would ambulate between mental hospitals, hostels for the mentally disturbed, and psychiatric outpatient clinics. She had taken 25 or so drug overdoses, some of them genuine suicide attempts according to her psychiatrist Dr Ann Guldberg at the Dingleton Hospital in Melrose. Ann Douglas told her that her life was worthless, and deplored that human beings were so very cruel: they killed and ate animals, waged war against each other, and constructed nuclear weapons. The best thing for her would be to die, she said, and she knew some girls in Edinburgh who could get hold of heroin and give her an overdose.

In 1984, the 26-year-old Ann Laird and the 20-year-old Alison Scott, both of them intravenous drug addicts, were living in an Old Town flat at 13 Cornwall Street. On March 14, Ann Douglas was found dead in this flat, and the other two girls were taken into police custody and charged with murdering her. Ann Laird had a long history of psychiatric disease, and she had met Alison Scott in the drug addict ward at the Royal Edinburgh Hospital. The murder trial of the two girls began in July 1984, although not all members of the legal profession were convinced that the charge was a proper one. They both denied murdering Ann Douglas and blamed each other for giving her a heroin overdose. The problem was that these two muddled females had been 'high' much of the time, and that their recollection of events was far from crystal clear.

Ann Laird testified that Ann Douglas had come to the Cornwall Street flat, declaring that she wanted to buy some heroin. Since she had £90 with her, they went out to purchase a gram of heroin, before returning home and injecting a quarter of a gram each. Ann Laird had hoped to inject Ann Douglas with the drug, she said, but she was 'high' and could not find a vein, so it had been Alison Scott who had performed the injection. Ann Douglas soon felt unwell and was put to bed. Keith Murray-Tait, the boyfriend of Alison Scott, had seen her there, before taking a 'shot' of heroin and going to bed himself. He was awakened by Ann Laird, who said that the girl had stopped breathing and looked like if she was dead, and it had been he who had telephoned for an ambulance.

After much contradictory evidence from drug addicts and mental nurses, the charge was reduced to one of culpable homicide. Ann Laird had by this time been made an inmate of the State Mental Hospital in Carstairs for her psychotic illness. In the end, both girls were found guilty, although their punishment would be lenient. Alison Scott was put on probation for three years, under strict supervision to prevent her from using illicit drugs. Ann Laird was out of Carstairs in late August 1984 and was freed at the dock of the High Court, becoming a voluntary outpatient at the Andrew Duncan clinic for psychiatric patients. The wisdom of putting these two muddled young females on trial for murder seems very dubious today.[18]

II.

THE NEW TOWN

Plans to drain the polluted Nor Loch and construct a New Town of Edinburgh began in earnest with an architectural competition in 1766, won by the young James Craig with a simple and ingenious plan. The main thoroughfare was to be George Street, named after King George III, with Queen Street to the north and Princes Street to the south. Two minor service streets, Rose and Thistle Street, were to supply the grand new houses with delivery access and servant's accommodation. The three streets traversing the grid; Castle, Frederick and Hanover Streets, were named after the view to the Castle, the name of the King's father Frederick Prince of Wales, and the name of the royal family. The Second, or Northern New Town was constructed between 1800 and 1830, extending Edinburgh northwards towards the Water of Leith; its elegant Georgian terraces largely remain intact today. The next extension to be built was the Earl of Moray's estate north of Charlotte Square, which was not finished until the 1850s. The Third, or Eastern New Town, was constructed after Regent Bridge had traversed the ravine between Princes Street and Calton Hill in 1819.

With a few notable exceptions, the fashionable streets of the New Town were inhabited by wealthy and law-abiding people, meaning that the murder rate was low. Rose Street and the other service lanes, inhabited by servants and other impecunious types, became hotspots for crime in late Victorian times, as did the humble Stockbridge terraces, filled to the rafters with working-class people, with an entire family occupying a single basement room. The New Town houses were very well built and have withstood the passage of time with impressive tenacity. An exception was Jamaica Street, to the west end of the Second New Town, which was entirely pulled down in a slum clearance, with new houses constructed; thus went the historic murder house at 40 Jamaica Street, where Philip Murray murdered William Ronald Cree in 1923. Largely spared the attention of Decay and the Luftwaffe, the Developer has been their main enemy, with perfectly good houses in Princes Street and Rose Street, among other New Town terraces, being wantonly pulled down to allow the construction of various modern monstrosities. Several murder houses in Rose Street were lost in this manner, as well as a historic Princes Street murder hotel. Still, due to its considerable size and well preserved architecture, the New Town is home to a not inconsiderable population of murder houses: read about Edinburgh's second oldest murder house, a humble shop in Frederick Street, the extraordinary double murder hotel in Princes Street, the two murder houses in Thistle Street and the three murder houses in Scotland Street...

THE SECOND OLDEST MURDER HOUSE IN EDINBURGH, 1863

The oldest murder house in Edinburgh is of course Holyrood Palace, notorious for the murder of David Rizzio in 1566. The hunt for the second oldest murder house in the Capital was not a straightforward one. In the 17th and 18th centuries, Edinburgh was still a relatively small city, and its murders took place in various Old Town closes and pends off the Royal Mile, the majority of which are no longer standing today. House numbering was in its infancy back in those days, and the newspaper indication of the exact situation of the murder house often very diffuse indeed. In 1827, Mr Mark Dow, a well-to-do Edinburgh shoemaker was found dead lying at the bottom of the common stair at 13 Bank Street, which is still standing. This would have been a perfectly good murder house had the gang of thieves responsible been prosecuted for murder, but they got off on a lesser charge. The gradual construction of the New Town meant a considerable increase in the size of the capital, but not an increase in its murder rate, since the people inhabiting its comfortable Georgian houses were well-to-do and law-abiding. Thus the elegant New Town terraces, the majority of which are still standing today, were largely spared the spectre of Murder, whereas the crowded closes of the Old Town, the majority of which have been done away with in various development schemes and slum clearances, saw bloodshed with regularity.

Alexander M'Millan was a native of the county of Monaghan in Ireland, born there in the early 1830s. He ran away from home as a young lad and lived with his grandfather in Lancashire for a while, before becoming cabin-boy on a vessel plying between London and Hull; he ended up tramping all the way up to Glasgow, where he changed his name to Alexander Milne and fell in with some very bad company. Escaping from the police, he found work in an Edinburgh printing office, but soon quarrelled with the foreman and was discharged. He took lodgings in Rose Street, where he fell in with some travelling Swedish hair-plaiters who found him useful as an interpreter. In return, they taught him their trade, and since there was a demand for hair-plaiters in the New Town at this time, things started looking up for young Milne. He took apartments at 47 Cumberland Street, where he had a successful hairdressing salon. He married a wife named Ellen Lawson and went on to become the father of three children: the daughter Helen Louisa, born in 1855, the son William Alexander, born in 1856 at Milne's new shop at 20 George Street, and the son James Lawson, born in 1858 at yet

1. The murder shop at 31 Frederick Street as 'Chiquito' in 2009.

another small shop at 29 Frederick Street. By early 1863, Milne had relocated into the shop at 31A Frederick Street, consisting of two small rooms, with a front room and a kitchen in the basement below to house the entire family. By this time, the now 29-year-old Milne was a chronic alcoholic who had celebrated Hogmanay with such enthusiasm that he seemed to verge on delirium tremens. On January 5, he was visited by a doctor, who prescribed some medicine and censured him for his debauchery. How Milne could at all do his work under these circumstances remains a mystery, and it is not surprising that he was losing the confidence of his fellow tradesmen. Nor was he a particularly attractive individual: short, stout and powerful, with coarse and flabby features.

On January 7, the 28-year-old working jeweller James Paterson, of 5 St James Square, sent his shop assistant George Graham to Milne's shop to inquire about some hair mounts. Milne, who was sober and alert for a change, said that they were nearly done, but he asked that Mr Paterson should be sent along to his shop, since he wanted to see him. Milne and Paterson had been good friends for some time, but when the jeweller came along to his shop close to mid-day, Milne had purchased a sharp dagger from a shop. He admitted Paterson, who said 'How are you today?', and got the taciturn reply 'Just come in.' All of a sudden, Milne assaulted Paterson in front of his two young sons who were in the back shop: he gave him a push down the stairs to the kitchen of the flat below, before bounding after him with the dagger. The 8-year-old Helen Louisa Milne, who was sitting in front of the fire in the front basement room, was astounded when Paterson came running into the room and out into the area, with his umbrella underneath his arm, and shouting 'I am stabbed!' He made it all the way up the stairs, but collapsed in the street holding the railings, exclaiming 'Oh! I am stabbed!' and pointing at the left side of his chest. He never spoke again.

The chemist Bruce Allen, who happened to be passing by in Frederick Street, saw Paterson collapse and helped him into Alexander Forrester's baker's shop at No. 31. He saw Milne emerge from his own shop, saying 'The fellow has been poisoning my wife and my children! I have got him in bed with my wife!' Allen gave Milne a push back into his own shop, saying 'Go into your shop, sir, and do not attempt to escape!' When Constable John Stewart came to the scene, he found that Paterson was already dead; when he seized the dagger and took Milne into custody, the Frederick Street desperado exclaimed 'He was a blackguard for running after married men's wives in that way!' Being examined at the police-office, Milne said that he had suspected that Paterson was having an affair with his wife, armed himself with the dagger, and challenged his presumed rival with the words 'Now, what is this about my wife? What have you been doing with her?' When Paterson had responded with a derisive laugh, Milne could not stand it any longer: he stabbed his rival hard in the chest. After Milne had been removed to a cell at Calton Jail, he seemed calm and sober, and quite unconcerned about the 'accident' he had caused, since Paterson had been making advances to his wife. At midnight, he leapt out of bed, frightening the other prisoners with a terrible outcry of 'Murder! Murder! Oh, my wife and children!' Fearful of delirium tremens, the turnkey put him in the padded cell, but Milne did not become delirious.

There was widespread curiosity throughout the New Town that a murder had been committed in one of its most fashionable streets. Throughout the day of the murder, and for weeks afterwards, crowds of people came to see the murder shop. Although Mrs Milne pulled down the shutters of the shop, "The morbid curiosity of the inhabitants was not however in any way diminished by this proceeding, for during the whole day an immense throng congregated around the shop, and narrowly inspected its exterior", as a newspaper rather disapprovingly expressed it.

The trial of Alexander Milne for murdering John Paterson opened at the High Court of Edinburgh on February 7. George Graham described how he had gone to Milne's shop and set up the meeting with Paterson. Ann Wilson, the landlady of the murdered man at 5 St James Square, said that she had advised Paterson not to go near Milne, who was an excitable and crazy-looking man who was very fond of strong drink. Milne's little daughter gave evidence about what she had seen, as did the resourceful Bruce Allan, Constable Stewart and William Cowan, the lieutenant of police.

There was no doubt at all that the prisoner Milne had stabbed John Paterson to death, but had he been sane at the time? The defence called a number of witnesses who described Milne's strange behaviour in the weeks prior to the murder: he had been fearful of being robbed, thought his entire family were being systematically poisoned, and imagined that Paterson was having an affair with his wife. The doctors who had examined Milne in prison agreed that he was not labouring under delirium tremens and that he was not feigning insanity; instead, they suggested that he had been under the influence of paranoid delusions against Paterson when he committed the murder. After a lengthy and impartial summing-up from the Lord Justice Clerk, the jury was out for an hour before returning a majority verdict of guilty of murder, albeit with a recommendation to mercy since three of the jurors had been of the opinion that Milne had been insane. Sentence of death was pronounced, and the execution date set to March 4. There was widespread opposition to this harsh sentence, and a good deal of writing in the medical press debating whether Milne had been insane at the time of the murder. His solicitor sent a memorial to the Home Secretary, who replied on February 26 saying that he had come to the conclusion that the recommendation of the prisoner to mercy by the jury was entitled to more than ordinary weight, and that the sentence should be commuted to penal servitude for life. Milne is said to have been very grateful for this last-minute respite, on account of his wife and family.[1]

When I first saw it in 2009, the murder shop at 31A Frederick Street was part of the 'Chiquito' Mexican restaurant. It was still possible to see that there had once been two shops on the premises, although the door to Milne's former shop had been replaced with a large window, the entrance to the restaurant being through the (original?) door to Forrester's shop, on the floor of which Paterson had expired. I spoke to the headwaiter of this restaurant, who expressed amazement at the former notoriety of his establishment as the New Town's premier murder shop. The place was not haunted. The entrance to the basement floor, where the Frederick Street murderer had eked out a miserable existence, with a family of five living in two small rooms, had long since been paved over. In very recent times, the shopfront has been changed around after the restaurant and the former jeweller's shop at 29 Frederick Street have been converted to a large steakhouse; the opinion of the restless spirits of Milne and Paterson on this wanton rearrangement of two traditional New Town shops was never consulted by the developers.

THE DEMON FRENCHMAN OF
GEORGE STREET, 1878

According to his marriage certificate, Eugène Marie Chantrelle was born at Nantes in 1838, the son of the ship owner Jean Etienne Chantrelle and his wife Marie Anne, born Martinet. He had a maiden aunt in Nantes named Marie Martinet, who was alive as late as the 1870s. According to his marriage certificate, he was born in 1838, but his biographer Mr A. Duncan Smith prefers the year 1834. He is likely to have received some degree of a university education, since he knew excellent Latin and Greek, and good English and German, and since his medical knowledge was better than what could be expected from an uneducated layperson. According to his own account, he studied medicine in Strasbourg for four years. He had taken part in the Paris riots of 1851, being wounded when fighting on the barricades, for the republican side. He then claimed to have gone to America for a while, as a teacher of languages.

In 1862, Eugène Chantrelle turned up in England, visiting Newcastle, Leicester and other places as a teacher. According to an article in the *Edinburgh Evening News*, published after Chantrelle's downfall, he was sentenced to nine month's imprisonment in Brighton for sexually assaulting a young lady, presumably one of his pupils. In 1864 or 1865, Eugène went on to Edinburgh, where he took a comfortable house at 81A George

2. A postcard showing George Street looking towards the west, stamped and posted in 1908. The Chantrelle murder house is further down in the terrace to the right.

Street, living on the second and third floors above a shop. He advertised for private pupils in the *Scotsman* newspaper of January 4 1865. Since Eugène was a rather handsome, elegantly dressed man, and obviously a person of learning and culture, he was employed at several schools, including the private Newington Academy, where he began work in December 1865. Here, he met the pretty 15-year-old schoolgirl Elizabeth Cullen Dyer, who came from a distinguished Edinburgh family. After a short acquaintance, Eugène seduced and impregnated her; when she showed obvious signs of pregnancy, a shotgun marriage ensued on August 11 1868. On their marriage certificate, the bride's age is wrongly given as 18 and the groom's age is underestimated as well. Elizabeth moved into 81A George Street, where she gave birth to her eldest son Eugène John later the same year. A second child was born in 1870 but did not live long.

Initially, Eugène and Elizabeth Chantrelle got on well

3. A cabinet card showing Eugène Chantrelle.

together: he kept teaching at various schools and she minded her surviving son. There was a schoolroom in the house where he taught private pupils who wanted to brush up their French or Latin. In 1875, he published *Reading Lessons in Latin with Practical Exercises*, a scarce and privately published book not held by any library, although his biographer William Roughead had a copy of it, which is today in the Signet Library. But soon the marriage of the two Chantrelles was breaking up. Eugène drank French wine and champagne with enthusiasm, but he also developed a taste for the Scottish national drink, emptying a bottle of whisky per day. He beat and mistreated Elizabeth, and sometimes kicked her out into the common stair at night, forcing her to take refuge in the flat below. He cursed her in bloodcurdling terms, saying that he would shoot her with a loaded pistol he used to carry around, or that he would make use of his medical knowledge to kill her with a poison that could not be detected. Fearful for her life, she wrote to her mother complaining of her abusive husband, but old Mrs Dyer advised her to stay with him. There was by now three little Chantrelles to feed, with Louis being born in 1871 and James Ernest in 1876, and she did not want the family to be split up. A man of voracious sexual appetite, Eugène was a regular at a fashionable brothel in Clyde Street, where he drank champagne and caroused with the harlots, sometimes firing off his pistol to make them jump.

In 1877, Eugène left his pistol lying about when the family was visiting Portobello: his son Eugène John grabbed it and fired off a shot that went through the hand of his brother Louis, before lodging in the fleshy part of Eugène's thumb. The Frenchman gave

4. *A portrait of Eugène Chantrelle, from A.D. Smith (Ed.), Trial of Eugène Marie Chantrelle (Edinburgh 1906).*

a fearful yell when a local doctor came and extracted the bullet. This narrow escape from being shot dead by his own son made Eugène consider insuring his life, or so at least he claimed: in October 1877, he took out £1000 policies on both his own life and that of his wife. Elizabeth was fearful that Eugène would murder her now when her life was insured, but her mother, who seems to have been entirely devoid of common sense, pooh-poohed her concerns. On New Year's Eve 1877, everything seemed normal in the Chantrelle household. The jovial paterfamilias had lately run into debt due to his extravagant life, but still he drank wine and champagne like if it had been water. When twelve o'clock was striking, the family listened to the band of the Castle garrison playing festive hymns, having invited their servant Mary Byrne to join them.

On the morning of New Year's Day, Elizabeth felt a little unwell, complaining of a slight headache. Eugène sent his eldest son out to purchase a duck for dinner, but Elizabeth vomited and did not eat anything. After she had been put to bed, Eugène took all three children into his own bedroom and left his wife some lemonade, grapes and an orange to eat. The following morning, the servant Mary Byrne rose before seven to make a cup of tea for her mistress. When she was lighting the kitchen fire, she heard a moaning sound from Elizabeth's room. The door to the room was open, whereas it was regularly kept shut; the gas was turned off and there was no smell of gas in the room. Elizabeth was lying on the bed moaning piteously, and the pillow and bedclothes were stained with vomit. The tumbler of lemonade was empty and only two small portions remained of the orange. In the parlour was a large, empty whisky bottle. When Eugène was roused, he went to see his unconscious wife, who did not stir. He asked Mary Byrne if she could smell gas in the room, something she denied. He then said that the baby was crying and asked her to look after it, but when she came into the other bedroom, she found all three children sleeping peacefully. Returning to the sick-bed, she could see her master coming from the window of the room. Summoned by Eugène, Dr Carmichael, of 42 Northumberland Street, arrived at 8.30 am. He could smell gas in the room and suspected coal-gas poisoning. He brought some brandy to inject as a stimulant, but the thirsty Eugène drank much of the contents of the bottle when the doctor was not looking.

Dr Carmichael called in the police surgeon Dr Littlejohn, and Mrs Dyer brought her own family doctor along to see Elizabeth, who was now deeply unconscious. The doctors tried artificial respiration but to little avail, and the patient died at the Royal Infirmary soon after. The histrionic Eugène exhibited grief and rage, accusing the doctors of murdering his wife. When the gas company was called in, they found that a gas pipe behind one of the shutters of Elizabeth's bedroom had been wrenched

5. *Madame Chantrelle, from A.D. Smith (Ed.), Trial of Eugène Marie Chantrelle (Edinburgh 1906).*

loose by some person. But the doctors no longer thought the symptoms were those of coal-gas poisoning; Dr Gordon, who had seen many poisoning cases before, instead thought the patient had died from the administration of some narcotic poison. And indeed, the post-mortem examination demonstrated the presence of opium in the vomit on the patient's nightdress. When Elizabeth was buried, there were distressing scenes when the frantic Eugène tried to fling himself into the open grave. But after it had been established that on November 25 1877, he had purchased sixty grains of opium, he was arrested for murdering his wife. A strange matter was that her urine had an alcoholic odour, suggesting that he might have administered the poison in some of the whisky from the empty bottle found in the parlour.

The loose gas pipe had just been a clumsy attempt to make the death look like an accident, so that he could cash in the life insurance money without any demur.

The trial of Eugène Chantrelle began on May 7 1878, before Lord Moncrieff. Mr William Watson, the Lord Advocate, led for the prosecution, and Mr John Traynor led Chantrelle's defence team. The maid Mary Byrne gave her damning evidence clearly and without contradiction: it suggested that after poisoning his wife, Eugène had lured her out of the sickroom to be able to sever the gas pipe and simulate an accident. She further described his heavy drinking and angry outbursts, screaming

No. 81a George Street, Edinburgh, where
E. M. Chantrelle resided.

6. The murder house in 1906, from A.D. Smith (Ed.), Trial of Eugène Marie Chantrelle (Edinburgh 1906).

'Go to hell!' and 'I will kick you out!' at his wife in the presence of the servant. There was then a painful interlude as the little boy Eugène John described how his papa used to call mamma bad names, swear at her, strike her, and make her cry. Papa had also freely cuffed and kicked the children when they made a noise, although he had never administered a proper thrashing. A former maid in the household described how, in 1876, she had rescued Madame Chantrelle from her abusive husband; when they had reported the matter to a police constable, the furious Frenchman had screamed, prophetically as it turned out, 'I will do for the bitch yet!' Yet another maid described how Eugène had kissed her and tried to take liberties with her, only desisting when she threatened to tell her mistress. The amorous Frenchman had just 17 shillings in the bank and he owed £200 to various tradesmen.

The medical evidence pointed in favour of opium poisoning, the very same poison the prisoner had purchased a quantity of just weeks before the murder. The defence had a difficult task, mainly concentrating on finding witnesses that corroborated some of the prisoner's statements, and persons who could testify that he was not always violent and abusive to his wife. The jury returned a verdict of guilty and Lord Moncrieff sentenced the prisoner to death. For a scoundrel of his calibre, there was no hope of a reprieve: after hearing that he was a doomed man, the demonic prisoner had exclaimed 'Would that I could but place a fuse in the centre of this earth, that I could blow it to pieces, and with it the whole of humanity! I hate them!' In the scrapbook on the trial of M. Chantrelle held by the National Library of Scotland are preserved two letters from the prisoner to the governor of Calton Prison, asking for a glass of whisky per day and a supply of tobacco and cigarette paper. When asked, on the night before the execution, whether there was anything he wanted, the prisoner said 'Send in three bottles of champagne and a whore!', a request that was denied him. Unrepentant to the last, he breakfasted on coffee and eggs, washed down with a glass of brandy, before smoking a cigar. Eugène Chantrelle was hanged by the executioner Marwood on May 31, the first execution in Scotland to be conducted in private, inside the prison grounds. The Edinburgh murder enthusiasts swarmed like bees on Calton Hill, but they were unable to see more than the Black Flag being hoisted from the turret flagstaff in the bright spring sunshine.[2]

When my old friend, the late Richard Whittington-Egan, was researching his biography of William Roughead, he found a letter directed to Eugène Chantrelle by Miss Ellen Lucy Holme, the daughter of a clergyman and a native of Cromer. When she had lived in Edinburgh in early 1867, she had gone to Chantrelle's house in George Street to answer an advertisement for a housekeeper. Chantrelle had flung her down on the floor and raped her, before sending her packing. She had given birth to a healthy son, born in Cromer on September 22 1867 and still living in 1877. Miss Holme wrote to Chantrelle asking that he should recognize the boy as his son, since he was 'very like his father', but the cruel Frenchman snubbed her. After Chantrelle had been arrested for murder, the timid Miss Holme made her predicament known to the prosecuting council, but they decided not to call her as a witness, since she was a feeble woman who would not withstand a hostile cross-examination. Since it turns out that no child with the name of Holme or Chantrelle was born anywhere in Norfolk at the relevant time, it must be presumed that the murderer's bastard child went by an alias, since I cannot see any reason for Miss Holme to make up such a story. William Roughead had a pair of white linen cuffs that were said to have belonged to Elizabeth Chantrelle; these later came into the possession of his biographer Richard Whittington-Egan, as a part of his criminal museum.

There was a collection for the three parentless Chantrelle children, securing £500 in a few months. The children were taken care of by the Dyer family and changed their name to Nelson to avoid their father's notoriety. The eldest son, Eugène John

7. The murder house at 81A George Street today.

Chantrelle alias John Cullen Nelson, became a sailor before the mast, but he committed suicide through blowing out his brains with a pistol shot in Glasgow in 1890. The second son, Louis Chantrelle alias Henry Nelson, also became a mariner, sailing the world with some success, and possibly moving to the United States. The youngest son, James Ernest Chantrelle alias James Ernest Nelson, stayed ashore and tried a variety of occupations. In 1897, he married Christina Guthrie at Newington, describing himself as an insurance agent and giving the name of his father as 'Eugene Marie Nelson, Teacher, Deceased'. But Christina had to enter an asylum after a few years, and she died there from general paralysis of the insane in 1912. James Ernest became a tobacconist but was hounded out of the shop after his true identity had become known; he then kept an Edinburgh bicycle shop for a while, before moving to Glasgow. He remarried Mary Baird there in 1919, this time describing himself as a commercial traveller and giving the name of his father as 'John Nelson, School Teacher, Deceased'. He never returned to Edinburgh, even to pick up an inheritance from a friend of his mother who had mentioned him in her will. He supported himself by various menial jobs and supported his large family of four sons and three daughters as well as he could. At least one of his sons had issue himself, meaning that Eugène Chantrelle, the Demon Frenchman of George Street, has a living descendant in Glasgow today.

CHILD MURDER IN NORTH EAST CUMBERLAND STREET LANE, 1879

In 1879, the 43-year-old widow Helen Edmondstone lived in a flat at 9 North East Cumberland Street Lane, with her numerous brood of children. The eldest son, 21-year-old John, worked as a stonemason, and his 19-year-old brother William was an unemployed gentleman's servant. They both lived at home, but the 14-year-old son George was a drummer with the 7th Regiment of Highlanders. The youngest son, 10-year-old Robert, had refused to go to school, and become an inmate of the Original Ragged School as a result. The 17-year-old daughter Ann worked as a book folder, but also assisted her mother in her work as a charwoman and cleaner at the Internal Revenue Office in Waterloo Place. Although Helen Edmondstone was rather fond of strong drink, she was a hard and willing worker, who gave satisfaction to the office housekeeper. She was a religious woman, who worked as a pew-opener at St Paul's Episcopal Chapel.

But although she was old enough to know better, Helen

8. The entrance to the murder house at 9 East Cumberland Street Lane.

Edmondstone had embarked on an intrigue with a man named Douglas, who worked as a porter at the Internal Revenue Office. When she became pregnant, he promised to marry her, but afterwards he reneged on his pledge; as a result, she was alone in the world, with a numerous family to feed and a baby on the way. When she was unable to keep on working, the housekeeper Madeline Deans did not discharge her, but kept on paying her salary and welcomed her back after her baby had been born. Helen Edmondstone gave birth to a healthy girl on December 10 1879. The creature Douglas is recorded to have come to see the baby the day after.

Helen Edmondstone became very depressed and despondent after giving birth, although her baby was a jolly little creature, very popular among her children. She despaired of ever being able to go back to work, and her unemployed son William had to help her run the household. On December 30, William Edmondstone went out a little after 9 am, leaving his mother alone with the baby. He returned at 10.15 am, to find the baby floating in a tub of water, quite dead. "Oh mother, what's this you've done?" he exclaimed in horror, before running to fetch the neighbourwoman Mrs Margaret Watson. Mrs Watson took the baby out of the tub and put it on a table, but it was dead and cold. She did not think Helen Edmondstone, whom she had known for three years, looked like if she was in her full senses. Mrs Watson sent William for the police, and he returned with criminal officer William Milne, who saw the baby and the tub and took Helen Edmondstone into custody.

When Helen Edmondstone was on trial for child murder at the High Court of Edinburgh on March 8 1880, her children William, John and Ann gave evidence describing their mother's miserable life. Both Mrs Watson and the housekeeper Madeline Deans could verify that after giving birth to her daughter, Helen Edmondstone had become very depressed. Dr Henry Duncan Littlejohn and Dr Benjamin Bell, who had performed the autopsy, found that the baby, who was otherwise healthy and fit, had died from drowning; Dr Littlejohn, who had seen the mother after her crime, added that she had been a weakly woman, depressed but not obviously insane. A plea of guilty to culpable homicide was accepted and Helen Edmondstone was sentenced to imprisonment for 12 months; hopefully, the wretched woman could enjoy this enforced rest cure behind bars, with no dirty rags, cleaning brooms or hungry children, without being haunted by the screams of a ghostly baby.[3] The man Douglas hopefully felt thoroughly ashamed of the tragedy he had caused, in one of the poorest dens of the fashionable New Town.

THE MURDER OF A POLICEMAN
IN ELM ROW, 1881

In 1881, David Rintoul and John Henry Shewan were two young seamen on board the fishery cutter HMS Vigilant, based at Granton Harbour. David was born in 1862 and had both his parents alive in Edinburgh; John Henry was born in Leith on August 13 1863, but both his parents had died early and he was taken care of by his grandfather, the old sailor James Smith, who lived at 2 West Cromwell Street. On board the Vigilant, David had a good character, whereas John Henry could be dour and discontented. On March 13 1881, HMS Vigilant had docked at Granton Harbour after inspecting some fisheries, and the two young sailors went ashore. David Rintoul lived with his family at 17 Union Place, whereas John Henry Shewan went to see his grandfather in Leith. John Henry had a friend living at 2 Elm Row, Leith Walk, the apprentice plumber James Aird who lived with his family at top floor flat at this address. In the evening of March 14, the two sailors made their way towards 2 Elm Row, where they forced the main door and rummaged around in the hall. Rintoul forced the door leading to the basement, allegedly to find a water closet to relieve himself, but in reality with burglary in mind. But as he was searching the basement cellars, the policeman on the beat, the 21-year-old George Low, came into the common stair to check for burglars. He had been an Edinburgh constable for four years and had an excellent service record. George Low saw the intruder in the basement and went down and collared him, saying that he would be taken to the police office for this offence. But John Henry Shewan, a strong and sturdy lad, came running down the stairs to defend his friend and shipmate: he produced a sharp dagger and stabbed George Low three times in the chest, eight times in the back, and one time in the side. David Rintoul wrenched an iron bar from a cellar window and used it to beat the policeman around the head. Their murderous work done, the two sailors left 2 Elm Row, with expedition.

It turned out, however, that the frenzied Shewan had stabbed his friend Rintoul twice by accident, right through the fleshy part of the left hand. They decided to go back to 17 Union Place to get the hand bandaged. The squeamish Rintoul, who cared more for his own blood than that shed by the policeman at Elm Row, opened a water tap to clean his wounds. The house painter Alexander Rintoul and his wife Agnes were of course greatly alarmed that their son had been wounded. When they demanded to know the reason, Shewan politely apologised, saying that it had been a mere accident: when he had seen his friend in the grip of a large policeman, he had decided to interfere with his dagger drawn. Alexander Rintoul went to get a doctor for his son, but he then went on to the St James Police Station to give information about the two miscreants. Sergeant John Butcher made sure that two constables went to 2 Elm Row, where George Low's body was recovered from the basement. A sergeant and a constable were dispatched to 17 Union Place, where

J. R. Burnett,   ELM ROW AND LONDON ROAD, EDINBURGH   : Antigua St. Edinburgh.

9. A postcard of Elm Row, showing the door to the murder house at No. 2.

Rintoul and Shewan were taken into custody. The local newspapers were full of the Elm Row sensation: it was not every day that an Edinburgh police constable was murdered on duty. The 22-year-old George Low was a native of Tillyfourie near Alford, Aberdeenshire, where his parents were still alive; he had joined the Edinburgh police in 1877, and lived at Prince Albert Buildings, Dumbiedykes.

In June 1881, David Rintoul and John Henry Shewan stood trial for murder at the High Court of Edinburgh. Mr John Veitch was the owner of the grocery shop at 1 Elm Row, at the corner with London Road. The common stair of 2 Elm Row, leading to the dwelling houses above, was adjoining the shop. The policeman on the beat held a key to 2 Elm Row to be able to control the premises. John McIntoch, porter to Mr Veitch, said that he made it a habit to keep the door to the cellars, one of which belonged to the shop, securely locked. Thomas Pennycuick, baker and confectioner of 2 Elm Row, had a shop which also adjoined the common stair, with access to the cellar and bakehouse from a set of stairs inside the shop. James Aird, an apprentice plumber, lived at the top flat at 2 Elm Row with his father and family; he knew John Henry Shewan, who had often visited him there, and had manufactured a dagger and sheath for him. The sailor James Smith, grandfather of John Henry Shewan, had seen him go out in the evening of March 14, dressed in civilian attire; the following morning, he had been informed that his grandson was in custody for murdering a policeman. He identified a felt hat and a dagger and sheath left behind at the scene of crime as those belonging to his grandson. Several other people identified the chisel and dagger left behind as belonging to John Henry Shewan. Several people living at 2 Elm Row had heard a 'howling' from the basement, and the outcry 'Oh Good Lord!', before they heard the front door shut behind the two miscreants. Alexander and Agnes Rintoul both gave evidence in court, as did a police inspector who said that after being arrested, David Rintoul had said that Shewan had stabbed the police constable, and himself by mistake, before the two young sailors had escaped from 2 Elm Row.

10. The entrance to the Elm Row murder house today.

The jury was out for 43 minutes, before finding Rintoul guilty of assault and Shewan guilty of culpable homicide. Rintoul got away with just 18 months in prison, but his fellow sailor was sentenced to 15 years behind bars. After his release, David Rintoul became a house painter and married a woman named Alice Howie, but although the High Court had been lenient, the Grim Reaper stood ready to smite him: the wretched man died of tuberculosis in 1892, aged just 31. As for the creature Shewan, who had shown that he was a criminal worth reckoning with by his murderous exploits, there is nothing to suggest that he died in prison, or that he expired under his own name anywhere in Scotland or the United Kingdom; he may well have been 'exported' abroad to the colonies after serving his sentence, either to become a carefree 'Wild Colonial Boy' who robbed and stole with impunity until one day his number was up, or a gloomy Ancient Mariner who had to carry the Albatross of Murder around his neck until the day he died.[4] The murder house still stands and has barely changed since 1881.

THE STOCKBRIDGE BABY-FARMER, 1889

Jessie Kean was born on March 27 1861 in the Anderston district of Glasgow, the daughter of the illiterate cotton yarn warper James Kean and his wife Grace. She had two brothers named Peter and John. Her mother died when she was just 18 months old and her father expired when she was in her late teens. Her schooling was very defective and she would remain illiterate throughout her life. She became a mill worker for a while as a youngster, but hard work and honest toil did not agree with her. We next encounter her at the Magdalene Asylum, a home for fallen women in Edinburgh, where she was an inmate for 18 months and learnt the trade of a laundress. She worked in laundries in Glasgow and Edinburgh, but once more her natural indolence and fondness for the lads got her into trouble: this time, she was sent to prison for several months for concealment of pregnancy. A man named King, whose name she adopted, is likely to have played a part in her life at some stage or other, albeit not with any permanence.

Once out of prison in 1886, Jessie got a job as an ironer at a Causewayside laundry and moved into the house of the 56-year-old Thomas Pearson, a Glaswegian man of mystery who used three different names and did no work at all. The wreck of a man as the result of chronic alcoholism, he had once been a tobacco merchant, but now he led a vegetating existence; he had once been married to a certain Janet Baillie, but she had ceased to play any part in his miserable life. Instead, Pearson was cohabiting with an angry, jealous woman who called herself 'Mrs Taylor', who did not at all like Jessie joining the household. But in May 1887, Pearson and Jessie moved into 24 Dalkeith Road together, his other paramour having died mysteriously in the meantime. Later the same month, Jessie gave birth to a little daughter named Grace, who disappeared without trace soon after. Jessie and Pearson made it their business to take care of unwanted illegitimate children of unmarried women. They lived in the

11. *The Stockbridge Baby-Farmer at work,*
from the Illustrated Police News, March 2 1889.

Edinburgh slums, where children came and went without any
person taking much notice: from the Dalkeith Road lodgings,
they moved on to Ann's Court, Canonmills, and then to a room
in Cheyne Street, Stockbridge.

On October 26 1888, some boys were playing football
with a curious bundle they had found in Cheyne Street. One
of them had a look inside and found a dead baby. The police

were communicated with and the mummified baby taken to be examined by the pathologist Dr Henry Littlejohn: since the cause of death was wilful strangulation, the Stockbridge police had a case of child murder on their hands. The Cheyne Street plasterer James Banks became suspicious when he heard that a baby had been found murdered near his house. Four months ago, he had let a room to a couple calling themselves Mr and Mrs Macpherson, to whom babies had been mysteriously delivered more than once. When Inspector Clark visited 'Mrs Macpherson' alias Jessie Kean, and threatened to search the room and its coal closet, she screamed 'Get a cab! Take me to the police station! It is there! I did it!' And indeed, the shocked policeman found a dead baby girl inside the closet, as well as tell-tale signs that the other baby had been stored on the premises before being used as a football in Cheyne Street.

When the police detectives made a trawl of the babies 'farmed' by Jessie and Pearson, three definite instances of unmarried mothers giving babies over to them emerged; one of them was the baby found in the coal cellar, another the tiny corpse used as a football in Cheyne Street. The Dalkeith Road lodgings were searched and the floorboards lifted, but without any more corpses coming to light. There was also the matter of a dead baby that had been found inside a bonnet box at Abbeyhill Station. Jessie Kean was found guilty of child murder, sentenced to death, and executed in the Calton Jail on March 11 1889. She was the last woman to be hanged in Edinburgh. Squeamish people had suggested that it was 'not cricket' to execute a woman in these enlightened times, but a forthright Edinburgh fishwife, who had no sympathies for child murderesses, instead offered her services as executioner. The executioner Berry thought Jessie Kean had met her end with courage. Her little son Thomas Kean, the solitary infantine survivor from the Cheyne Street house of horrors, was given over to a Roman Catholic priest. When asked by a journalist whether he had used a new rope to execute the Stockbridge baby-farmer, Berry said 'Oh, dear, no. I have executed several with that rope. One good rope does a large number.'⁵

Today, feminist elements have expressed sympathy for the wretched Jessie Kean, a downtrodden woman who had been dealt such a poor hand of cards by the Almighty, being driven to murder by hunger and desperation. With some reason, they have questioned the role of the creature Pearson, who had been freed by Jessie's confession that she had been solely responsible for the murders, and who had acted as Queen's evidence against her just like Hare had done against Burke. After Jessie had been executed, Pearson moved back to Glasgow, where he died mysteriously from a fractured skull in 1890; did he fall over when drunk, or had some Edinburgh vigilante ended his career?

From the viewpoint of a murder house detective, the Jessie Kean case is a particularly difficult one. There is a 24 Dalkeith Road today, but I doubt whether this solid-looking tenement was there as early as 1887. Ann's Court, Canonmills, is no longer on the Edinburgh map. I have been to Cheyne Street, Stockbridge, not to kick a baby's corpse around as a football, but to have a look at the houses. One of the terraces remains from the time of Jessie Kean; the other has largely been demolished. Furthermore, the number of the Cheyne Street murder house was never disclosed in the media, meaning that the Stockbridge baby-farmer is not represented among the Murder Houses of Edinburgh.

WIFE MURDER IN CLARENCE STREET, 1890

The old soldier John Adamson had served with distinction in the Crimea and the Indian Mutiny, being awarded several medals and good conduct badges. He retired in 1875 and settled down in Edinburgh. After some years, he moved in with the widow Mary Turnbull in the tiny flat at 30a Clarence Street, two stories below the ground and consisting only of a kitchen and a small bed closet. The couple married in 1887 and Mary's son, the apprentice confectioner Malcolm Turnbull, was allowed to live with them in the flat. After receiving his quarterly pension, John Adamson used to go on a prolonged drinking binge. The tough old soldier lived peaceably when sober but beat and abused his wife and stepson when drunk.

On October 1 1890, John Adamson drew his pension and started drinking in his usual manner. A week later, his wife Mary sported two formidable black eyes. On October 10, the furious old soldier damned and blasted his stepson Malcolm in such a manner that the lad left the flat in disgust. The following day, when Malcolm returned to check on his mother, she was lying drunk in bed with a bruised cheek. John Adamson was sitting by the fire. Two other men were in the flat: the labourers Peter Reid and John Kelly, the latter of whom brought old Adamson two pint bottles of whisky. The following day, the washerwoman Sarah Webber, the neighbour of the Adamsons at 32a Clarence Street, was dismayed when John Adamson came lurching into her flat at 11 am, asking for whisky. When she said that she had none to give him, he looked quite morose and disappointed. He said that his wife was ill in bed and needed a drink to cheer her up. An hour later, he returned to Mrs Webber's flat, exclaiming "Will you come in and look at my wife for I think she is dead!" And indeed, Mary Adamson was lying motionless in bed. Another neighbourwoman, Miss Webber's married sister Mrs Margaret Dingwall, spotted blood on her abdomen and cried out "That woman is murdered!"

John Adamson changed his vest before going to fetch a doctor, but the suspicious Mrs Dingwall could see blood on his hand. But instead of going to Dr Murray's house at 1 Brandon Street, he went to see his brother-in-law, the night watchman Alexander Dingwall, asking for a pipe of tobacco. Puffing away at the pipe, he said that he was in trouble, and asked Dingwall to hide him away, but the night watchman had too much respect for the law to engage in such a criminal enterprise. John Adamson lurched back out into the mean New Town streets: we do not know what dark thoughts tormented his soul, or whether he pondered flight or self-destruction. Dingwall went to the Stockbridge police station, where Sergeant Joseph Gretton made haste to the murder flat, sending a constable to fetch Dr Littlejohn, of 24 Royal Circus. Detective officer Joseph Clark was alerted via the telephone that there had been a suspicious death in Clarence Street; as he was examining the body, John Adamson returned home. Officer Clark made sure that he was arrested and sent to the Stockbridge police station, and that the body was sent to the mortuary.

On trial for murdering his wife at the High Court of Edinburgh in November 1890, things did not look good for John Adamson. The autopsy had shown that Mary had died from a stab wound to the abdomen, injuring the liver. The wound matched a sharp knife with a white bone handle, which many people had seen at the Adamson flat. No other person had been in the flat at the time of the murder. Dr Henry Duncan Littlejohn described the medical evidence, declaring the knife to be a very likely instrument to have caused her death. John Adamson entered a plea of culpable homicide, which was accepted. As he was awaiting sentence, a *Scotsman* journalist visited the murder flat, a double sunk area two stories below ground level; was it strange that a person living under such miserable circumstances, a stone's throw from some of the finest houses in the New Town, had been driven to drink, desperation and murder? But Lord Young had no kind words for John Adamson when passing sentence, declaring that since leaving the army, his life had been a disgrace. Although his age and insobriety were taken into account, he would have to serve seven full years of penal servitude, and his army pension should be stopped. The prisoner received his sentence apparently unmoved.[6]

ANOTHER MURDER IN GEORGE STREET, 1894

In 1894, the 45-year-old Scotsman Donald Macdonald was employed as a messenger and caretaker at the Royal Insurance Company, situated at 13 George Street, to the immediate east of St Andrew's Church. A native of Greenock, he had been in Edinburgh for five or six years, working in various menial capacities; he had been at the insurance office for about 18 months, but no person knew much about him, due to his surly and taciturn nature. He lived in the caretaker's flat at the Royal Insurance Company, situated in the basement and approached through a sloping lane between the church and the insurance building; it had a door and a number of heavily barred windows looking out at the dustbins in this dismal yard. He shared this flat with his sister Miss Johana Macdonald, whose duties included keeping house for him and cleaning the insurance building.

On July 17 1894, the police was notified that Donald Macdonald had gone missing. Since he had been in trouble for stealing stamps from his employer, and recently given a week's notice after being suspected of stealing money, it was conjectured that he might have left Edinburgh to return to his home town, or even that he had committed suicide inside his flat. The constables picked the lock to gain entry to the basement flat at 13 George Street. The place was very dirty, the blinds of the windows all drawn, and the inside door between the offices and the flat had been securely locked. In the kitchen was a recess bed, on which a pair of ice-cold feet protruded from a pile of clothes, on top of which had been placed the wooden cover of a sewing machine. Suspecting that Donald Macdonald had destroyed himself by some stratagem or other, the constables called in a detective, and also the police surgeon Dr Littlejohn. But when the doctor removed the pile of clothes and the blanket from the bed, it was seen that it was Johana Macdonald who had been murdered: her head had been partially battered in, and her throat cut in a ghastly manner.

EDINBURGH: GEORGE STREET LOOKING EAST

12. A postcard showing George Street looking east, with the murder house at No. 13 in the left-hand terrace, behind the building with the pillars.

Once notified that there had been a murder right in the heart of Edinburgh's New Town, Chief Constable Henderson and Superintendent Bain came to see the murder flat. The bed and its walls were liberally sprinkled with blood. It was presumed that Johana Macdonald had been struck a series of heavy blows on the head, perhaps when she was soundly asleep in the bed, and that the murderer had then cut her throat with a formidable knife. There were no depositions to take from any witness, since the only living creature inside the murder flat was a light grey cat. The murder had probably taken place several days earlier, since the body was stiff as a plank and since there was some mould on the pool of blood underneath the bed. A few days earlier, when a woman had come asking for Miss Macdonald, her brother had brusquely told her that she was not at home. The obvious murder suspect was of course Donald Macdonald himself, since he had absconded from the flat without telling any person where he was going. Since the murder weapon was nowhere to be

13. The murder house at 13 George Street today.

found, he had probably taken the knife with him. In addition to being dismissed from his job on account of a suspected theft, he had led an irregular life for some time, being addicted to drinking chloral hydrate. A number of letters addressed to either of the Macdonalds were found inside the flat, but none of them contained any clue as to his present whereabouts.

A police advertisement poster was printed, reproducing a photograph of Donald Macdonald found in a box inside the flat, informing the readers that he was 45 years old, with dark hair turning slightly grey, a small moustache and a long reddish brown beard, an aquiline nose, regular features and a sallow complexion. His body was thick-set and his gait clumsy; he used to jerk his body and swing his arms a good deal when walking, and spoke with hesitancy. Since the photograph of him was reproduced in the *Edinburgh Evening Dispatch*, the police had high hopes that if he had remained in the Capital, he would shortly be tracked down due to his distinctive appearance. The problem was that the fugitive had quite a head start

*14. The tell-tale crest betraying the sinister origin
of the building at 13 George Street.*

on the police, having left the murder flat several days ago, quite possibly tramping in the direction of Glasgow. Although presumed to be a man of limited intellect, he had succeeded in committing the perfect murder, claiming his own sister as a victim without any discernible motive, and then successfully escaping from the police.

On July 19, there was an alarm in Carlisle, to the effect that a man answering the description of the murder suspect Donald Macdonald had been seen at St James' Vicarage, begging for relief. The Chief Constable ordered a thorough search of the town, without the fugitive being discovered. The following day, a Glasgow house-painter who knew Macdonald saw him at Glasgow Green. When aware that he had been recognized, the fugitive took off, leaving the detectives behind. The police were now aware that their man was in Glasgow, where soup-kitchens and lodging-houses were searched, and tramps and vagabonds rounded up. But early in the morning of July 25, a body was found in the Clyde by the assistant harbour master at the Queen's Dock. He made the body fast and called in the river police, who removed the corpse to the mortuary at Stobcross Quay. Since a brick was found in one of the man's pockets, and since a heavy piece of coal had been tied to his right arm with a handkerchief, it was concluded that he had committed suicide. His pockets contained, among other things, an Edinburgh time-table, a notebook with the names of several Edinburgh streets, and entries like 'Brown, against fire, 5s.', a quantity of stamps and a formidable-looking knife with coagulated blood and hair adhering to the blade. He did not possess any money at all, not even a penny. When an insurance clerk from 13 George Street, who had known Donald Macdonald well, was sent to Glasgow to see the corpse, he had no doubt in identifying it as that of the former caretaker, who had destroyed himself after being on the run for several days for murdering his sister.[7]

SHOCKING TRAGEDY IN A PRINCES STREET HOTEL, 1899

The young Peterhead man Charles Stephenson worked as a traveller for Messrs Baume & Co., wholesale watch manufacturers, of Hatton Gardens in London. He was a gloomy and taciturn fellow, although appreciated by his employers as an able and trustworthy servant. In early 1899, Charles Stephenson wanted to marry the 26-year-old Annie Mary Florence, another native of Peterhead, and he was accepted by her family as a promising suitor. In February, the couple travelled to Edinburgh to get married there, taking a room at the Central Hotel at 121 Princes Street. By her family, Miss Florence had been given a set of brand-new luggage, a fine dressing-case and a handsome umbrella bearing her monogram.

15. The western end of Princes Street, a postcard stamped and posted in 1914, although the image is older than that.

On Thursday February 16, Charles Stephenson and Annie Florence breakfasted together, before going out for a stroll and returning a few hours later. In the afternoon, the hotel staff became fearful that the couple had absconded from the hotel to avoid paying the bill. They knocked at the door but there was no answer. It was decided to break down the door, but "the servant who first entered the apartment rushed back in a state of alarm and consternation with the ghastly intelligence that a horrible tragedy had been committed", as the breathless and sensationalist *Illustrated Police News* informs us. On the blood-soaked bed were the lifeless bodies of Charles Stephenson and Annie Mary Florence, with their throats terribly cut. He had murdered her, before committing suicide.

Charles Stephenson's pocket-book contained a wedding ring and several letters, one of them addressed to 'someone in authority', with the words: "The end is near. Keep everything as quiet as possible; make no fuss, spare us newspaper publications.

SHOCKING TRAGEDY IN AN EDINBURGH HOTEL.
LOVERS DIE TOGETHER ON THE EVE OF MARRIAGE.

16. The dead couple are found in the Princes Street murder hotel, from the
Illustrated Police News, February 25 1899.

Trusting to receive the free pardon of all entailed in our troubles."
In Peterhead, where both the Stephenson and the Florence families
were well known, there was widespread grief. There was much
newspaper publicity about this seemingly motiveless murder and
suicide, although the name of the murder hotel was scrupulously
omitted.[8] The death certificate of Annie Mary Florence contains
the relevant address, however, but this historic murder hotel has
since been wantonly destroyed: the ghosts of Charles Stephenson
and Annie Mary Florence today have to walk the sterile corridors of
the newly constructed Premier Inn hotel, an ugly building if there
ever was one, and wholly unsuited to dignified old Princes Street.

MURDER IN CLARENCE STREET, 1902

17. *A portrait of
Andrew Nicoll,
from the Edinburgh
Evening News,
August 18 1902.*

Andrew Nicoll, an elderly man of
respectable appearance, lived at 16a
Clarence Street, Stockbridge, with his wife
Janet. They had a son named Andrew Jr
and a daughter named Jane, who had died
in 1901. Andrew Nicoll spent much of
his time drinking whisky in his damp and
miserable little basement flat and beat his
wife up with regularity. Andrew Jr used
to come round twice a week to make sure
all was well with his parents. Old Andrew
Nicoll was a strong and sturdy man,
whereas his wife was short and frail; she
was a gloomy woman, prematurely aged
and marked by many years of ill-treatment, and mourning her
prematurely deceased daughter bitterly.

On August 16 1902, Janet Nicoll went out shopping. Her
husband came home half an hour later, having drunk much

18. The dismal basement flat at 16A Clarence Street.

whisky. For no apparent motive, he kicked her out of the flat into the area shouting 'Out you go!' and proceeded to kick and stamp on her. A crowd of children was attracted by the heavy thuds of the kicks and the moaning of poor Mrs Nicoll; when they jeered and hooted at the assailant, he bounded up the stairs and chased them away. Police Constable Archibald McConechy was on patrol in Hamilton Place, when a little girl came up to him and said that a woman was being kicked in Clarence Street. The constable made haste to the scene, when the public-spirited girl pointed out Andrew Nicoll, who was walking away. Constable McConechy arrested the miscreant and took him back to 16a Clarence Street, where his wife was lying unconscious in the area. Detective John Brodie Craib came to the scene and made sure that the woman was taken to the Edinburgh Royal Infirmary, where she expired a few hours later. Andrew Nicoll said that he had punished his wife for behaving badly, and that she had been quite insane since her daughter had died.

On trial for murdering his wife at the High Court of Edinburgh, things were not looking good for Andrew Nicoll. Although quite venerable-looking, with a long beard and a bald head, he was clearly a brute of a man who had made his poor wife's life a misery for many years. Andrew Nicoll Jr had seen a crowd in front of the flat inhabited by his parents, and been told that his father had murdered his wife. Janet Nicoll had been 58 years old at the time of her death, and very feeble both mentally and bodily. A number of witnesses had seen Andrew Nicoll drag his wife out of the flat and kick and jump on her without mercy. One of the neighbours, who had helped her into the flat, had heard her exclaim 'I'm done for this time!' Constable McConechy described how he had apprehended the prisoner, and Detective John Brodie Craig told of his encounter with the wife-beating old man, finding traces of blood on his shoes, and bloodstains inside the flat. Dr Harvey Littlejohn testified that death was due to shock caused by direct violence to the ribs, lungs and other parts: six ribs were broken, and both lungs collapsed. Andrew Nicoll was found guilty of culpable homicide and sentenced to imprisonment for 20 years.[9]

A ROSE STREET HOUSE OF HORROR, 1917

Rose Street was built from 1770 until 1781 as a narrow, secondary street running between Princes and George Streets, from St Andrew's Square to Charlotte Square. It is today known for its many bars and pubs, and for the rowdy nightlife of those parts. But back in Victorian times, blood and not beer stained the Rose Street cobbles: a street for the poor, and home to various needy and desperate characters, it was several times visited by the fell spectre of Murder. In 1863, the chimney sweep Thomas Skirving beat his wife to death with a poker at 122 Rose Street; he was found guilty of murder and sentenced to imprisonment for life. Three years later, the retired sergeant major James Boyd was suspected of murdering his wife at 15 Rose Street. In 1882, a certain Mrs Gibson stood accused of murdering an old woman named Jessie Reid in the sunk flat at 43 Rose Street. In 1929, the picture frame finisher James Brown Marr was found guilty of the culpable homicide of Mary Ann Mills at 114 Rose Street North Lane, and sentenced to penal servitude for 12 years. The original three-story vernacular houses in Rose Street, much less grand than those in the surrounding streets, have been severely decimated by the passage of time and the construction of large and ungainly buildings wholly unsuited to the area. But although the four murder houses listed above are all gone, the main Rose Street house of horrors still frowns upon the passer-by ...

Joseph Wilmot was born in Oakham, Rutland, in 1889. He joined the army as a young man and served three years as a batman and waiter in the Royal Field Artillery, with an exemplary record, before being discharged in 1912 and becoming a miner in Cockenzie, East Lothian. Here he met Annie Grant, the daughter of a fellow miner, and married her in September 1912. They soon had a healthy son named William, born in Cockenzie in June 1913. At the outbreak of the Great War, Joseph Wilmot was called up as an army reservist, but he was found medically unfit for service. He instead became a fitter's labourer at the North British Railway and moved into the top flat at 120 Rose Street South Lane, consisting of three rooms, a kitchen, and two small lumber rooms. His second son Charles Wilmot was born here in December 1916. But by this time, all was not well with Joseph Wilmot's health. Although still a young man, he complained of unsteadiness on his legs and a feeling of paralysis. In February 1917, he had to give up his work, and was left with five shillings per month from the insurance company, not even enough to pay the rent. Since his wife nagged him and the children went hungry, he was becoming increasingly desperate.

19. The house of horrors at 120 Rose Street South Lane.

The butcher Duncan Forbes lived in the second flat at 120 Rose Street South Lane, just below the Wilmots. On May 28 1917, he heard a strange sound from above stairs, like if some person was walking about and breaking coal in the upper flat. The following day, Joseph Wilmot was nowhere to be seen, nor did his family stir. Two days later, when Constable Alexander Mackenzie was on patrol in Castle Street, Glasgow, Joseph Wilmot came up to him and said that he had murdered his wife and two sons in Edinburgh. He was taken to the police office, where he explained that he had hit Annie on the head with a hammer and cut her throat with a razor, before treating William in a similar manner and smashing the baby's skull in with the hammer. He carried an empty whisky bottle and smelt of drink, saying that he had intended to leap into the canal, but was worried that some person was watching him.

The Edinburgh detective officer Alexander Little received notice from Glasgow on May 30 that Joseph Wilmot had been captured. He went to 120 Rose Street South Lane, where he found the three bodies in a bloodbath; since there were no sign of a struggle, they had clearly been murdered in their sleep. Joseph Wilmot had written letters to his parents in Melton Mowbray, and to the Edinburgh police, telling them that he had murdered his wife and sons, and that his body would be found in a canal in Glasgow, but since he had never posted them, they were found in his pocket. On trial for murder at the High Court in August 1916, the defence council of Joseph Wilmot did not have a leg to stand on, since the prisoner stood convicted by his own admissions to the police. But Dr Harvey Littlejohn, professor of forensic medicine, who had carried out the autopsies on the three victims, had also examined the murderer himself. He found evidence that Joseph Wilmot was suffered from locomotor ataxia, a disagreeable disease of the spinal cord causing jerky and unsteady walking, that was sometimes a sign of tabes dorsalis caused by tertiary syphilis. He also considered that the Rose Street desperado had not been of sound mind when he murdered his wife and sons, and the court followed his advice: Joseph Wilmot was found guilty of murder but insane at the time, and was ordered to be detained during the King's pleasure. He died at the Lunatic Department of HM Prison Perth on September 10 1926, aged just 36, from disseminated [multiple] sclerosis and asthenia according to his death certificate.[10]

THE LETHAL ABORTIONIST OF
EYRE PLACE, 1919

In 1919, the young South African medical student John Moir du Toit was active at Edinburgh University. He had a girlfriend,

20. The former home of the lethal abortionist of Eyre Place.

the 23-year-old typist Mona Dunn, and in June 1919 there were signs that she was pregnant with their child. John du Toit had no intention of marrying her and she did not want to keep the child. He suggested that she should see a doctor discretely, but it turned out that she had been introduced to a woman who offered to carry out the abortion, Nan Main of 3 Eyre Place. John du Toit was not happy that the abortion would be performed by a person who entirely lacked any medical education, but still he went along with Mona to a pharmacy, where they bought various items the Eyre Place abortionist said she needed for the operation.

On June 18, Mona Dunn came to 3 Eyre Place to have her abortion, but Nan Main bungled the procedure badly, and her patient quickly bled to death. The abortionist was arrested by the police and charged with murder, in accordance with the law of the period. Standing trial at the High Court in September 1919, Nan Main pleaded not guilty. Mona's father, the butcher James Dunn, said that he had not known that she was pregnant when she took two weeks off work in mid-June. John Moir du Toit denied ever promising to marry Mona, although admitting that he had been very friendly with her. They had once spent the night in the same house, as he expressed it. He had told her that the abortion was a dangerous procedure, which should not be performed by a layperson, but she had begged him to come with her to the pharmacy and purchase the supplies needed. He had afterwards heard that Mona had died.

The medical evidence spoke in favour of death being due to a bungled abortion; it had not been a spontaneous haemorrhage. It was rightly considered culpable that Nan Main had made no attempt to call a doctor, or an ambulance, to 3 Eyre Place. Miss Anne Smith, a woman staying in the same house as Nan Main, said that Mona Dunn had made a friendly call at 3 Eyre Place, when she suddenly complained of feeling very sick. She was taken to the bedroom, where Nan Main brought her some hot water. Anne Smith had not seen any suspicious-looking instrument in the bedroom. She had walked out to escort an old woman home, and when she returned, Nan Main told her that Mona had just died. Lord Scott Dickson asked the jury if they believed that the deceased had come to Eyre Place for an illegal operation, and that instruments had been kept there on purpose, or if they believed the version told by the defence, namely that Mona Dunn had died from a haemorrhage brought on by violent sickness and natural consequences. The jury was out for ten minutes before returning a verdict of culpable homicide, and Nan Main was sentenced to imprisonment for five years. She was not the only bungling abortionist in Edinburgh, but she will represent them all in this book.[11]

INFANTICIDE IN SCOTLAND STREET, 1920

Marion Stone was born on April 28 1897, as a daughter of the West Calder miner Robert Stone and his wife Jane. After rudimentary schooling, she went into Edinburgh to become a domestic servant. In early 1920, when she was 23 years old, she was working for the egg merchant Mr John Wightman and his wife Helen, of 16 Scotland Street in the heart of the New Town. Mr Wightman was very satisfied with her service and planned to employ her long-term.

But by this time, Marion had got into serious trouble. She had enjoyed an affair with a man from Shotts, but after she had become pregnant, he had said that he was not the father and she could do what the hell she liked with the baby. This uncouth recommendation appears to have been carried out almost to the letter. At 8 am on April 24 1920, Mr Wightman saw Marion hiding in the coal cellar. With her was a newly born baby girl with considerable bruising around the throat and neck. Mrs Wightman telephoned for a doctor and Marion was taken to hospital, but since the post-mortem on the baby indicated that it had been suffocated to death, she was indicted for murdering her child the very same day.

On trial for infanticide at the High Court of Edinburgh on July 19 1920, Marion Stone was ably defended by Mr Chisholm QC. She pleaded not guilty to killing the child, claiming that she had done nothing to it after it had been born. She told her pathetic story about the wicked man who had deceived her and cast her aside. Since no person had witnessed the unsavoury proceedings in the Scotland Street coal cellar, the medical evidence was of primary importance. Professor Harvey Littlejohn testified that death had been due to suffocation produced by manual constriction of the throat, but under cross-examination from the clever Mr Chisholm, he could not rule out, with absolute certainty, that the marks on the throat had been caused by the wretched woman's

21. The murder house at 16 Scotland Street.

efforts to deliver herself. The jury, which sympathised with the woman at the bar, unanimously returned a verdict of not guilty, and Marion Stone left court in triumph, although the applause from the audience were instantly suppressed.[12]

After her fortunate reprieve in 1920, Marion Stone's life returned to normality: she did not murder any more defenceless little babies, or adults for that matter. She married the coal miner Joseph McBirnie and moved to Lanarkshire to lead a humdrum life for many years, surviving her husband and parents before suddenly falling ill in 1969 and dying from a 'cardiac collapse' at the Law Hospital, Carluke.

THE BUCKINGHAM TERRACE MATRICIDE, 1926

John Donald Merrett was born in New Zealand in 1908, the son of the consulting engineer John Alfred Merrett and his wife Bertha. His parents split up before the Great War: John Alfred went to work in Russia for a while, but Bertha went to Switzerland to nurse wounded British officers, taking her son with her. John Donald attended a good school in New Zealand, where he excelled in modern languages and became a champion boxer, before he finished his education at Malvern College in Worcestershire, once more doing well and excelling as a pugilist. Mrs Merrett took the first-floor flat at 31 Buckingham Terrace in Edinburgh's New Town, sharing it with her son who had registered on a Master of Arts degree course at Edinburgh University. John Donald had been kept in tight reins at his schools, without getting any opportunity to do mischief, but the temptations of the Edinburgh night life soon became too much for him. He liked dancing at various clubs, drinking and carousing with various attractive but expensive 'hostesses', making his escape from the family flat through jumping down from the small cast iron balcony just outside his bedroom. His mother became aware that he was neglecting his studies and getting into debt, something that displeased her, although her relations with her son remained good on the surface.

On March 17 1926, Bertha Merrett was sitting in the front sitting-room at 31 Buckingham Terrace, with her son. The daily help, Mrs Henrietta Sutherland, was busy in the kitchen, when she suddenly heard the report of a gun. A few seconds later, the 18-year-old John Donald came into the kitchen, calmly saying 'Rita, my mother has shot herself!' And indeed, the startled domestic got the impression that Mrs Merrett had just attempted to destroy herself. John Donald just stood around uselessly, making no effort to make his mother comfortable, until Police Constables David Izatt and Thomas Gray Middlemiss arrived on the scene. From the beginning, both of them seemed to take the suicide scenario for granted. When Izatt asked whether Mrs Merrett had shot herself because of financial troubles, John Donald said that she had in fact been well off. Izatt found it odd that he was just standing about when his mother was writhing in agony on the floor. They all went to the hospital, where Middlemiss again asked John Donald why he thought his mother had tried to commit suicide. "Money matters" the suave lad answered. "What do you mean by 'money matters' – too much or too little?" "No, just money matters." The obtuse policeman made no further questions.

Poor Mrs Merrett was taken to the Royal Infirmary, where she was held as a prisoner charged with attempting suicide. She gradually recovered consciousness but remained very weak, with paralysis of the left side of the body. When asked by one of the nurses whether she had had a pistol handy when sitting in her flat, she answered in the negative. Her son had been standing beside her, she remembered, waiting to go and post the letter she had been writing. But John Donald remained cool, calm and collected: no person could discern any motive for him to murder his mother, and he had given several people the impression that he had been quite fond of her. Moreover, the policework in the case had been scandalously incompetent, from the start. No person had bothered to examine the flat or to collect and catalogue the evidence there; the letter Mrs Merrett had been writing was discarded, and the discharged cartridge case lost; since no fingerprints had been dusted for, it could not be established who had held the pistol when it was fired.

22. *Poor Mrs Merrett in happier days, from W. Roughead, Trial of John Donald Merrett (Edinburgh 1929).*

23. John Donald Merrett at the time of his trial, from W. Roughead, Trial of John Donald Merrett (Edinburgh 1929).

Mrs Merrett died from meningitis secondary to her injuries on April 1 and was buried at Piershill Cemetery.

The distinguished Edinburgh forensic pathologist Professor Harvey Littlejohn, who had initially supported the suicide hypothesis, was getting second thoughts as he pondered the details of the case, however. There had been another person in the room, namely Bertha Merrett's son John Donald, and although he seemed a benign presence on the surface, nobody knew for sure what he might have been capable of. Professor Littlejohn consulted his Glasgow colleague Professor John Glaister and made an ambitious series of experiments firing the pistol used in the shooting, loaded with identical bullets, at cardboard or at human skin, to observe the amount of powder marks. There had been none on the skin of Mrs Merrett. But Professor Littlejohn found that if the weapon was fired less than three inches from the skin, there were clear powder marks. This indicated that the bullet that killed Mrs Merrett had been fired from some distance, by another person. Since there was consensus that John Donald had been the only other person in the room, he became the prime

24. *The murder house in 1929, from W. Roughead, Trial of John Donald Merrett (Edinburgh 1929).*

25. *The murder weapon, and a court sketch of the murder room, from W. Roughead,* Trial of John Donald Merrett *(Edinburgh 1929). Mrs Merrett's bureau found its way into Roughead's criminal museum.*

murder suspect. After it had been discovered that he had been forging his mother's signature on cheques for large amounts of money, he was arrested and charged with murder.

It was clear to young Merrett's legal team that things were looking far from good for him, and that they must employ a crack team of forensic witnesses to shake the findings of Littlejohn and Glaister. Their choice was a good one: the eminent pathologist Bernard Spilsbury and the experienced London gunsmith Robert Churchill. Defended by the eloquent Craigie Aitchison, John Donald made a favourable impression in court, although there was good evidence that he had been forging his mother's cheques.

But had he also murdered her to prevent her from discovering his serial frauds? Spilsbury and Churchill had made experiments of their own, however, with results directly contradicting those of Littlejohn and Glaister: the lack of powder marks did not rule out that the show had been fired at close range, by Mrs Merrett herself. Handled skilfully by Craigie Aitchison, these two managed to obscure the matter of the medical evidence, planting doubt in the minds of the jurymen. The verdict in the murder trial was 'not proven', but for the cheque forgeries, John Donald was sentenced to be imprisoned for 12 months. The legal luminaries and forensic experts helped themselves to some generous fees from the money held in trust for John Donald after the death of his grandfather, congratulating themselves that they had saved their client from a dire fate indeed. Many independent observers, not the least of whom the distinguished Edinburgh criminologist William Roughead, believed that a murderer had evaded justice thanks to the quality of his defence team.

John Donald Merrett was released from prison in October 1927. He left Edinburgh with rapidity and changed his name to Ronald John Chesney, apparently without any person having a clue as to his real identity. After once more spending time in prison after being caught for a cheque forgery, he married the heiress Isobel Bonar in January 1929. Later the same year, he came into the legacy from his grandfather, enough money to keep him going for many years to come. The Buckingham Terrace Matricide led a comfortable life, eating and drinking well, and becoming a useful yachtsman. In 1940, he became a temporary Lieutenant RN, leaving his wife and mother-in-law to run an old people's home in Ealing, West London, as he went on to serve afloat on various small craft, not without distinction. After the fall of Tobruk in 1942, he was captured and taken to an Italian prisoner of war camp, making three attempts to escape before being repatriated in March 1943. He returned to sea and served for the remainder of the war, being promoted to temporary Lieutenant Commander but not winning any medal for gallantry.

After the war, Chesney served on as a naval officer in Germany. Having tired of his wife, he enjoyed affairs with various German floozies. After his discharge from the Royal Navy, he became a professional smuggler, initially with some success, although he was later caught and sent to prison more than once. In 1954, he got the idea to murder his estranged wife to claim the inheritance money, something that would also enable him to marry his German girlfriend. He clandestinely travelled to the old people's home at 22 Montpelier Road, Ealing, entered through a back window, and sneaked up to the bedroom where Mrs Isobel Chesney was lying in bed drunk. He seized hold of her with a hearty goodwill, dragged her to the bathroom and drowned her in the bath, cunningly putting some soap in her hair to make it appear that she had suffered an accident falling over in her cups.

After stealthily sneaking downstairs, he was dismayed to be confronted in the hall by the old mother-in-law, who of course recognized the hulking cad her daughter had been unwise enough to marry. But Chesney seized hold of a heavy coffee pot and whacked the old woman about the head until she was well-nigh dead, before murdering her through strangulation. Chesney successfully fled the country after committing the double murder, but he realized that he was a hunted man and that his luck was running out with rapidity. Back in Germany, he blew out his brains with the pistol he always carried. When the London detectives asked for evidence that the flesh from underneath the fingernails of the mother-in-law, who had fought for her life with desperation, matched the injuries to the arms of the suicide, the Germans cut off both his arms and sent them to London for examination; the injuries were a perfect match, and the arms are still kept at Scotland Yard's Black Museum. But for the Buckingham Terrace murder house in Edinburgh, which still stands in good order, these gory relics are the only remainders of a strange and wasted life wantonly saved back in 1927, only for two other innocent women to suffer at the hands of the callous murderer.[13]

26. The Merrett murder house today.

MURDER IN REGENT TERRACE, 1927

Jeanie Ross Holden was born in March 1892, daughter of the Blackburn cotton manufacturer George Pickup Holden and his wife Annie. She made an advantageous marriage in 1915, to Lieutenant Richard James Paget, of the Canadian Army. He was a commission agent in civilian life and came from quite a wealthy and distinguished old English family. They had the son Richard Holden Paget, born in Bromsgrove in 1920, but the couple divorced in 1923.

In the years following her divorce, the life of Jeanie Ross Paget steadily went downhill. Her mental health left much to be desired and she became a drug addict. In August 1927, she and her little son visited a family friend, Lieutenant Commander John Henry Jauncey, who lived in the comfortable house at 30 Regent Terrace, in Edinburgh's fashionable Eastern New Town. On August 11, she was going to give Richard a bath, but Commander Jauncey and his wife noticed that she was absent for some considerable time. She eventually emerged from the bathroom, in a state of collapse, having just drowned her little son in the bath.

Jeanie Ross Paget was arrested by the police and placed in the Royal Edinburgh Asylum in Morningside Drive. On October 21, she was brought before the Edinburgh Sheriff's Court to be formally charged with murder. Described as a tall woman with bobbed hair, she was dressed very quietly. She fainted just as the court officer opened the gate of the dock, but was caught just in time by this official, and suffered no injury. On October 31, when she stood trial for murder at the High Court of Edinburgh, the defence lodged a plea that the prisoner was insane and incapable of pleading to the indictment, and also insane at the date of the commission of the alleged crime.

The medical witnesses, Professor George Matthew Robinson and Dr William McAlister, who had examined Mrs Paget at

27. 30 Regent Terrace.

the asylum, were both of the opinion that she was insane and irresponsible for her actions. She had no desire to injure her son, but had been driven to murdering him by insane delusions and forebodings as to his future. The Lord Justice-Clerk ordered that she should be kept in strict custody until His Majesty's pleasure be known.[14] It is not known how long this was, but we know that Jeanie Ross Paget died at Gillespie Crescent, Edinburgh, in 1981 aged 89, from deep vein thrombosis and pulmonary embolism according to her death certificate. Commander Jauncey, the owner of the Regent Terrace murder house, went on to enjoy a distinguished wartime career, becoming a Captain RN and winning the DSO and Bar.

MURDER IN ST STEPHEN STREET, 1953

In 1953, the 60-year-old railway greaser William Wilson Smith lived at 97a St Stephen Street with his wife Elizabeth. The couple had one adult son alive, and she also had another son from a previous relationship. William Smith was a decent, hard-working man, and normally on good terms with his wife, but unfortunately, both of them had a great fondness for drinking beer and gin. When intoxicated, they were both angry and argumentative, although there had not been any serious fighting between them prior to September 12 1953. That day, William Smith had been out drinking at various public houses from noon until 3pm. He then reeled home to his basement flat in St Stephen Street, to be welcomed by his termagant wife, who had also been out on an early afternoon pub crawl. An angry quarrel ended with him seizing hold of her throat and strangling her to death.

As soon as he realized what he had just done, William Smith went to a police box nearby, and was promptly taken into custody.

28. A postcard showing St Stephen Street.

On November 20, he was committed for trial at the High Court, and when the trial began 10 days later, he pleaded not guilty to murder, but guilty to culpable homicide. His legal counsel pointed out the heavy drinking by both parties and argued that there had not been any premeditated intent to kill. Both the son and the stepson of the accused had gone to see him in prison, and both were convinced there was no motive for him to deliberately murder his wife. Smith claimed to have no recollection at all of the events of September 12, and this was accepted by two medical specialists. Lord Thomson, the Lord Justice Clerk, sentenced William Smith to six years in prison for culpable homicide, perhaps a salomonic compromise given the circumstances of the killing.[15]

THE MONSTER OF
MARSHALL'S COURT, 1953

On December 11 1953, everything seemed normal in the crowded slum tenements off Greenside Row, situated not far from the fashionable, brightly-lit Leith Street. The little girls Lesley Sinclair, aged four years and a half, and Margaret Johnston, aged three, went out to play at three in the afternoon, near Lesley's family home at 5 Marshall's Court. At shortly after five, they were nowhere to be seen, so Lesley's mother mobilized the neighbours to look for them. She knew that her husband John Sinclair was in the local pub having a pint and went to fetch him there. Another drinker in the pub, the unemployed Irishman John 'Paddy' Lynch, a native of Dublin, offered to buy her a port and lemon to help her calm down, since he saw that she was beside herself with worry. Keen to look for her little girl, she turned his offer down. Himself, Lynch had another drink before joining the search party.

29. The remaining rump of Marshall's Court, photographed in 2009.

The search for Lesley and Margaret went on for five hours without the girls being found. But when a woman broke down the door to the communal toilet at 5 Marshall's Court, the two girls were found in there, severely beaten and quite dead. The woman gave a terrible scream and a large crowd gathered, aghast at what they were seeing. An autopsy later showed that they had been strangled to death, and that Lesley had been raped by the murderer. John Lynch uttered dire threats against the child murderers, promising to find and kill them. He reeled about the murder scene and interrupted the police with his ramblings, exclaiming "Take my name! I'll show you how it was done" His unbalanced behaviour caught the attention of the police, who decided to keep a watch on the flat where he lived at 5 Marshall's Court, with his common-law wife, the kitchen-maid Annie Hall. When the police came calling at just after 2 am, intent on questioning Lynch about his activities the previous evening, he called out, in a frenzy, "Take me! I did it!" The police did just that, and his flat was thoroughly searched for technical evidence.

The trial of John Lynch opened at the High Court of Edinburgh on March 23 1954, before Lord Thomson. John Lynch's neighbour at the top floor of 5 Marshall's Court had heard him talking to himself in the stairs at around 5 pm the day of the murder, and she had also heard the lavatory door slam shut. Horsehair of the kind used to stuff mattresses was found on the clothing of both girls, on the clothes of Lynch, and in his flat. Hairs from both girls were found on Lynch's clothes, and there were stains of blood and vomit on his shirt sleeve. It was presumed that Lynch had invited the two girls into his flat some time after 3.10 pm, when they had last been seen, raping Lesley and murdering both of them, before dumping them in the lavatory around 5 pm and jamming the door. The jury was out for 55 minutes before returning a unanimous verdict of guilty to murder, Lord Thomson sentenced Lynch to death, and he was hanged at Saughton Prison on April 23 1954.[16]

There was still a Marshall's Court in 2002, when newspaper criminologist Sandra Dick came calling, although only 1-3 Marshall Court remained, the other two houses having been flattened for the construction of a car park. When I went murder house detecting the following year, the three sad-looking, neglected houses were still there, a memorial of a sordid and brutal double murder in the heart of Edinburgh; today they no longer stand, and few must be missing them.

THE STOCKBRIDGE STABBING, 1964

The 47-year-old joiner Jack Murray lived alone in the rented top flat at 8 Cumberland Street, Stockbridge. He was living apart from his wife and two children. He kept very much to himself and was known to like drinking whisky. On March 7 1964, Jack Murray was found dead in his flat: he had been stabbed 39 times, and the murder room resembled a slaughterhouse. The Edinburgh City Police murder squad was soon on the premises, amidst much local uproar, and started making inquiries in its usual effective manner. Murray had been alive at a quarter to midnight on March 6, when he had been observed parking his Lambretta scooter in Cumberland Street South Lane. A number of sightings of mysterious men had been made in the early hours of March 7, in Cumberland Street and its vicinity. One of them turned out to be the 21-year-old meat porter William Martin Campbell, of no fixed address.

When Campbell was taken into custody by Chief Inspector Reid at a public house in Jamaica Street, he freely admitted that Murray had invited him to call at his flat for a drink or two. He had come knocking in the evening of March 6, when Murray was away, and again at midnight, when Murray had just returned home. The joiner was pleased to see his young friend, but as they sat drinking whisky together, he made homosexual advances to the younger man. When Campbell angrily stood up and asked him to 'cut it out', Murray seized up some object and aimed to hit him on the head. He had the 'walked into' the knife that Campbell had pulled up to protect himself.

William Martin Campbell was arrested and charged with murder. When he was on trial at the High Court on June 16, he pleaded not guilty with a special plea of self-defence, but things were not looking good for him. The object seized up by Murray had in fact been a hot water bottle made of rubber, and the medical evidence spoke in favour of a ferocious assault. Campbell was found guilty of murder and sentenced to imprisonment for life.[17]

CUMBERLAND STREET AGAIN, 1967

In 1967, the young office workers Marion Ward and June Briggs shared a flat at 68 Cumberland Street, Stockbridge, with another girl. On February 3, when their respective boyfriends Graham Strachan and Ian McLaren came to visit, Marion was making them all some tea when there was suddenly a hard knock on the door. It was the two young hooligans Billy Capener and Brian Hand, who held a grudge against the two boys inside the flat. The apprehensive McLaren seized up a poker, and all four went to the door, hoping to dissuade the two hooligans from forcing an entry. McLaren and Capener exchanged threats through the letterbox, and the excited Brian Hand shouted that they should have a fight there and then, in the street.

All of a sudden, Capener and Hand kicked the door hard; it burst open, and they came bounding into the flat. When Capener gave Strachan a hard punch to the side of the face, knocking him down, Marion Ward ran into the bedroom to take cover. Capener then seized hold of McLaren's arms, as Hand punched him. All of a sudden, Hand came reeling into the bedroom, exclaiming that he had been stabbed, before falling down. Since he was of a 'horrible white colour', Marion suggested that a doctor should be called, but when this eventually happened, Brian Hand was already dead.

The 17-year-old cooper Ian McLaren was arrested by the police and charged with murdering the 16-year-old Brian Hand. Although not all of the legal fraternity were convinced that this was really a case of murder, McLaren had to stand his trial at the High Court, before Lord Robertson. He pleaded not guilty and lodged a special plea of self-defence. The prosecution called 35 witnesses. The dead boy's father, Mr Owen Hand, wept as he gave his evidence, saying that Brian had left school at 15, to become a warehouse assistant. Marion Ward gave a blow-by-blow account of the fight inside the flat, although she had

30. The murder house at 68 Cumberland Street.

not seen Hand being killed. Ian McLaren said in evidence that the stabbing was accidental. He had dropped the poker when Capener seized hold of him, and Hand punched him hard in the face. He had then managed to get free, and seeing three knives on the floor, he had grasped one of them. Capener pushed him hard against Hand, who then seemed to collapse, exclaiming 'I don't want to die!' McLaren then explained how he had taken the knife into the kitchen, cleaned it and put it back in a drawer, before going for help to the dying boy. The jury was out for an hour and a half, before returning a verdict of not guilty, and Ian McLaren was discharged.[18]

MURDER IN MONTGOMERY STREET, 1967

The 53-year-old Miss Mary Rennie lived in the ground floor flat at 9 Montgomery Street, off Leith Walk. She worked as a clerkess at the Edinburgh Royal Infirmary, and also as a waitress at the Ristorante Luna in Elm Row three nights per week. She was a quiet, hard-working woman, who had four sisters and a brother alive. She sometimes bought chips at the fish shop at 5 Montgomery Street, but never stopped to chat. On Thursday January 26 1967, when Mary Rennie's sister Mrs Morna Durrand came to call, she found her lying dead on the floor.

When the CID officers came to take possession of the murder flat, they found that a basement window had been broken, indicating that the murderer had entered the flat by that route. Miss Rennie's rings were missing, indicating that the murderous burglar had stolen them. After an ambitious police investigation, aimed to find sightings of the murder victim returning home from work, and of suspicious-looking men loitering in the street, the 38-year-old scaffolder William Bannon was identified as the main suspect. He had a formidable police record: 14 previous convictions, five of them for violent crime. At the High Court, he pleaded guilty to murdering Mary Rennie and stealing her effects, and he was sentenced to imprisonment for life.[19] In December 1968, he was again on trial for three assaults on the prison officers at Perth Prison, and sentenced to 18 more months in prison, to take effect from the date of his release.[20]

BODY IN THE BATH AT THISTLE STREET, 1968

The 25-year-old Edinburgh salesman John Albert Hope lived with his parents at 8 Beaverbank Place. On January 17 1967, when he disappeared without trace, his mother called in the police.

31. The murder house at 62 Thistle Street.

Hope was allegedly spotted around the city more than once by people who thought they knew him, but the police were unable to track him down. His parents were fearing for the worst and became increasingly distraught as the weeks and months went by with no news forthcoming.

On June 18 1968, the 35-year-old wire weaver George King telephoned his brother, saying that he wanted to confess to a terrible secret he had been hiding for many months. On January 17 1967, he had been lying in wait, in his attic flat above an antiques shop at 62 Thistle Street, to catch the man with whom his wife Colette was having an affair. Without warning, he had bounded into the living room and confronted the guilty pair. Infuriated when the man had tried to ignore him, he had knocked him down and strangled him to death with a belt. He had then dismembered the body into little pieces, which he put in an old zinc bath in the flat's spare bedroom.

George King did his best to continue his life as well as he could, having disguised the door to the spare bedroom by putting a couple of heavy bookcases in front of it. After Mrs King had left him and taken their three children with her, George was sitting alone in the rather smelly flat, pondering what he had accomplished, until one day he became desperate and telephoned his brother. Having listened to this extraordinary story, the brother persuaded George to give himself up to the police: he was taken into custody, and the dismembered body in the bath at 62 Thistle Street identified as that of John Albert Hope, who had disappeared back in January the previous year. For a while, the police suspected that the homicidal George King had murdered his wife and children as well, but they were found alive and well, having taken refuge in Leeds.

As he faced trial for murder at the High Court in September 1968, the previous life of George King was recapitulated. He was a former member of the Leith Corps of the Salvation Army, and a valued and reliable labouring man at the Granton Wire Works. A rather taciturn, moody fellow, he had never had much to do with his workmates there, but he had always done his work to the satisfaction of his superiors. Nor had he ever committed any crime before that awful glut in the Thistle Street attic flat. After pleading guilty to the murder of John Albert Hope, George King was sentenced to imprisonment for life.[21]

THE ROYAL BRITISH HOTEL IS ON FIRE! 1971

The Royal British Hotel in the Princes Street has a favourable position: it is one of the first buildings people see after ascending the Waverley Steps. Back in the 1970s, the Royal British Hotel had a very different kind of notoriety, however: it was Edinburgh's leading 'murder hotel'!

In May 1971, when there was a staff shortage in the kitchen at the Royal British Hotel, the 25-year-old Glaswegian chef Robert Collins Docherty was given temporary employment there. He had only been on the premises for two days when there was a suspicious fire near the hotel's rear fire escape. The following day, there was a full-scale fire in the old hotel; although the staff led the guests away to safety, the 49-year-old Glasgow resident Mrs Margaret Bowman was overcome by the fire and smoke, and died in her hotel room. Since Robert Collins Docherty had been behaving suspiciously nearby, he was arrested by the police before being released on bail.

The Edinburgh detectives were cheered to find that Docherty was wanted by their Glasgow colleagues, on a charge of fraud; after standing trial there, he was sentenced to 18 months in prison. He was thus a prisoner at Barlinnie when sent to the High Court of Edinburgh in March 1972, for trial on three charges of starting fires, one of which had resulted in the culpable homicide of a hotel guest. Docherty pleaded not guilty to all charges. While in police custody, he had admitted starting the small fire on the premises, although he said that the big fire had not been intentional: he had carelessly thrown a lighted cigarette in a box full of rubbish in an empty room. A firemaster testified that in his opinion, the fire had been deliberately started, however, and the jury found Docherty guilty of arson and culpable homicide. Lord Grant said that this had been a reckless, wicked and wilful act, and sentenced him to imprisonment for nine years, adding that he had been fortunate to escape a more serious charge. Docherty served his time and never did anything newsworthy again; he may well still be alive today.[22]

THE ROYAL BRITISH HOTEL AGAIN, 1977

The 25-year-old Irishman John Dwyer worked as 'house father' at the Madonna House children's home at Blackrock just outside Dublin. He took his work seriously, and was a valued member of staff, who was never accused of any wrongdoings, paedophilia included. In May 1974, the young Irish lad Tommy Hayden was placed in the home, along with his two brothers, after allegations of neglect and ill-treatment by their mother. John Dwyer became very fond of young Tommy, and the mischievous young lad used to tell the other attendants at the children's home that they would be reported to the 'house father' if they punished him. Tommy was a very naughty boy, however, and in 1977 he was transferred to St Kieran's Children's Home in Rathdrum, Co. Wicklow, a stricter institution that had the resources to discipline recalcitrant youngsters. Tommy was very unhappy here, and it did not take long before he escaped and travelled all the way back to Dublin to see his great friend John Dwyer.

John Dwyer, an awkward-looking, long-haired character according to his newspaper photograph, was greatly affected by his young friend's account of his miserable life at the strict Rathdrum children's home. But Tommy, who was just nine years old, told him that if in the future he might bust out of the home once more, they could escape together. Dwyer thought this an excellent idea: he sold his car for £1000 and made plans to go to London with his young friend. When Tommy again escaped from the children's home and came to Dublin, Dwyer booked tickets for them to go to London as father and son; they took a room at the Post House Hotel at Heathrow Airport, under the names John and Thomas Dwyer. Fearful that the police would track him down, the child-abducting Irishman moved hotels twice, before deciding that London was too hot for him: to put their imagined pursuers off the track, they travelled to Edinburgh by train and took a room at the King James Hotel under the name Delaney.

Telephone No.: 26086

20 Princes Street.

Edinburgh .... 192 ...

ROYAL BRITISH HOTEL

32. An old postcard showing the Royal British Hotel.

The timid John Dwyer was becoming fearful and despondent, however: he regretted this foolhardy escapade, which would surely end his career within the Irish child care system, and land him in prison as a kidnapper. They changed hotels once more, this time moving into Room 117 at the Royal British Hotel near Waverley Station, the leading murder hotel of Princes Street. By this time, the creature Dwyer was a nervous wreck, fearful of the police and journalists, and despairing of ever finding a job, or a flat, among the hostile Scots. In the end, the desperate Irishman put a 'Do Not Disturb' sign on the door and drowned Tommy in the bath. He then went to inform the hotel deputy manager that his 'son' had perished in a bathing accident, but the hotel doctor saw that Tommy had in fact been murdered and called in the police. Dwyer told the detectives that his young friend had died accidentally when they had 'played' in the bathroom, and that he himself had taken an overdose of some unspecified medicine to commit suicide, but they did not believe him.

It turned out that nobody had missed Tommy at the St

33. The Royal British Hotel today.

Kieran's Children's Home, a strange and blameworthy state of affairs, since the boy had after all been gone for nearly three weeks. Thus the creature Dwyer had no foundation at all for his craven fear of the Irish police and newspaper journalists, but his rash and foolhardy deed was done, and poor Tommy would never return to the Irish child care system. On trial for murder at the High Court of Edinburgh in December 1977, John Dwyer pleaded not guilty, but the evidence against him was overwhelming. The jury found him guilty of murder, and Lord Stewart, who rightly described the case as a 'strange and tragic story', sentenced him to imprisonment for life.[23] No person appears to have mentioned the word 'paedophile' during the trial, but today we are aware that in the 1970s, the Irish child care system employed a variety of unsavoury types who preyed upon the vulnerable children. Although his contemporaries thought him just foolish and muddled, there might well have been a dark secret behind this remarkable escapade, which ended in the bathroom of Room 117 at the Royal British Hotel. After its unwanted notoriety in the 1970s, the hotel has been murder free, and it is still operational today.

MURDER AT THE ST VINCENT WINE BAR, 1982

At 11.30 pm on April 4 1982, the St Vincent Wine Bar at 9 St Vincent Street was closing down for the day. Three of the four barmen were busy clearing up the premises, as the fourth of them, the 40-year-old male nurse Ron Lockhart, was playing a fruit machine. All of a sudden, two masked men came bursting into the wine bar through the side entrance, brandishing sawn-off shotguns. They struck one of the barmen on the back and herded all four into the toilets. Three of the barmen were shut into one of the toilet cubicles, and Ron Lockhart was to be pushed into another, when there was suddenly a tremendous explosion, followed by the sound of swiftly running feet, and a car taking off at speed.

When the three barmen managed to free themselves from the toilet cubicle, they found Ron Lockhart dead on the floor. He had been blasted in the back with both barrels of a powerful shotgun, from point-blank range. The Edinburgh police were soon on the scene, and Detective Chief Superintendent Brian Cunningham took charge of the murder investigation. The surviving barmen told the police that one of the robbers turned murderers had been aged around 30 and of normal build; the other one had been younger and slightly taller. They had spoken in a local accent. The police appealed for witnesses who had

34. The St Vincent wine bar today.

been in the vicinity of the St Vincent Wine Bar between 11.30 and 11.45 to come forward. They also appealed for help to track down a large, dark-coloured car seen parked near the side entrance to the wine bar and travelling at speed along Circus Lane after the murder.

Interviewed by an *Edinburgh Evening News* journalist, the manager of the St Vincent Wine Bar, Mr John Cole, said that Ron Lockhart had worked this particular evening to give himself the night off. The wine bar was normally a quiet place, and did not carry much cash money, rendering it an unlikely target for a pair of armed desperadoes. A total of £250 had been left behind in the unmanned till. He had known Ron Lockhart for many years, and the quiet, bushy-bearded nurse turned barman did not have any enemies who wanted to put an end to his existence. The police agreed that the murder was most likely the result of a robbery gone wrong. But had the armed robber gunned down Ron Lockhart to intimidate the other three barmen, or had the shotgun gone off misadvertently? The latter version seemed the more likely, since the robbers had fled empty-handed.

On April 13, the St Vincent Wine Bar robbers and murderers were still walking free. The police had manned a caravan at the crime scene, questioned pedestrians and motorists who might have been in the area, and investigated known criminals known to have good access to firearms. The latter line of inquiry soon concentrated on the 30-year-old Fife gangster James Baigrie, who was awaiting trial for illegal possession of shotguns and ammunition. The police speculated that he had intended to flee Scotland before going on trial and wanted to rob the St Vincent Wine Bar to get some travel money. They found out that he had associated with a young apprentice gangster, the 18-year-old hoodlum John Watson. When this youngster was 'leant on' by the police detectives, he freely admitted being the second armed robber at the wine bar, although it had been James Baigrie who had gunned down Ron Lockhart.

Arrested by the police, James Baigrie and John Watson appeared at the Edinburgh Sheriff Court on April 14, to be charged with the murder of Ron Lockhart. The police found out that Baigrie was quite a 'Mr Big' in the Fife gangster world: he liked making audacious plans for robberies and wage snatches, and had accumulated an arsenal of shotguns and other weapons. He had worked as a craneman in Leith Docks for a while, and been an oil platform worker, but honest toil and hard graft was not for him. He had also been an army soldier but had bought himself out after three months. The foolish young John Watson had fallen for Baigrie's big talk, imagining that through consorting with such an experienced and ruthless gangster, he could get rich quick. They would get at least £30 000 at the St Vincent Wine Bar, Baigrie had promised, and this would enable them to go to Greece and live in luxury there.

The prosecution promised John Watson a lenient deal if he agreed to give evidence in court about James Baigrie, and the young man, who belatedly seems to have regretted his foolish actions, willingly agreed. On trial at the High Court in late July 1982, Watson blamed Baigrie for everything, including the murder of Ron Lockhart. Mr Robert Henderson, QC for Baigrie, suggested that Watson was the real murderer, and that he blamed Baigrie to hoodwink the police and prosecution, but the young hoodlum convincingly denied this. After a three-day trial, James Baigrie was found guilty of murder and was sentenced to imprisonment for life. Although the fatal shot might not have been fired with intent to kill, Lord Hunter pontificated, his crime had been a premeditated and dastardly one, culminating on the death of an innocent man. Baigrie was also sentenced to ten and a half years in prison for a separate series of theft and firearms offences, and Lord Hunter ordered the forfeiture of his arsenal of firearms and ammunition. As for the creature Watson, he was sentenced to six years in a young offender's institution.[24]

But this story does not end here. James Baigrie was a very tough character, and the prison was not built where he could safely be confined. In October 1983, he made use of a smuggled hacksaw to break out of Saughton Prison and went on the run for many months to come. The dismal 'squealer' Watson, who had been instrumental in getting Baigrie convicted, probably praised his luck to be incarcerated in a prison where his erstwhile gangster colleague could not get hold of him. In March 1985, the police received a tip that James Baigrie was in London, and they tracked him down to a van in Philbeach Gardens, Earl's Court. After a lengthy siege by armed police, the Edinburgh desperado blew his brains out with a shotgun, ending his life of crime with a bang rather than a whimper.[25]

THE MURDER OF ALAN BORWICK, 1987

The 50-year-old former merchant seaman Alan Borwick was a very fine specimen of a kind of man today almost threatened with extinction: the good old-fashioned Edinburgh drunk. Divorced, unemployed and unemployable, he lived in a room at the boarding house at 56 Dublin Street. Having received his unemployment benefit, he regularly got 'stone drunk' on beer and whisky, reeling about in the pubs and liquor stores in the Broughton Street area; unwashed and scruffy-looking, he played his mouth-organ to all who would listen. Angry and argumentative in his cups, he often screamed abuse at complete strangers in the street and made a nuisance of himself.

On May 8 1987, Alan Borwick was found murdered in the common stair of 75 Broughton Street, with severe head injuries from a brutal beating from a blunt instrument. Immediately prior to the murder, he had been seen quarrelling angrily with a young man, possibly a teenager, with fair hair and wearing a baggy light green sweatshirt with long sleeves. This individual was nowhere to be found, however, and the witness observations were not distinct enough to track him down. Since Alan Borwick was well known to the Broughton Street publicans and shopkeepers, it had been easy to reconstruct his final evening alive: at 8.30 pm, he was seen in Barony Street, already very drunk; half an hour later, he was at the Phoenix Bar in Broughton Street, before going on to the Barony Bar across the street, and buying a fish supper at the Deep Sea in Antigua Street. At just after 10 pm, he was playing his mouth-organ in Forth Street, and shouting and swearing at a young man; ten or so minutes later, these two were still arguing, standing at the crossing of Forth Street and Broughton Street.

The months went by without any noteworthy progress in the hunt for Alan Borwick's murderer; the mystery teenager remained elusive, and there were no other worthwhile clues. But ten months after the murder of Alan Borwick, the 17-year-

35. The murder house at 75 Broughton Street.

old John Verth was apprehended by the police on a charge of housebreaking. In spite of his youth, this individual had a very impressive criminal record, totalling sixteen offences of dishonesty since September 1986. The constables were amazed when without provocation, Verth made a statement about being involved in the murder of Alan Borwick, although claiming it had been an accident. On trial for murder at the High Court in June 1988, Verth pleaded self-defence: the night of May 7, he had attended the dog races at Powderhall Stadium, before purchasing a fish supper on his way home. The drunken Alan Borwick had tried to snatch his bag of chips and attacked him with his fists after an angry altercation, pulling him into the stair of 75 Broughton Street. He had then thrown a large stone at Verth, but the tough youngster picked up the stone and gave the old drunk the beating of his life with it. A pathologist testified that Borwick had drunk the equivalent of fifteen pints of beer the night of the murder; the cause of death was severe head injuries and seven fractured ribs, consistent with repeated blows from a stone in a frenzied assault. One witness thought that Verth vaguely resembled the youth he had seen arguing with Alan Borwick. In the end, Verth was found guilty of murder and sentenced to imprisonment for 12 years.[26]

The sentence would probably had been longer had it not been known that the street pest Alan Borwick had such a short temper when drunk; he might well have attacked John Verth with his fists, only to find out, to his detriment, that in spite of his youth, Verth was a tough career criminal and a dangerous opponent in a fight. There is reason to believe that Verth made it out of prison alive, paying a heavy price for his unwisdom in blabbering to the police, after successfully keeping his crime a secret for ten months. It appears likely that he was the 33-year-old John Archibald Verth who died in 2003, from acute alcohol intoxication according to his death certificate; short and evil were his days, and wholly uninvigorated by any spark of genius.

THE MURDER OF ABDUL RASHID, 1988

The 42-year-old Pakistani immigrant Abdul Rashid lived with his family at Smith's Place, Leith, and ran the Fair Deal Stores at 32 Rodney Street in the New Town. He was a decent and hard-working man, who managed to make his shop in busy Rodney Street quite a success. In May 1988, when his wife and children were on holiday in Pakistan, he hoped to join them there within the next few weeks.

36. Rodney Street, a postcard stamped and posted in 1905.

On May 25, Mrs Catherine Campbell went into the Fair Deal Stores just after 1 pm. She noticed some red footprints on the floor but thought someone had stepped in a spilled bottle of wine. When she went to look over the counter, she saw Abdul Rashid lying on the floor, Noticing that the shop's cash register was missing, she ran to alert the fishmonger Robert Cunningham whose shop was next door. She then returned to the Fair Deal Stores to help Abdul Rashid, but when she lifted his shoulder to turn him around, she saw a knife sticking out of his chest.

Detective Superintendent Tom Wood, the officer leading the hunt for the Rodney Street murderer, made an appeal for witnesses near the Fair Deal Stores from 12.50 pm, when Abdul Rashid was last seen alive, and 1.05 pm, when he was found dead. A scruffy-looking man had been seen leaving the shop around 1 pm, carrying the cash register with him, and it was likely that this was the murderer. House-to-house searches were in operation, and vacant sites nearby were searched by foot patrol teams with tracker dogs.

It turned out that the young drug addict Sharon McCallum had been seen near the Fair Deal Stores the day of the murder, and on May 28, detectives went to her flat at 76 Eyre Place nearby to question her. She was not at home, but the door was answered by her boyfriend, the 36-year-old heroin addict David Fleming. When the detectives had a look around in the flat, one of them found parts of the cash register hidden in a cupboard! Fleming sighed and said 'Aye, you are right, it was me.' He assured them that he had not intended to kill Abdul Rashid, just to frighten him, adding 'I am glad it is over because I have not been sleeping.'

On May 29, David Fleming and Sharon McCallum appeared at the Edinburgh Sheriff Court, to be charged with the murder of Abdul Rashid. On trial at the High Court in September 1988, Fleming wanted to plead guilty to the lesser charge of culpable homicide, but this was rejected by the Crown. Giving evidence, Fleming said that he had turned to heroin around three years earlier, after splitting up with his wife. The day of the murder, he had been in dire need of a 'shot' and very short of money. He had decided to rob the Fair Deal Stores, knowing that Abdul Rashid was often alone in there. The plan had been to frighten the shopkeeper with a knife and to snatch all the money from the till, but things went awry when Abdul Rashid leapt up and flailed his arms about. Fleming had punched him in the face, but the furious Pakistani bit him hard in the thumb. As the two were struggling, Fleming had slipped and fell, and Abdul Rashid fell down on top of him, onto the knife which entered his chest. Fleming had not been aware of the knife entering his body, he assured the jury, not had he driven it in. He had then taken the cash register, which he could not open on the spot, to his girlfriend's flat nearby, where he had dismantled it using a hammer and stolen the money inside.

Catherine Campbell gave her evidence without contradictions, breaking down in tears when she described the knife handle sticking out from the chest of the murdered shopkeeper. The pathologist Professor Anthony Busuttil testified that Abdul Rashid's body had cuts and bruises to the face, like if he had been punched. The lethal stab wound had been inflicted with great force, severing two ribs and going straight through the heart; it was not consistent with an accidental stabbing, or Rashid falling onto the knife. This damning medical evidence turned the course of the trial: by a majority verdict, the jury found David Fleming guilty of murder, and Lord Cullen passed sentence of imprisonment for life.[27] The murder shop at 32 Rodney Street, at the corner with Heriothill Terrace, is today the office of the Ravenstone Property estate agents.

37. The murder shop at 32 Rodney Street today.

THE MURDER OF RONALD TRIPP, 1993

The 65-year-old retired shopkeeper Ronald Tripp lived in the basement flat at 11B Buckingham Terrace. He had run a grocery store in the Fife village of Pittenweem, before going to Gibraltar. Returning home, he had stayed in Gullane for a while, before renting the flat in fashionable Buckingham Terrace. A quiet, reserved bachelor, he liked visiting charity and music shops, looking for records and electrical equipment.

On October 8 1993, Ronald Tripp was found dead in his flat by his brother, murdered in a brutal attack. He had been struck on the head at least 30 times, breaking the skull into little pieces. The police soon got a vital tip-off: a few days before the murder, Ronald Tripp had visited Murray's electrical shop in Dalry Road to get a quote for some work to be done to his flat. On October 6 1993, the part-time electrician Phillip Brummitt had come calling to do the work, for which he received £17 in cash. On October 11, the police went to Brummitt's Muirhouse flat. When confronted with his visit to the Buckingham Terrace murder flat, he sighed and exclaimed 'It is either talk to you or a priest, isn't it?'

It turned out that the 37-year-old Phillip Brummitt was an army veteran, who had served with the Royal Electrical and Mechanical Engineers in Germany, Ireland and the Falklands. He had left the army after nine years, with an exemplary service record. In recent years, he had got badly into debt, owing £700 or so. Seeing that Ronald Tripp had a good deal of money in his flat, he decided to return to the flat two days later and rob him. But Tripp had fought back, and Brummitt had gone berserk, striking him down with the heavy hammer from his toolkit. He had stolen £20 before leaving the flat. On trial for murder at the High Court in January 1994, Philip Brummitt pleaded guilty to murdering Ronald Tripp, and he was sentenced to imprisonment for life. 'Life for the £20 Killer!' exclaimed the headline of the

38. The murder basement flat at 11b Buckingham Terrace.

Edinburgh Evening News, although there was later newspaper speculation that Ronald Tripp had been a homosexual, and that he had invited Brummitt to his flat for sex.[28]

AGONY AUNT IN KNIFE HORROR, 1998

The 54-year-old Mrs Catherine McCaskill worked as an 'agony aunt' for the *Edinburgh Evening News*, under the pen-name Kit Dallas, and also acted as the Scottish press officer for Sir James Goldsmith's Referendum Party in the run-up to the general election. She lived in a luxury top-floor flat at 35 Scotland Street, in the heart of the New Town., with her 57-year-old husband Commander Simon McCaskill, a retired naval officer who was a Falklands veteran. In June 1998, when an *Edinburgh Evening*

News reporter called on Catherine McCaskill at her flat to ask her about the controversial *Trainspotting* author Irvine Welsh, who had just moved into one of the flats below, she seemed her usual jovial self, making jokes that she hoped he would not bring drugs into the house.

The great sorrow in the lives of Catherine McCaskill and her husband was their 26-year-old son Kenneth, who suffered from severe schizophrenia and could behave like a complete madman at times. On June 21 1998, Kenneth was taken to visit his grandmother, before the family returned to 35 Scotland Street. When he told his mother that he was Lucifer, she told him to stop reading books about devil worship. When his father eventually joined them, Kenneth was becoming increasingly excited: he told his parents that he was Lucifer, and that they should leave for good since he wanted the flat for himself. When Kenneth demanded the car keys, his father refused to give them to him. This made the lunatic absolutely furious, and he threw a crystal ashtray hard into the wall, breaking it. Seeing a block of kitchen knives, he seized one of them and fiercely attacked his father, stabbing him hard in the chest several times. Since one of the stabs hit the heart, Commander McCaskill died in the hall a few minutes later. Catherine McCaskill picked up a frying pan and hit Kenneth on the head several times, but the cracking impacts against the lunatic's rock-hard skull did nothing to slow him down. Instead he turned his attention to his mother and stabbed her hard in the arms, back, neck and chest. He left her with the 12-inch knife blade completely embedded in her chest, thinking that she must be dead.

People living in the surrounding flats at 35 Scotland Street heard the screaming emanating from the top floor and called in the police. Commander McCaskill was declared dead at the scene, but his wife was still alive in spite of her injuries. Aghast at what he had just accomplished, Kenneth McCaskill gave himself up to the police. On trial at the High Court in October 1998,

39. The McCaskill murder house at 35 Scotland Street.

two psychiatrists agreed that he had been insane at the time of the Scotland Street patricide, but that he was now able to plead. They recommended that Kenneth McCaskill should be sent to the State Mental Hospital, Carstairs, without limit of time, and this advice was acted upon.[29] Catherine McCaskill is said to have recovered completely from her physical injuries and moved back into the murder flat at 35 Scotland Street. She may still be alive today, and the same goes for the demented Kenneth, who hopefully received the psychiatric care he needs, and is restricted from knives and other sharp instruments. Hopefully, Irvine Welsh did not move away from his new flat at 35 Scotland Street, in the belief that this was a very dangerous neighbourhood where knife-wielding lunatics were constantly on the prowl.

ST STEPHEN STREET AGAIN, 1998

At 6.30 am on March 3 1998, the body of the 42-year-old mother of five Mrs Margaret Reid was found in a skip in Henderson Place Lane. This skip was owned by the City of Edinburgh Council, and placed in a small private car park, situated behind office blocks in nearby Dundas Street. Since her throat had been cut, the police immediately knew that this was a case of murder. The autopsy showed signs of a sustained, vicious and savage attack. She had not been murdered in or near the skip, but the body had been transported there, quite possibly in a motor vehicle, it was thought. Led by Detective Chief Inspector Pat Byrne, the police were busy searching the streets nearby, as well as all drains and parcels of rough ground between Mrs Reid's home at 120 St Stephen Street, Stockbridge, and the place where her body had been found. CCTV recordings from cameras in Dundas Street and elsewhere was closely examined.

The husband of Margaret Reid, the 41-year-old unemployed painter and decorator Thomas 'Tam' Reid, told the police that his wife had suffered from a severe bowel condition for many years, until she had recently been cured by a successful operation. Her failing health had not prevented her from giving birth to five healthy children, who were all alive and well. The three eldest were in the process of leaving the parental home. Tam Reid had last seen his wife at mid-day on March 2, he said, but he knew that she was planning to go out and meet friends in the evening, to see the blockbuster film 'Titanic'. He had gone out to search for her after she had failed to return home. Speaking to an *Edinburgh Evening News* reporter, the grieving Tam Reid said "How will I bring up my bairns now? She was a wonderful woman, she wouldn't have harmed anybody. She was a good mother to my bairns. I don't know what they are going to do without her." Several neighbours and family friends described the Reid family as very happy, although the children could sometimes be boisterous; Margaret had lived contentedly with her husband and had never gone missing from the family hone before.

40. The murder house at 120 St Stephen Street.

But after the police had seen Tam Reid acting suspiciously on a CCTV recording near the BUPA House office block in Dundas Street, the husband became the prime suspect. He was arrested on the third day of the murder inquiry, after traces of the blood of the murdered woman had been found in the kitchen at 120 St Stephen Street. After pressure had been put on Tam Reid behind bars, he broke down and confessed murdering his wife. After the bowel operation, she had become a changed woman, he explained, taunting him about his lack of sexual prowess and speaking of affairs with other men. On March 2, he had attacked her in a furious rage, after she had threatened to leave him for another man, stabbing and battering her to death. He had hidden the body in an underground recess to the kitchen, done his best to clean up all the blood, and then acted the part of the concerned husband to perfection. Later, when all the children were asleep, he had stuffed the body of his short, thin wife into a large rubber bag and carried it through the streets until he reached the skip in Henderson Place Lane. On trial at the High Court in August 1998, Tam Reid, whose hair had turned grey since his arrest, broke down and cried when the post-mortem findings were read out in court. There was no doubt concerning his guilt, and his confession neatly fitted what was known about the murder; he was sentenced to imprisonment for life.[30]

THE MURDER OF SUZANNE PILLEY, 2010

In 2010, the 38-year-old Suzanne Pilley lived in Edinburgh and worked as a book-keeper at Infrastructure Managers Ltd, a company based at 11 Thistle Street. On May 4 2010, she failed to turn up for work, having previously been a very reliable employee. After she had been reported missing by her parents, the police began studying CCTV recordings from the New Town area. At shortly before 9 am, she was spotted leaving the St Andrew Square branch of Sainsbury's on her way to work, and a few minutes later, she was in North St David Street, about to turn into Thistle Street. Thus there was evidence that she had either been kidnapped and abducted just by her workplace, or actually murdered on the premises before reaching the company's second-floor offices.

There was soon a prime suspect to the murder of Suzanne Pilley: her workplace colleague David Gilroy, with whom she had enjoyed a turbulent on-off affair for about a year's time. Gilroy was an obsessive character who used to send Suzanne more than 50 text messages per day. He had led a double life, having a wife and family at Silverknowes. The day after the disappearance of Suzanne Pilley, he had adjusted his diary to get an excuse to make a long car journey to Argyll. When he returned, there was damage to the suspension of the car, and vegetation was stuck underneath it, suggesting that it had been driven off road. The detectives suspected that Gilroy had lured Suzanne Pilley down into the basement of 11 Thistle Street and murdered her there. When he had reappeared in the company offices, he had been sweaty and dishevelled, with scratches to his hands and face. He had then collected the body after work and taken it out to his car and kept it in the car at Silverknowes overnight, before driving up to Argyll and burying it in forest land up there.

David Gilroy was arrested on June 23 and charged with the murder of Suzanne Pilley. The police were searching the Argyll forests, with dogs and specially trained teams of constables, but without finding anything of interest. They did a good job of tracing the movements of Gilroy's silver Vauxhall Vectra, however, finding that on his journey to Lochgilphead to inspect a school, he would have had time to dispose of the body on the way. He was committed for trial on July 1 2010, but due to the complexity of the case, it would take until February 20 2012 for the trial to begin, at the High Court of Justiciary, with Lord Bracadale presiding. A team of constables explained that they had allowed some specially trained cadaver dogs, which could sniff out blood and human remains, to have a rummage round 11 Thistle Street, and inside Gilroy's car. They had identified three areas of interest: one in the basement area of the offices, two in the boot of the car. A forensic imagery expert could testify that after studying some indistinct CCTV images from Thistle Street, she had made a definite sighting of Suzanne Pilley, just 20 metres from the entrance door to the offices.

A police sergeant and a forensic pathologist described the scratches on Gilroy's face, hands and wrists when he was examined on May 6 2010. A search for DNA evidence at 11 Thistle Street, and in the boot of Gilroy's car, had failed to

41. The Pilley murder house at 11 Thistle Street.

provide any traces of the DNA of the murdered woman. After recreating the journey made by David Gilroy from Edinburgh to Lochgilphead, using CCTV footage, the detectives had found that he had taken two hours longer than expected each way, and that 124 miles of his journey were unaccounted for. The defence case lasted for just half a day, with a number of witnesses from Infrastructure Managers Ltd saying that they had noticed nothing out of the ordinary the day Suzanne Pilley had disappeared. Gilroy had the opportunity to give evidence in his own defence, but he declined to make use of it. The closing speech for the prosecution, delivered by advocate depute Alex Prentice QC, was a powerful one. The case for the Crown was that David Gilroy had murdered Suzanne Pilley in the basement of 11 Thistle

Street, before hiding the body in a recess and transporting it to a lonely grave in Argyll the day after. After her disappearance, she had made no contact with any person, there had been no activity on her credit cards, and she had made no arrangements for her pet cat and fish. Nor had the obsessive Gilroy sent her any further phone or text messages after her disappearance, was this not because he knew she was dead and he had her phone? For the defence, Jack Davidson QC urged the jury to assess the evidence dispassionately; he said it would be unsafe to convict his client of murder since the evidence was circumstantial in nature. Many people must have been fearing an anticlimactic ending to the case, with a 'not proven' verdict, but the jury returned a majority verdict of guilty and Lord Bracadale sentenced him to imprisonment for life with a minimum custodial sentence of 18 years.[31]

David Gilroy has continued to maintain his innocence, but the various appeals he has made have all been turned down. In March 2018, Suzanne Pilley's mother and sister appealed to him to tell them where he had buried the corpse, but he did no such thing. In June 2019, Gilroy's wife and children were reported to have changed their name to escape the notoriety of the case.[32] The 'murder basement' of 11 Thistle Street was put up for rent in May 2012 and is still there today, with the offices of Infrastructure Managers remaining at the second floor.

THE CURSE ON SCOTLAND STREET, 2016

In late 2016, the two young Welshmen Ashley Hawkins and Kieran Davies drove all the way from Barry near Cardiff up to Edinburgh for a holiday. They planned to live in a flat at 7 Scotland Street owned by a relation to Hawkins. Ashley Hawkins was an unemployed drug addict, wanted for burglary and suspected

42. The murder house at 7 Scotland Street, completing the hat trick for the New Town's leading murder street.

of stealing a vehicle in Cardiff. Kieran Davies used drugs with moderation, but he also had a criminal past, and was known as a tough character who did not take any nonsense from anybody. To begin with, the two friends and cousins got on well together, but the short-tempered Davies disapproved of his friend's incessant drug taking. Once, when he had injured himself on a needle left behind by his muddled friend, he got seriously annoyed with him, and another time, he seized hold of Hawkins and held a knife to his throat.

On December 2 2016, the neighbours in Scotland Street heard repeated heavy thuds from the flat occupied by the two

Welshmen, and they called the police. In a furious rage, Davies had beaten up his friend with a hammer and a metal pole, before repeatedly jumping on his head, screaming 'Fucking idiot!' When the police arrived, Davies seemed to be 'high' on some substance; he himself said that he had taken heroin and ecstasy, although he tested positively only for benzodiazepines and cannabis. His clothes were saturated with blood and spattered with brain tissue after the horrific attack. At the police station, he tried to knock down a police sergeant who had annoyed him and had to be forcibly restrained. On December 6, he was charged with murder at the Edinburgh Sheriff Court.

On trial for murder at the High Court in July 2017, Davies pleaded not guilty and seemed to show little remorse for his actions. His guilt was not in doubt, however, due to the impressive technical evidence against him, and all the defence could achieve was to plead that the murder had not been premeditated, but the result of a sudden rage. A psychiatrist had declared the prisoner fit to plead, and to stand trial for his crime. After the expected guilty verdict, Lord Boyd sentenced the Welsh ruffian to imprisonment for life, adding that he should serve at least 19 years before becoming eligible to apply for release on parole.[33]

III.

SOUTH AND EAST
EDINBURGH

The more salubrious area of South Edinburgh consists of the suburbs immediately south of the Old Town: Viewforth, Merchiston, Bruntsfield, Marchmont, Sciennes and Newington. Their solid Victorian or Edwardian houses were usually inhabited by a better class of people and seldom visited by the spectre of Murder, apart from the occasional family tragedy or violent burglar. In contrast, some of the most notorious slums of these parts, like Potterrow and the North and South Richmond Streets, have long since been cleared and rebuilt with better quality houses. Moving south, we come to several former villages incorporated into the city, like Colinton, Liberton and Gilmerton, and also some of the city's toughest housing estates, constructed in the 1960s and 1970s, and home to a variety of violent juvenile criminals, robbers and gangsters. Read about the 1865 double murder in Dalrymple Crescent and the horrible 1915 triple murder in Falcon Avenue; from modern times, we have the 1968 child murder in Colinton Mains Drive, the Frogston Horror of 1991, and the Marmion gangster murder of 2006 …

MURDER AT DALRYMPLE CRESCENT, 1865

The well-to-do sculptor and builder Robert Hunter was born in Roxburghshire in or around 1797. At the time of the 1841 Census, he was living in the Old Town with his wife Marion and their ten children, but twenty years later, the Hunters were living at 4 Lord Russell Place, Newington. In the following years, Robert Hunter purchased land at 6 Dalrymple Crescent, Grange, and erected a detached villa for himself and his wife, large enough to accommodate the sons David and John and the unmarried daughter Elizabeth. John Hunter was born in 1838 and had shown early signs of a disturbed mind. He had worked as a mason for a while, but had tramped down to England and slept rough in the hedges for several weeks, until retrieved by his brother. In 1865, he was living at the family home but doing no work. He was seen as a harmless lunatic, whose ideas were very odd: he spent much time reading the Bible and was under the impression that he was a great prophet himself. He imagined himself to be very strong, a virtual Samson among men, and never cut his hair since that would surely make him less powerful. Since he had never struck or threated any person, it had never been considered that he should be put under restraint in an asylum.

On October 5 1865, the household at 6 Dalrymple Crescent followed its regular morning routine. Robert Hunter and his son David went to work, leaving the two women with John. The 14-year-old girl Mary Stewart Robertson, who lived at Lauder Road, had a good view of the front gardens of some of the houses at Dalrymple Crescent. She saw John Hunter pull up an iron rod and strike his mother a series of blows on the head. When Elizabeth came running out of the house, she was treated in the same manner, falling over her mother's recumbent body. 'O Mamma, that man is killing his mother and sister!' screamed Mary Stewart Robertson, calling the attention of her brother and sister, who both saw John Hunter and the two bodies. The mason Joseph Brown, who saw

*1. The oldest murder house in South Edinburgh, 6 Dalrymple Crescent,
where John Hunter murdered his mother and sister in 1865.*

John Hunter attack his sister Elizabeth when he came walking
past the murder house, called out 'Murder!' and ran up to the
two bodies, but neither of them breathed or moved. The surgeon
Henry Newcombe, who lived next door at 5 Dalrymple Crescent,
had a servant who heard Joseph Brown's outcry and saw the two
bodies; he walked over to the murder house and declared the two
women dead. The police constable John McManamin came to
6 Dalrymple Crescent after being told of the double murder: he
arrested John Hunter, who was skulking in the back garden, and
took the iron rod away from him. When charged with murder by
the Sheriff Substitute, the lunatic remained silent when questioned
about his horrible deed. A large crowd soon congregated outside
the murder house, and two police constable had to be posted on
the premises to prevent lovers of criminal curiosities carrying off
some blood-stained garden stones.

John Hunter faced trial for murdering his mother and sister at the High Court of Justiciary on November 27 1865. A number of eyewitnesses identified him as the murderer. No motive for his sudden attack could be discerned, although there was speculation that the two women had tried to stop him from wandering off again; his father and brothers denied that he had previously shown any violent tendencies. "I have led a life of great vexation on account of his state of mind, but I did not apprehend any danger from him", the dignified Robert Hunter exclaimed. Dr Littlejohn, who had spoken to John Hunter at length, gave examples of his odd religious ideas: he was a mighty prophet, superior to the Saviour, since he was under the influence of the Holy Spirit. Dr Littlejohn pronounced him a dangerous lunatic and he was ordered to be kept in strict custody during her Majesty's pleasure.[1] Robert Hunter sold the murder house in December 1865, remarried a much younger wife, and lived on until 1877. The house at 6 Dalrymple Crescent still stands, although it has been subdivided into flats.

MURDER IN CLERK STREET, 1890

The 50-year-old fireman Alexander Anderson lived in a flat at 14 Clerk Street, with his much younger 'wife' Marion Johnston. He used to call himself 'William Johnston', but this was an assumed name to hide that he was living in sin. Marion had a living husband but he had deserted her. 'William' and Marion were said to have two living children, but neither of them were staying at the Clerk Street flat.

On October 21 1890, Alexander Anderson was lighting his pipe in the reception room at Clerk Street. Marion was with him and so was her machinist friend Ellen Cameron. The pipe would not light up, however, and Alexander got furious when he

2. Clerk Street, a postcard stamped and posted in 1903.

thought his 'wife' was making fun of him. He turned her chair over and sent her sprawling on the floor, before kicking her hard in the private parts from behind. Marion was bleeding severely and Ellen Cameron was trying to help her up. Aghast at what he had just accomplished, Alexander Anderson ran out of the flat and took refuge in a pub next door. Fearful that he would return with more ill-usage, Ellen Cameron helped Marion into the flat of the neighbourwoman Jessie Miller. A doctor was fetched but when he arrived at 14 Clerk Street, Marion had bled to death from her injuries. Jessie Miller stopped the police constable Alex. Yeats in Clerk Street, explaining how her friend had just been done to death, and he went into the pub and took the inebriated Alexander Anderson into custody.

When Alexander Anderson stood his trial for murder at the High Court of Edinburgh on December 15, Dr Harvey Littlejohn declared that Marion Johnston had been five months pregnant when she had been assaulted. Her death was due to syncope caused by the loss of blood from a large lacerated wound to her private parts. Ellen Cameron had seen the assault and Marion had told Jessie Miller that she had been kicked by Alexander Anderson. He pleaded guilty to culpable homicide and was sentenced to imprisonment for 12 months.[2] No explanation for his cruel and cowardly assault on a pregnant woman who was said to be the mother of his children ever emanated.

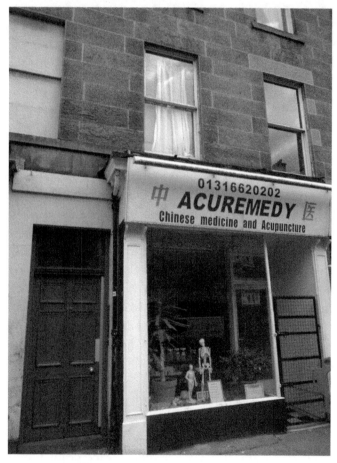

3. The murder house at 14 Clerk Street today.

MURDER IN BRUNTSFIELD PLACE, 1899

Frederick Warwick was born into a working-class Whitechapel family in 1854, one of several children of Henry and Mary Ann Warwick. He left the crowded family home as soon as he could, to train as an electrician. In May 1882, when he was living in Lisbon, Portugal, he married the 21-year-old spinster Ada Saunders, the only daughter of Captain W.G. Saunders, in Southsea. He later moved on to Malta, where he advanced to become superintendent of telephones. He remarried Margaret McGregor in the late 1880s, and fathered the two sons Charles and Arthur, and later the little daughter Katie as well. In early 1899, when Frederick Warwick was feeling quite broken down in health, he decided to move back to Britain to recuperate. For a while, he and his family resided in Elie, Fife, but in late June, they moved on to two rooms in the lodging-house at 215 Bruntsfield Place, Edinburgh. Mr Warwick and the two boys slept in one room, Mrs Warwick and Katie in the other. On July

4. A postcard showing Bruntsfield Place.

5, the landlady gave the family notice to leave the premises, for good, and this snub seems to have disrupted Frederick Warwick's fragile intellect, to murderous effect.

Just after five in the morning of July 6 1899, Frederick Warwick went out of bed and grabbed hold of a loaded revolver. He pointed it at his 9-year-old son Charles, and blew his brains out as he slept in bed. He then took aim at his eldest son, 11-year-old Arthur, but the lad had woken up when his brother was murdered, and he threw himself out of the way when he saw the smoking revolver pointed at his head; the shot missed, although the lad's face was singed by the flame, and the bullet hit the wall. Frederick Warwick then sat down on the bed and blew his own brains out. When the landlady heard the revolver shots and rushed upstairs to investigate, she heard Mrs Warwick scream 'My husband is dead!' in a terrible voice. And indeed, both Frederick and Charles Warwick were stone dead, although the lad Arthur had survived his gruelling late-night adventure well-nigh unscathed. He is said to have tried to comfort his distraught mother, exclaiming 'You know, mother, God does nothing without reason!' The little daughter Katie also entered the murder room, and appeared to understand the magnitude of the tragedy that had just occurred; she knelt down and prayed for the souls of her father and brother. The landlady went out to call Dr Carmichael, who lived across the road, but he could do nothing but declare that the murder victim and the suicide were both dead from their terrible injuries. It was considered curious that all the neighbours, although briefly roused by the revolver shots, went back to sleep again without trying to investigate; they found out about the Bruntsfield Place tragedy only the next morning.

The Bruntsfield Place murder and suicide was one of the saddest tragedies to have struck Edinburgh for many a year, and it is said by the *Edinburgh Evening News* to have marred the visit to the city by the Prince of Wales. There was lewd speculation that

A FATHER'S MAD CRIME IN EDINBURGH.
HE ATTEMPTS TO MURDER HIS FAMILY AND SHOOTS HIMSELF.

5. Frederick Warwick shoots his son dead before committing suicide, from the Illustrated Police News, July 15 1899.

Frederick Warwick had planned to gun down his entire family, although other newspapers emphasized that he had always been very fond of his wife, and an affectionate father. Frederick Warwick had left behind letters to Mrs Warwick's sister, and to a Mr Brown in Glasgow, asking them to come at once, since the worst had happened; he had signed them both 'Maggie' to seem that they had come from his wife. He left a handsome legacy, of more than £2 200, to the physician Joseph McGregor Robertson. On July 9, the two Bruntsfield Place victims were taken from the City Mortuary to the Grange Cemetery. A troop of relations and friends of the deceased arrived in town at the Princes Street Station and joined the funeral cortege in Rutland Street, but otherwise people paid very little attention to the cortege on the way to the cemetery.[3]

MERCHISTON LANDLADY MURDERED, 1902

Colin Sinclair Murray Brown was born in 1865, the son of a crofter living in the hamlet of Basta on the island of Yell, Shetland. He had five living brothers and four living sisters; unlike them, he showed a precocious intellect and a talent for studies since an early age. He went to study at Edinburgh University, graduating as a Master of Arts in 1896, before aiming for a career in the United Free Church. While serving as a Licentiate in this church, he studied hard for his divinity degree at the university during the weekdays, and preached in churches at Shetland and Forfar on the Sundays.

In 1902, Colin Sinclair Murray Brown took a bedroom and a parlour at 11 Rochester Terrace, Merchiston, a house owned by the 70-year-old widow Mrs Mary McIntosh. Although he was quiet and respectable, as becoming a clergyman, he had a strange manner and often exclaimed 'I want no more of that!'

Mary McIntosh and her daughter Grace, who also lived on the premises, did not like him much due to his queer mannerisms. He studied hard every day and went out preaching in the weekends. On August 6 1902, Colin Sinclair Murray Brown went stark raving mad. He shouted and screamed in his room, saying that he was the rightful King and should be crowned. After the neighbours had complained, Mrs McIntosh called in the family doctor. Dr Robert Thin was admitted into Brown's rooms, where the lunatic calmed right down, saying that he had studied very hard for his exam, and was not feeling well. Although his family was in Shetland, one of his sisters had married Mr Magnus David Thomson, manager of the Danish Butter Co., who lived at 14 Comely Bank Avenue. Dr Thin promised to fetch the brother-in-law, with whom Brown was on good terms. But when the doctor went calling at Thomson's house, he was not at home, although the doctor left his card at the butter shop.

Mary McIntosh, who had been promised that someone would be coming to help pacify the lunatic, was dismayed when no person made an appearance. She tried to persuade Colin Sinclair Murray Brown to go to bed, but he started howling again and went out into the lobby. When she tried to impede him, he knocked her down and jumped on her. When Grace McIntosh went to see what had happened, she was horrified to find the lunatic jumping on her mother's motionless body, dressed only in his nightshirt. She called Dr Thin and the police, and the former managed to pacify Brown and persuade him to go to bed, until Constable James Scott came to apprehend him. Mary McIntosh was quite dead, with many fractured ribs. The forensic specialist Dr Harvey Littlejohn came to the murder house, where he spoke to Brown, who was lying in bed partially dressed; the lunatic told him about the terrible dreams he had been having.

When charged with the murder of Mary McIntosh in the Edinburgh Sheriff's Court, Colin Sinclair Murray Brown smiled inanely, and did not seem to realize his position in the slightest degree. When he was on trial for murder at the High Court in September 1902, Grace McIntosh and Dr Thin gave evidence against him. Mr Thomson said that he had not seen his brother-in-law for 13 months, until Brown had come to the butter company on August 1, talking incoherently about church affairs. Dr Littlejohn testified that the cause of death had been due to the fracture of the sternum and of multiple ribs, caused by blunt trauma. He had examined the accused and found him a person of unsound mind, and unfit to plead in a court of law. Brown was sentenced to indefinite incarceration in a lunatic asylum.[4] He died in the Montrose Royal Asylum on January 10 1923, from chronic nephritis and uremia according to his death certificate.

DOUBLE MURDER AT SURGEON'S HALL, 1902

William Ivison Macadam was born in 1856 and educated at Heidelberg University in Germany. He followed in his father's footsteps and became an analytical chemist and lecturer, teaching both medical and veterinary students, publishing many valuable papers, and becoming a member of a number of learned societies, both in Edinburgh and in London. He also took an interest in antiquarian pursuits, was an enthusiastic Freemason, and become an officer in the Army Volunteers. He set up a company of volunteers of the Royal Scots Guards in Portobello, and exerted a wholesome influence of good in Edinburgh military circles. A dapper-looking man with a large bushy moustache, he advanced to become Colonel in 1896, taking command of a battalion of Royal Scots Guards volunteers.

In 1902, Colonel Macadam's battalion was just about to embark on a ship to London, to attend the parade for the coronation of Edward VII. On June 24 1902, dressed in his military uniform, he visited his laboratory at Surgeon's Hall

6. A postcard showing Surgeon's Hall.

to make some experiments. All of a sudden, the 46-year-old former soldier David McClinton, who worked as a porter in the laboratory, seized up his army rifle and fired two shots at Colonel Macadam, killing him instantly. When the laboratory assistant James Kirkcaldie came into the laboratory to see what was going on, McClinton fired at him with the outcry 'Here is another one I will shoot!' Kirkcaldie lived to fight another day, however, taking a leap to safety. When a student named James Bell Forbes, who had not noticed the gunfire, next came into the room, McClinton fired two rounds at him; the mortally wounded student died in hospital a few hours later. Stevenson Macadam, the brother of the murdered Colonel, bravely confronted the gunman, eventually succeeding in persuading him to surrender his rifle and ammunition.

The funeral of Colonel Ivison Macadam was one of the finest ever seen in Edinburgh. There was widespread grief that one of the leading citizens of the Capital had been gunned down in such a pointless and cowardly manner. More than 1000 troops took part in the funeral parade, and there were many carriages; the spectacle was followed by tens of thousands of townspeople, as the procession went from Colonel Macadam's house in Lady Road to the family grave in Portobello Cemetery. His son, Sir Ivison Macadam, later had a distinguished career in London and became the first Director-General of the Royal Institute of International Affairs.

Taken into custody by the police, Daniel McClinton faced trial for double murder in September 1902. He was a native of Lismoine, Ireland, and a married man who lived at 31a Windsor Street with his wife Jessie. He had been discharged from the Highland Light Infantry in 1895 after 21 years of service. A veteran army volunteer and an excellent marksman, he had been a good and reliable servant since employed at the Surgeons Hall laboratory in 1897. The last few years, he had seemed very paranoid and worried that people were spying at him or following him around. It had been suggested that he should be seen by a doctor, but McClinton continued his duties at the laboratory, and at the shooting range, until he made the decision to gun down Colonel Macadam; the murder of the student Forbes seems to have been spontaneous and not planned, although McClinton had planned to get even with two other servants at Surgeons Hall, who had annoyed him in the past.

In the end, David McClinton was convicted of culpable homicide, sentenced to imprisonment for life, and sent off to spend 20 years at HM Convict Prison, Peterhead. He was a willing worker there, although peculiar and erratic; since he was a sly and undependable character, and since his mental health was far from good, he was never considered for release. In 1920, he developed the delusions that his food was poisoned to do him harm, and that the son of Colonel Macadam was serving five years in prison at Peterhead under an assumed name. He was formally declared insane in February 1921 and transferred to the Criminal Lunatic Department at Perth.[5] David McClinton died from peritoneal cancer at the Perth prison infirmary in July 1923, aged 67.

7. Surgeon's Hall today.

MURDER AND SUICIDE IN
WARRENDER PARK TERRACE, 1908

Robert Mauchline was born in Edinburgh in 1846 and trained as a schoolmaster. The 1861 Census has him living with his parents, James and Mary Mauchline, at 19 St James Place, and working as a 'pupil teacher'. As a young man, he taught in a school at the West Port, but after graduating from the Training College, he went to Carluke, Lanarkshire. Teaching at the local school, he met Miss Jessie Pettigrew Russell, daughter of the prominent local mason Robert Russell, and married her not long after. They moved back to Edinburgh, where Mr Mauchline became headmaster at the

8. A postcard showing Warrender Park Terrace.

Old Assembly School, under the Heriot Trust. When this school was closed down, he transferred to the Torpichen Street School as an assistant master, teaching English, history and geography. He would spend many years at this school, rising to become first assistant master, with a good salary. He had a great interest in military music and liked visiting Edinburgh Castle to listen to the bands playing there. He could play the cornet and the flute himself, and had even written some musical compositions. He was able to save some money, and to give his wife and son a comfortable life in their flat at Warrender Park Terrace.

The 1901 Census has the 54-year-old Robert Mauchline living at 36 Warrender Park Terrace, with his 46-year-old wife Jessie and their 20-year-old son James. In early 1908, when Mr Mauchline was 62 years old, he was still teaching at the Torpichen Street School. But his colleagues noticed that the normally so jovial schoolmaster was looking quite sad and gloomy. When asked whether Mrs Mauchline might be suffering from a cold, or even influenza, he admitted that she had recently had delusions. The headmaster told him that he could take the rest of the day off, to spend it with his ailing wife. But Mr Mauchline returned to the school, where he conducted his classes with his usual ability.

On July 15 1908, a friend of the Mauchlines, in Tarvit Street, received a letter from Mrs Mauchline, to the effect that she should come to 36 Warrender Park Terrace, and bring a doctor. Since the note included instructions where to find the keys to the flat, and what steps should be taken in the event of an accident, the family friend got hold of a doctor and went to the Mauchline flat straight away. They found the two Mauchlines in bed, both of them stone dead. Robert had shot Jessie through the chest, before committing suicide by shooting himself through the head with a revolver, which was found next to the two corpses. 'Murder and Suicide in Edinburgh!' exclaimed the headline of the *Dundee Courier*, and the *Scotsman* also wrote several articles about the tragedy. Mrs Mauchline had been in ill health for some time, but her husband was known for his genial and kindly disposition, and he was regarded by his colleagues as about the last man to be involved in a tragedy of this kind.[6]

THE MURDER OF WEE FRANKIE DEMEO, 1909

Frankie Demeo was born as Francesco Demeo, at 21 High Street, Peebles, on November 27 1902. His father was recorded to be the Italian master confectioner Philip Demeo, and his mother the Scotswoman Elizabeth Mackay; there is nothing to suggest that his parents were married. Wee Frankie had a younger sister named Caterina alias Catherine, born at Peebles in 1905 and dead at Morningside in 1908. Since Philip Demeo had a relative who was in business in Edinburgh, he soon took his common-law wife and two children with him there.

In 1909, Elizabeth Mackay and the now six-year-old Francis Demeo were lodging at 3 Home Street at Tollcross in Edinburgh. In the early evening of March 22, Wee Frankie was playing outside the house, venturing out through the busy traffic to the railings of the Tollcross public lavatory. When a stranger approached him, they spoke together for a little while. But all of a sudden, the stranger hoisted Frankie up in the air, and flung him over the railings into the lavatory below. Wee Frankie landed on his head, and his skull was severely fractured. There were many people out and about in the Tollcross that particular evening, and although they had first thought that the stranger was the boy's father, who was playfully hoisting him up onto the railings, the real horror of the situation soon became apparent. Some of the onlookers grappled with the stranger, and managed to overpower him, while others carried Francis Demeo's limp body up from the lavatory and took him to the Royal Infirmary, where the doctor on duty declared that the severity of the boy's head injuries gave no hope of him surviving. Blameless Wee Frankie Demeo died just a few minutes after his admission to the hospital.

The cab proprietor Robert Henderson Moffat shouted 'Police!' when he saw Wee Frankie hurtling towards his death, and the brewery worker Donald Rowley tripped the murderer up and held him down until the police had arrived. The murderer was taken into custody by two sturdy police constables and conveyed to the City Police Office. He seemed quite insane and sang all the way to the police station. His name was John O'Neil, and he was a farmer from the village of Dromod, County Leitrim. A tall, thin man, he seemed to be of mediocre intellect, and he could not provide any motive for his murderous frenzy at the Tollcross. For reasons he could not explain to the police, he had moved from rural Ireland to Edinburgh just a few days earlier and had stayed in a lodging-house at the Grassmarket. Earlier the day of the murder, he had attempted to destroy himself by jumping in front of a tramcar, but unfortunately for Francis Demeo, a

9. The stairs down to the public lavatory, Tollcross, a postcard stamped and posted in 1912, three years after Wee Frankie Demeo had been murdered here.

bystander had been able to dissuade the Irish desperado from such rash actions. Described by a newspaper journalist as a tall, gawky-looking man, whose eyes had a wandering, restless look, he was committed to stand trial for murder.

On May 10 1909, John O'Neil stood his trial at the High Court of Justiciary in Edinburgh, for the murder of Francis Demeo. The Irishman looked quite despondent in court and appeared to feel his position keenly. Lord Guthrie stated to the jury that a special defence was to be put forward, to the effect that at the time he committed the crime, the accused was insane. Professor Harvey Littlejohn testified that he had twice spoken to John O'Neil, and that the move from the quiet Irish countryside to the busy streets of Edinburgh had clearly had a pernicious effect on his feeble intellect. The day of the murder, O'Neil believed he had seen mysterious strangers murder his brother, by shooting him and tearing off his arm, and that he had seen his own blood flowing in the street. When it had been explained to him that he had just murdered a little boy, he had wept and said he was sorry for the mischief he had caused. Dr Hay, the prison doctor, corroborated Professor Littlejohn's findings. In accordance with Lord Guthrie's directions, the jury acquitted John O'Neill on the capital charge of murder, on the grounds that he had been insane at the time. Lord Guthrie issued an order that O'Neil should be confined to Perth Prison until his Majesty's pleasure was known. When the prisoner heard this, he raised his head and stared directly at his Lordship, before relapsing into his former state of oblivion.

Elizabeth Mackay, who was heavily pregnant at the time of the murder, felt the loss of Wee Frankie very keenly. She rushed to the Royal Infirmary to be with him and collapsed when she became aware that he was dead. Since there is no mention of Philip Demeo, the boy's father, in any of the newspaper reports of the murder, he might well have deserted his family by that time. Francis Demeo was buried with much pomp on March 27. There was much interest in the brutal murder of a blameless little boy among the citizens of Edinburgh, and a crowd of more than a thousand people gathered in the Tollcross, obstructing the busy traffic. All the windows in the surrounding houses had their blinds drawn. There was a sudden hush among the crowd as the little white coffin was carried out of 3 Home Street and placed in the hearse. The men in the crowd removed their headgear, and some of the women wept aloud, as the procession passed slowly down Lothian Road, which was also lined with spectators. The funeral procession continued up Queensferry Road, and across Dean Bridge, to reach the burial-ground at Comely Bank. A force of police was in attendance, and the general public was excluded from the graveyard. The Rev. R.L. Jeffery, of St John's, conducted the service, and the grave was marked by a large marble cross subscribed by the general public.[7]

Elizabeth Mackay gave birth to a daughter on April 3, just a few days after Wee Frankie had been buried. Well-nigh unhinged by the tragedy of losing her beloved son, she did not want anything to do with her little daughter. Elizabeth, as the child was named, was left with an old drunk and his wife, and later passed through a number of foster homes, workhouses and children's homes. She was visited, for a while, by a man who told her to call him 'Papa', but we do not know if this was the elusive confectioner Philip Demeo, or perhaps some other dodgy cove. In 1931, Elizabeth managed to track down her biological mother, who was then running a lodging-house in Portobello, and cohabiting with a man who had both his legs amputated below the knees. They lived together for a while, before the volatile Elizabeth Mackay once more got tired of her daughter, beat her up and threw her out. Young Elizabeth went on to become a domestic servant, before chronicling her sad life, which had been blighted by the murder of Wee Frankie Demeo, in her gloomy autobiography *A Discarded Brat*, published at Inverness in 1980.[8] Herself, she died in 1998, aged 89.

TRIPLE MURDER IN FALCON AVENUE, 1915

The young Boer William Juta came from a wealthy and influential family, being the son of Coenraad Jacobus Juta, High Sheriff of Transvaal, and his wife Renitte Johanna. Young Juta moved to Edinburgh in 1901, in order to study medicine. Financial support was not lacking, at least initially, to support his Caledonian medical career, and his wallet was kept well stocked with money by his family back home. After some linguistic tuition, Juta registered as a medical student in 1902, when he was 18 years old. The Edinburgh medical school was known for its high standards: the curriculum was a punishing one in those days, and the examinations very demanding. Since young Juta did not have the intellect to keep up with his studies, he soon fell behind the other students in his age group.

His academic difficulties did not prevent William Juta from having a good time in his adopted country. There was an established club for South African students at Edinburgh University, and in 1903, they went for an outing to Carnoustie, playing golf on the links there. Juta was a keen golfer, spending much time with his clubs; he moved in good society, and met several wealthy and respectable Scots from old Carnoustie families. One of them was the widow Mrs Jessie Jean Macgregor and her daughter Muriel. She had been married to the wealthy indigo planter William Macgregor, who had recently died in India. William Juta, described as a thick-set, well-built man of medium size, immediately became fond of the pretty young Muriel, who was one year younger than him. They played golf and tennis together, and he found her an excellent sportswoman, who shared his fondness for outdoor pursuits. She, in turn, was impressed with the wealthy young Boer, who would one day enjoy excellent prospects as a doctor, or so at least she hoped. They married in 1907 and set up house together at 21 Falcon Avenue, Morningside.

At the time of the 1911 Census, the Jutas had a little daughter named Muriel Renette, born in 1910. William was by now 27 years old and still a medical student, the 26-year-old Muriel did no work but looked after her little baby, and the 60-year-old Jean Macgregor lived with them in their comfortable, four-storied terraced house. Little Muriel Renette died from tuberculous meningitis and peritonitis in January 1912, but the Jutas had another child by that time, the healthy son William David Macgregor Juta, born in 1910. The problem was that William Juta was making very slow progress through the medical curriculum. In 1915, when he had been a student for 13 years, he still had several difficult examinations to pass before he would be taking his finals. His wife and mother-in-law were becoming apprehensive whether he would ever become a doctor, and aware that they could hardly support the household once the generous

FALCON AVENUE, EDINBURGH

10. Falcon Avenue, a postcard stamped and posted to Gibraltar in 1913.

flow of money from South Africa had been disrupted. Although William Juta did his best to keep up appearances, he was fast becoming a desperate man.

On September 17 1915, things looked blacker than ever for William Juta. His father had expired, and there had been murmurations from the direction of Transvaal that unless academic progress was made, and the final exams passed very soon, his allowance would cease, for good. Juta was now a man of 31, and he should have graduated as a doctor eight years ago. That very day, he had miserably failed an important examination, and this added disappointment seems to have removed his last mental inhibitions, and made him a murderous madman, determined to wipe out his entire family. Later that very day, Juta went back to 21 Falcon Avenue, where he loaded a pistol and shot his wife and little son dead. The mother-in-law Mrs Macgregor went into the kitchen to investigate when she heard the gunshots, but Juta stood ready for her at the doorway, and gunned her down as well.

11. The murderous William Juta makes it to the first page of the Illustrated Police News of September 23 1915.

12. The Falcon Avenue murder house today.

The demented mass murderer then reloaded his gun and went to the South African Student's Union at 14 Buccleugh Place, where he was one of the regulars. He read some books in the library and discussed the progress of the Great War with a friend. As Juta sat swigging from his glass of whisky, he suddenly called out "Good-bye boys! Forgive me for doing this. I want to die among my fellow-countrymen!" He then blew his brains out with a shot from his powerful revolver. The police found a letter where he had detailed the previous carnage he had wrought at the family house in Falcon Avenue, and they recovered the three bodies from the murder house. In his suicide letter, Juta asked that his wife and child should be buried at Morningside Cemetery; his wealthy brother in Pretoria would pay all the expenses. Controversially, the remaining members of the Macgregor family allowed Juta to be buried in the same grave. Three hearses were employed, the first carrying the coffins of Mrs Juta and her little son, the second that of Mrs Macgregor, and the third that of the triple murderer himself. The impressive funeral cortege was followed by a large crowd of people, as it passed the murder house in Falcon Avenue before entering the cemetery, where a grave had been prepared at the western end. The Rev. Mr Brown, of Morningside Parish Church, said a heartfelt prayer, and a troop of South African students stood to attention as the remains of the triple murderer of Falcon Avenue were interred in the same grave as those of his three victims.[9]

MURDER IN NICOLSON SQUARE, 1920

Nicholas Page Campbell was born in 1887, the son of the distillery worker Peter Campbell and his wife Hannah. He became a plumber and worked as an assistant in Mr Gilchrist's plumbing company. In 1907, he married the 19-year-old Margaret Hendry Paterson, the daughter of a mattress maker, and they soon had two sons: Nicholas Jr and Peter Campbell, and two younger daughters as well. When sober, Nicholas Page Campbell was a steady and industrious workman, but when drunk, he showed strong violent tendencies: in August 1910, he beat and kicked a police constable, being found guilty of assault and fined £2. He enlisted as a private soldier in the 5th Royal Scots two days after the outbreak of the Great War, serving with merit in Gallipoli and France, and being thrice wounded in action.

After being demobilized from the army, Nicholas Page Campbell carried on plumbing for Mr Gilchrist's firm. As fierce and angry as ever while in his cups, he was again convicted of assault in May 1919 after head-butting his wife hard in the face during a domestic argument, and fined another £2. In late July

1920, he was paid his gratuity for five years of army service, pocketing a total of £62 10s. To celebrate this windfall, he went out drinking whisky, consuming quantities of the Scottish national drink before lurching home to his wife Margaret at their ground floor flat at 8 Nicolson Square. He had bought six pies, which he planned to share with Margaret and the four children, but things soon turned nasty. Nicholas Page Campbell started cursing his wife, before striking her a series of blows to the face, sending her reeling to the floor. The 13-year-old son Nicholas, who had seen his mother being knocked down, was told to go to bed.

Old Peter Campbell, father of the wife-beating plumber, also lived in the small flat at 8 Nicolson Square, but at least he had a room of his own. From this humble abode, he heard Margaret scream 'Oh, dinna, Nicky!', followed by a loud crashing sound emanating from the kitchen, but he did not pay any notice. After a while, Nicholas Page Campbell came to tell him that his wife was unwell, inviting his father to come down to the kitchen to have a cup of tea. When old Campbell saw Margaret lying on the kitchen bed, her face very swollen and discoloured, he recommended that a doctor should be called, but his son pooh-poohed his concerns, saying 'There she is, lying there drunk!' It was not until the following morning, when he had sobered up, that Nicholas Page Campbell went to see his sister, but when a missionary and a doctor finally came to the flat at 8 Nicolson Square, all they could do was to certify the death of Margaret Campbell. Her husband was arrested for murdering her and ordered to stand trial at the High Court of Edinburgh.

The murder trial of Nicholas Page Campbell opened on September 28 1920. Nicholas Jr and old Peter Campbell gave accounts of their experiences the evening of the murder; the former described how his father, who was 'very bad in drink', had struck his mother down with great force. The post-mortem examination showed that Margaret Campbell had died from repeated blunt trauma to the head, resulting in intracranial haemorrhage, concussion and shock. The defence emphasized

13. The murder house at 8 Nicholson Square.

the impeccable military service record of the accused. When sober, he was very fond of his wife, they alleged. His veteran employer Mr George Gilchrist, for whose firm he had been working 16 years, found him a steady workman. Ten years ago, when he had been working on a construction site, he had been injured by a falling brick hitting his head; this experience had resulted in him getting very excitable while in drink, a medical witness alleged.

The jury was out for a quarter of an hour, before finding the accused guilty of culpable manslaughter, and he was sentenced to twelve years of penal servitude.[10] Nicholas Page Campbell served his time in prison, before carrying on working as a plumber in Edinburgh. He married a woman named Mary Ogilvie Ford in 1944, but died at the Royal Infirmary in 1954, from an inoperable carcinoma of the neck. His son and namesake also married and lived on until 1973.

MURDER IN ST PATRICK SQUARE, 1920

Samuel Thomas Fraser was a young Edinburgh man who had served as an army soldier from 1915 until after the Armistice. In 1920, when he was 25 years old, he was working as a brewery labourer. In April that year, he married the printing assistant Agnes Cree, the daughter of draper's traveller William Cree, who lived at 47 St Patrick Square. In May the same year, their little son Samuel Thomas was born, but the marriage was not a success and in August Agnes moved out of the flat where they had been living, at 9 Crichton Street, and went back to her father's little third-floor flat at St Patrick Square.

14. The Fraser murder house at 47 St Patrick Square today.

On August 21, Samuel Thomas Fraser came to see Agnes at St Patrick Square. He seemed very gloomy and despondent, but he was still taken into the parlour, where asked to see his little son. A quarter of an hour later, he asked Agnes to go and see what time it was, but she did not want to leave him alone with the baby and refused to go. He then pulled the window open, threw the child out, and then jumped himself. There was a 40-foot fall down to the unyielding flagstones of St Patrick Square: the baby died instantly, but the desperado Fraser lived on until the following afternoon, when he succumbed to his terrible injuries. 'Shocking Edinburgh tragedy!' exclaimed the headline of the *Edinburgh Evening News*; as for the possible motive for his rash act, it was pointed out that Fraser had been twice wounded in France, and that he might have suffered from shell-shock.[11]

TRAGEDY AT 'SUNNYSIDE', 1935

In the 1930s, the two-story villa 'Sunnyside' at 42 Alnwickhill Road, Liberton, was home to the 54-year-old Leith excise officer Frederick Campbell Baxter, his 40-year-old wife Jessie Agnes, and their 8-year-old daughter Kathleen Margaret. Mr Baxter was fond of studying languages, and a member of the French and German Circles; he was also an accomplished bowler, who played quite a few games for the local club. They had been living at Sunnyside for 10 years, and Kathleen had been born there. She was described as a particularly good-looking child, who found the schoolwork easy to cope with. The neighbours found the Baxters quite the model modern family.

But in late 1934, Mr Baxter's mental health had deteriorated: he became intensely self-centered and hypochondriacal, and depressed and despondent about his prospects in life. He remained devoted to his wife and daughter but was very concerned about

Robertson's Series.   *ALNWICKHILL ROAD, LIBERTON.*   Edinburgh & Liberton.

15. Alnwickhill Road, a postcard stamped and posted in 1913.

their future. When he saw, in a spiritualist magazine, a picture of two female figures who were stretching their hands out towards the sun, he realized that it was now his duty to help his wife and child to 'see the light'.

In the early hours of the morning of February 4 1935, Mr Baxter armed himself with a large hatchet and went on a rampage at Sunnyside. He hit Kathleen on the head, killing her instantly, before attacking his wife in a murderous frenzy, repeatedly hitting her about the face and head and mutilating her terribly. The demented murderer then washed the blood off his clothes and pondered what to do next. When a little girl came knocking at the door, to ask if Kathleen would come with her to school, he politely told her that his daughter had a cold and would be staying at home. But the sheer horror of staying in the blood-spattered family home must have been too much for him, since he quietly crept out to a public telephone kiosk and called the police. The City Police was promptly at the scene, and took Baxter

16. The murder house at 42 Alnwickhill Road. It has hardly changed at all since this contemporary photograph was taken.

into custody, as Professor Sydney Smith meticulously examined the murder house, with the two bodies still in situ.

On February 5, Frederick Campbell Baxter appeared at the Edinburgh Burgh Court, on a charge of murder. There was great public interest in the tragedy at Sunnyside, and many of the curious were unable to find seats for themselves. An *Edinburgh Evening Dispatch* journalist described the accused as a slight but wiry man, with thick dark hair greying at the temples, and a neatly clipped moustache. It turned out that Mrs Baxter's old parents were both still alive, and residing in Dunbar, where her nonagenarian father James Mustard had been station officer for the coastguards for many years.

On March 25 1935, Frederick Campbell Baxter stood trial at the High Court of Justiciary, charged with the murders of his wife and daughter. There was no question that he was the guilty man, but the psychiatrists Professor David Kennedy Henderson, of Edinburgh University, and Dr William McAlister, medical superintendent of the Bangour Mental Hospital in West Lothian, were both of the opinion that he had been insane at the time of the deaths of his wife and child, and that he was now insane and unfit to plead to the charge brought against him. The Lord Justice Clerk said that he was satisfied with the psychiatric evidence, and he sustained the plea of insanity in bar of trial.[12] The asylum doors closed behind Frederick Campbell Baxter, but not for very long, as it turned out; at the time of his death, from a cerebral haemorrhage, in March 1946, he was residing at 'Fife View', Alnwickhill Road, not far from the murder house.

A MATRICIDAL MEDICAL STUDENT, 1956

In 1956, the 60-year-old widow Mrs Christina Lees lived in the third flat at 75 Buccleuch Street, Newington, with her 35-year-old son Robert Black Lees, a former RAF navigator who had been studying medicine for quite a few years, with mediocre success. On Sunday June 24 1956, there was a '999' call from Mrs Lees' flat, and when the police arrived, they found her dead in bed. Several taps on the gas cooker were open, and the flat was full of gas. Robert Black Lees was also in the flat, unhurt apart from trifling cuts to the wrists. It was clear to the police that he had gassed his mother to death before staging a feeble suicide attempt.

After having his injuries seen to at the Edinburgh Royal Infirmary, Robert Black Lees was taken into police custody. The public benches at the Edinburgh Burgh Court were crowded when he appeared on a charge of murder on June 27. An *Edinburgh Evening News* journalist wrote that: "When he made his appearance at the Burgh Court, Lees, who is dark skinned and has black crinkly hair, was wearing a light grey pinstripe double-breasted suit and a white shirt. Asked by Mr J.G. Mitchell, Clerk of Court: 'Are you Robert Black Lees?' The accused replied clearly in a cultured voice: 'Yes, I am.'" At his trial at the High Court on August 27, medical evidence was presented that he had been insane at the time he had murdered his mother, and that he was unfit to plead to the charge of murder. Lord Wheatley ordered that Lees should be detained during her Majesty's pleasure under the Lunacy (Scotland) Act of 1887.[13] There is evidence that Robert Black Lees was out of the asylum by the early 1970s, however; he married in 1974, became a stereotyper, and died from a myocardial infarction in 1976 aged 56.

17. The tenement at 75 Buccleuch Street.

THE VIEWFORTH SHOOTING
TRAGEDY, 1957

On November 26 1957, all seemed well at 59 Viewforth, Merchiston. As the window cleaner Victor Murray was busy at Mrs Clark's first-floor flat in this tall tenement, he suddenly heard a bang, and then another one. He opened a window and leapt into the flat, only to find Mrs Clark standing leaning at the door to the stair, screaming 'There's a man with a gun out there!' Although the gunman had not aimed his weapon at her, but instead exclaimed 'It's all right, missus!' she had swiftly retreated into her own premises. When Murray alerted a crowd of schoolboys outside, it turned out that they had also seen the gunman escaping, so he sent them off to find a police constable since Mrs Clark did not have a telephone.

When the police arrived at 59 Viewforth, it soon became clear that the gunman had enjoyed good success in his murderous pursuits: the 46-year-old Mrs Martha Rutherford was lying dead across the doorway of her top floor flat, after being shot four times. The locals had thought Mrs Rutherford something of a mystery woman, who had arrived at the flat just two months earlier; she kept to herself and seemed to be guarding some secret. The police soon found out that she was in fact the mother of five living children, and the estranged wife of the miner William Rutherford, who lived at 40 St Clement's Crescent, Wallyford, with several of their children. When the police came knocking at this address, his son Kenneth told them that his father had gone missing and was not at home.

The hue and cry was now up for William Rutherford, the prime suspect for gunning down his estranged wife, but in spite of a diligent search, he was nowhere to be found. On November 27, his body was found in a disused hut in the yard of an Edinburgh scrap metal merchant, with a bullet through the head.[14] It turned out that 18 months earlier, Martha Rutherford had left the family

18. Bruntsfield Place and Viewforth, a postcard stamped and posted in 1911. Reproduced by permission of Mr G. Burgess, Dunbar.

home in Wallyford, to her husband's great chagrin, never to return. Rutherford had searched towns and cities all over Britain in his frenzied hunt for her, and spent a large part of his life's savings. Three weeks earlier, he had learnt that she was living in an Edinburgh flat ...

MURDER IN POLWARTH GARDENS, 1961

The 52-year-old stationery firm manager Dryden Alexander Brown lived in the ground floor flat at 27 Polwarth Gardens, Merchiston, with his 50-year-old wife Mona. On September 25 1961, a 999 emergency call was received at the police headquarters in the High Street. It came from Dryden Alexander Brown, who confessed that he had just killed his wife. The police officers promptly took Brown into custody, before they searched the murder flat minutely, and the forensic expert Dr F.S. Fiddes examined the body of Mrs Brown.

On trial for murder at the High Court in Edinburgh, Dryden Alexander Brown made a plea of culpable homicide, claiming that he had committed a 'mercy killing' when he strangled his mentally ill wife with a stocking. The bonhomous Lord Justice Clerk, Lord Thomson, accepted this plea after the evidence of two psychiatrists had been heard. Described as smartly dressed in a dark suit with a red tie, Brown got away with just 15 months in prison, a lenient sentence if there ever was one.[15] He went on to live a long and hopefully rewarding life, expiring in 2006 at the great age of 96.

TRIPLE MURDER AT OXGANGS GREEN, 1962

Marie Elizabeth Tucker was born in 1929. Her life was a sad and unfortunate one: her mother committed suicide when she was just five years old, and no person wanted to look after her; after travelling around Scotland for several years, she was finally admitted to a convent in Edinburgh. The nuns took good care of her, and in due course they managed to get her a job with an Edinburgh firm. Here she met, and later married, the electrician Michael M'Ginty. They moved into a small ground floor flat in a Corporation house at 2a Oxgangs Green and had a reasonably happy life together. With her feeble intellect, Marie M'Ginty was unable to handle the family finances, so her husband took care of the payment of the rent and the bills. The couple quarrelled regularly, and after one of these family disputes, in 1958, Marie made a half-hearted suicide attempt.

In December 1962, Michael and Marie M'Ginty still lived in their flat at Oxgangs Green. He had advanced to become branch manager of an Edinburgh TV shop, but she remained quite scatter-brained, and could only be relied upon to perform the most menial tasks. The marriage had been blessed with three children: four-year-old Susan, thirteen-month-old Michael, and baby Kevin who was just six weeks old. The family also had a budgerigar named Joey. On the morning of December 4, Michael M'Ginty was once more disappointed with his wife, after she had been unable to explain what had happened to a £6 maternity grant she had purloined. He angrily exclaimed 'I wish we did not have a family!' before leaving the house and going to work. His long-minded wife sat pondering this final insult, before taking swift and murderous action.

When Michael M'Ginty came home to the flat at lunchtime the same day, his wife had left him a sinister note: "Your last words this morning were 'I wish we did not have a family!' – Now you don't!" Lurching into the children's bedroom, he found them all dead, suffocated to death from plastic bags put over their heads. The distraught Mr M'Ginty ran off to St Mark's Chapel nearby, returning to the murder flat with Father Lynch and his curate Father McKessock. The two priests made sure that the police were called, and Mrs M'Ginty was soon taken into custody. Joey the budgerigar, the only living creature in the flat when the frantic father returned from work, was taken care of by an ornithophilic neighbour.

The drab-looking, bespectacled Marie M'Ginty wore a green coat in the dock as she appeared at the High Court in Edinburgh on January 22 1963. After medical evidence had been collected as to her mental state, the charge of murder had been reduced to one of culpable homicide, to which Mrs M'Ginty pleaded guilty. The Lord-Justice Clerk, Lord Grant, said that this was a most grave crime, although he was convinced that it had been emotional instability that had led to such a terrible tragedy. He sentenced her to life imprisonment, saying that this sentence would give the authorities the widest latitude to decide when it was appropriate in her own interests, and in those of other people, that she should be released.[16]

THE MURDER OF
WEE CATHERINE BROWN, 1968

In the evening of June 24 1968, the 7-year-old Catherine Brown left the family flat at 89 Colinton Mains Grove and went to the small grocery shop at 94 Colinton Mains Drive, where she played with her friend Anna Maria Andreetti in a sandpit at the back yard behind the shop. At 6 pm, the two little girls were happily playing in the yard; at 6.06, Mr Andreetti told them to come in and wash their hands; at 6.10, Catherine Brown was said to have left the house. But at 7 pm, Catherine's elder sister Alice came to the Andreetti shop to take her home, believing that she was still at the grocer's shop. Catherine Brown had clearly disappeared, and the police were swiftly called in. Little Catherine was not a flighty girl, and she had never gone missing before. Her father, the fruit market trader Bert Brown, told the police that his daughter did not have an enemy in the world; she was a bright and well-mannered little girl who was popular locally and did well in the school infant's class.

The police took the hunt for the missing Catherine Brown very seriously indeed. In one of the most ambitious missing person searches ever seen in Edinburgh, a task force of 80 policemen, including troops of mounted constables and dog handlers, was set to work searching every inch of Colinton Mains. The Scots Guards were also called in to help in the search operation, taking charge of the land towards the Pentland Hills, assisted by the police helicopter. Nothing interesting was found in spite of this great effort, and the following day the search party was scaled down to a troop of 30 policemen including detectives.

Speaking to an *Edinburgh Evening News* journalist from the upper flat at 89 Colinton Mains Grove, Bert Brown said the case was a great mystery. The local roads were quite busy, yet no person had seen little Catherine wandering about. He praised the police, army, and local community for their sterling efforts to find his missing daughter. Mrs Mary Brown, the mother of the missing girl, had left the family flat to stay with relatives, taking her two other daughters with her. The *Edinburgh Evening News* journalist also went to the Andreetti grocery shop at 94 Colinton Mains Drive, where he interviewed the 15-year-old son Ronald John Andreetti, who said that the day little Catherine had disappeared, he had shouted at the two little girls to come in and wash their hands, since his father was sitting in the lounge. After washing her hands in the upstairs bathroom, Catherine had shouted 'Cheerio!' and skipped off home.

The recruitment of detectives to the search party belatedly brought some superior brain power to the hunt for the missing Catherine Brown. Might the fact that no person had seen little Catherine in the streets not indicate that she had in fact never left the flat over the grocer's shop at 94 Colinton Mains Drive? And indeed, when the flat was searched on June 27, Catherine's dead body was found inside a large suitcase in the attic bedroom. The lad Ronald John Andreetti, who had been 'telling porkies' to the journalist just a few days ago, admitted that he had knocked her down, strangled her, stabbed her with a screwdriver, and attempted to ravish her.

In police custody, Ronald John Andreetti seemed quite apathetic, and he showed no reaction when he was charged with murder at the Edinburgh Sheriff's Court. Described as a stocky lad with dark wavy hair, he pleaded guilty to a charge of culpable homicide. On trial at the High Court, it was obvious that this 15-year-old lad had murdered little Catherine Brown. No other motive could be discerned but sexual perversion. Since there had been much speculation, the prosecution made it clear that no other member of the Andreetti family had taken active steps to protect the accused during the three days Catherine Brown had been missing; the discovery of the body in the attic room had come as a complete surprise to them. Two consultant psychiatrists gave evidence, saying that although Ronald John Andreetti was not clinically insane, he displayed a degree of mental abnormality

Mounted police taking part in the search for Catherine Brown ride past the shopping centre in Colinton Mains Drive. Mrs Andreettis' grocer's shop is arrowed.

19. A police patrol passing the Andreetti murder shop.

bordering on insanity. Considering what he had just proven himself capable of, he was clearly a very dangerous individual to have wandering at large, and it would be in the public interest for him to be indefinitely detained in the State Mental Hospital. Lord Grant, the Lord Justice Clerk, said that he was satisfied there was only one proper course open to him, and ordered Ronald John Andreetti to be detained at the State Mental Hospital, Carstairs, without limit of time.[17] He got out of there in the 1980s, moved to Livingston, married and became a joiner, but he died from a myocardial infarction in 1989, aged just 36.

The Andreetti family was said to have been completely devastated by the tragedy of their son murdering little Catherine Brown, for reasons of sexual perversion. Although the Andreettis had been quite popular before the murder, there was a good deal of local gossip that they had been trying to conceal the crime, and shelter their pervert son, and they soon sold their shop and flat and moved elsewhere. A contemporary photograph of the Andreetti shop at 94 Colinton Mains Drive shows its exact position in the row of shops that is today 76-90 Colinton Mains Drive. The following house is 98 Colinton Mains Drive, meaning that the number of the murder house is no longer in use today. But an experienced murder house detective is not fooled by such simple stratagems: the murder flat is situated above the Colinton Mains Pharmacy at what is today 86 Colinton Mains Drive.

HE MURDERED HIS GRANDMOTHER, 1968

Mrs Gwendoline Thompson married in 1946 and had not less than 10 children, eight of whom reached maturity. In 1967, when her marriage was breaking down, it was arranged that two of the children, the 17-year-old Alastair William Thompson and his 8-year-old sister Lynn, should go to live with their paternal grandmother, Mrs Margaret Swanson Thompson, in her ground-floor flat at 24 Colinton Mains Terrace. Gwendoline Thompson later left her husband and went to live in a flat at 19 Springwell Place. Her younger children were still at school, but Alastair was working as a banana packer at the Market Street fruit market. He did not get on with his grandmother, but there was no money for him to get a flat of his own. Alastair had always been a bad hat, cruel to animals and habitually dishonest.

On January 27 1968, the 71-year-old Margaret Swanson Thompson was found stabbed to death in her flat, by her 13-year-old grandson Patrick, who had climbed in through a window after she had failed to answer the door. The police soon found out that Alastair William Thompson had been living in her flat, and since they knew that he was a disreputable character who used to carry a knife, he became the main suspect. When the police came knocking at a known hideout for dubious young men in Leven Street, the young hooligans there lied that they did not know Alastair William Thompson, although he was in fact hiding in the flat. But in spite of this cunning trick, young Thompson was soon taken into police custody and charged with murdering his grandmother. When he was sitting in a room at the police station, guarded by a detective sergeant, he suddenly exclaimed 'It was her or me!' He went on to make the statement that his grandmother had been nagging him every minute of every day, and eventually he had had enough of her. He had hit her with a hammer and then murdered her with a knife as she desperately fought for her life. He had then looked through the flat for money but found none.

This incriminating statement to the police put Alastair William Thompson at a disadvantage when his trial opened at the High Court on May 7. His mother described her chaotic life, with children coming and going, and her son now standing trial for murdering her mother-in-law. The gang of young hooligans who had sheltered Thompson from the police received a stern talking-to, although they refused to admit that Thompson had put them up to this trick. Margaret Swanson Thompson had been stabbed 20 times, and her hands had been badly cut as she had desperately tried to defend herself from the frenzied murderer. Blood matching her blood group had been found on articles of clothing worn by young Thompson, and he had a cut to a finger that he was unable to explain. Alastair William Thompson gave evidence on his own behalf, denying everything, but he did not make a good impression in court. The jury took 90 minutes to reach a verdict of guilty to murder. Lord Wheatley told Thompson that he had been convicted of a brutal, vicious and dastardly murder, and sentenced him to imprisonment for life.[18] An appeal claiming that a girl had written a letter confessing to the murder, and a petition for a retrial claiming there was fresh evidence, both came to nothing.

Alastair William Thompson served sixteen years in prison, mostly in Perth, before being released in 1984. He married a female social worker he had met in prison, but the marriage soon ended in divorce and Thompson went to England for a while, before returning to Dundee, where he worked as a caterer's storeman, before becoming caretaker of the home run by the Scottish Association for the Care and Resettlement of Prisoners in Haldane Terrace. He had become a bisexual while serving his long prison sentence, and on Christmas Eve 1992, he met the homosexual Gordon Dunbar and took him to a flat in the high-rise block Butterburn Court. He threatened Dunbar with a knife and stole his bank card and personal identification number, before stabbing him to death. Thompson then dismembered the remains, and hid the bags of body parts away as well as he could, but they were found by an off-duty police dog and the murderous Scot received a second life sentence, this time serving seventeen years in prison before dying from atherosclerotic coronary artery disease at Perth Prison in December 2010, aged 61.[19]

MURDER IN CAPTAIN'S DRIVE, 1976

Mrs Jessie Moffat was a 82-year-old invalid pensioner, more or less housebound to her home at 79 Captain's Drive, Liberton. When her home help came calling on December 2 1976, the old lady was found throttled to death in the house. A young thug, the 19-year-old John Balsillie, appeared at the Edinburgh Sheriff Court on December 6, charged with her murder. He was also charged with attacking and robbing three other women not far from Mrs Moffat's home.

On trial at the High Court in March 1977, the charge alleged that Balsillie had pushed Jessie Moffat to the floor, punched and kicked her, and removed her stockings and underclothes, before throttling her to death. Weeping profusely, the craven Balsillie admitted attacking the defenceless old woman, kicking and punching her hard, before stealing two watches and a magnifying glass from the house, but he was certain that she had still been alive when he left with his swag. There was good technical evidence against him, and the pattern of his clogs fitted footprints found in the murder house. The jury brought a unanimous verdict of guilty to murder, and Balsillie was sentenced to imprisonment for life, but he would live to fight another day, and we will encounter him again in this book.[20]

HEAD-BUTTING AT THE GRAPES PUBLIC HOUSE, 1978

On July 22 1978, there was an angry altercation between two women at the Grapes public house, at 77 Clerk Street. When the 18-year-old John Morgan came forward to assist his mother in the argument, the son of the other woman, 33-year-old Thomas Restorick McCallum, head-butted him hard in the face. The two men then shook hands and had a drink together, as the two women continued quarrelling. But John Morgan, a feeble youth who suffered from haemophilia, was found dead the following morning.

Since it was believed that the head-butt he had received was the cause of death of John Morgan, Thomas McCallum was charged with murdering him at the Edinburgh Sheriff Court on July 31. But the autopsy showed that apart from his haemophilia, Morgan's skull was also seriously defective: it was 'paper thin' and only two millimetres thick in places. Thus even the slightest trauma to the head had the potential to cause a lethal intracranial haemorrhage, although Morgan might well have survived if

189

20. The Grapes murder pub at 77 Clerk Street still stands.

he had been taken to hospital with expedition. In the end, the case was heard in the summary criminal court of the Edinburgh Sheriff Court: McCallum pleaded guilty to a charge of assault and was sentenced to imprisonment for four months.[21] He may well have been the Thomas Restorick McCallum who died in Edinburgh in 2003, aged 53.

AXE MURDER IN MOREDUNVALE VIEW, 1983

In the early 1960s, the Edinburgh painter and decorator James Smith Weir married his wife Ethel. They were not particularly happy together, since James was a very angry, jealous man. In 1975, he was convicted of assaulting his wife in a bout of jealousy. In November 1982, this mismatched pair finally separated: Ethel stayed in the family home at 27 Moredunvale View, and James moved to a lonely bedsit at South Fort Street, Leith. He still stalked her whenever he could and spied on her movements from a high-rise building nearby. In January 1983, she obtained a court order to stop him molesting her, but he carried on regardless.

On April 7 1983, Ethel Weir was visiting her solicitor when she saw her bugbear husband lurking outside, spying on her. She became very distressed but was persuaded to return home. But James Smith Weir was also on his way to 27 Moredunvale View, having purchased an axe on the way. In a furious rage, he beat her up with the axe, inflicting horrific injuries, before throttling her to death. He then took the train to Newcastle but gave himself up to the police there. On trial for murder at the High Court in June 1983, James Smith Weir's long history of violence against his wife was exposed. A forensic psychiatrist described his condition as the 'morbid jealousy syndrome', adding that Weir would need treatment for a very long time, perhaps the remainder of his life. Lord Wheatley ordered him to be sent to the State Mental Hospital, Carstairs, without limit of time.[22] He was released in 1994 but is said to have committed suicide not long after.

MURDER IN GILMORE PLACE, 1984

On July 21 1984, the 42-year-old Mary Kane was found stabbed to death in the guesthouse at 14 Gilmore Place, near Tollcross. Another guest, the 24-year-old Malcolm Mackay, was taken into police custody since he had been behaving suspiciously nearby. He had just been released following a two-year prison sentence for indecent assault, imposed at the Stornoway Sheriff Court in August 1982.

On trial for murder at the High Court in November 1984, Malcolm Mackay pleaded guilty to the lesser charge of culpable homicide, but this was rejected by the Crown. Mackay testified that Mary Kane had come to his room demanding sex, but he had been incapable of performing intercourse. She had become angry, slapped his face, and threatened to tell his girlfriend, so he told her to put her clothes on and get out. She had then attacked him with a knife, and in the struggle that ensued, she had been accidentally stabbed in the chest. He had drunk much vodka, he admitted, and his recollections were very muddled.

But since Mary Kane had in fact been stabbed nine times in the back, Mackay's story was not believed. The jury found him guilty of murder, and Lord Murray sentenced him to imprisonment for life.[23] The murder house at 14 Gilmore Place is today the Emmaus House guesthouse.

THE FROGSTON HORROR, 1991

For many years, the retired district tax inspector Robert Steven lived contentedly in the detached house at 25 Frogston Road West, with his wife Florence. He had two vintage cars, which he maintained himself, and she was keen on gardening and antiques collecting; their front garden was the finest in Frogston Road West, and the house was tastefully furnished with valuable art and antiques. But old age crept up on the two pensioners: he got cancer and became an invalid, and she was house-bound and very frail. The vintage cars were sold, the garden neglected, and no one answered the door at 25 Frogston Road West when some public-spirited neighbour came calling. The Edinburgh burglar fraternity found out that the unprotected house was full of art and antique furniture, and in 1991, it was broken into not less than five times.

In October 1991, when Robert Steven was 82 years old and his wife 84, the reclusive couple still lived at 25 Frogston Road West. On October 3, the next-door neighbour Miss Ann Tod, of 27 Frogston Road West, received a call that the 'meals on wheels' people could not get into No. 25. On her lunch break, she went back home and entered 25 Frogston Road West. The hallway was littered with packages wrapped in brown paper. Robert Steven was tied to his bed, shouting for help. He had been handcuffed and gagged, and his hearing aid had been removed. In the room next door, Florence Steven was lying in her bed, tied up, gagged and quite dead.

Detective Superintendent Norman Henderson took charge of the murder investigation, leading a force of more than 40 officers. Robert Steven was taken to the Edinburgh Royal Infirmary, where he gradually recovered from his ordeal, although the handcuffs had led to permanent nerve damage to his hands. He told the police that two masked men had entered the house, shining a torch at him, robbing him of £80 in cash, and tying him up. The couple's only son, the Jersey brewery director Ian Steven, was flying back to Edinburgh to be at his father's bedside.

The Frogston Road West murder had clearly been committed by two professional burglars, who had ruthlessly gagged and tied up the elderly householders, with such force that the frail Florence Steven had expired. It turned out the police had struck very lucky, however. The night of the murder, two police constables on patrol in Frogston Avenue had spotted two men carrying large bags at 1.45 am. Clearly a pair of burglars, the constables rightly deduced; when challenged, the two men put down their bags and ran off. The older suspect was arrested, but his younger colleague managed to escape, running hard in the direction of the Princess Margaret Rose Hospital.

The arrested burglar was identified as the 58-year-old Birmingham career criminal David Tustin, who had an impressive police record, including lengthy sentences for safe-blowing and burglary. He was known to have been 'working' with the younger Edinburgh burglar Michael Cushion, and when this individual was arrested by the police, the two Frogston Avenue constables identified him as the man they had seen running away. Tustin and Cushion were brought before the Edinburgh Sheriff Court to be charged with the murder of Florence Steven.

On trial for murder at the High Court in March 1992, Tustin and Cushion pleaded not guilty. Ann Tod describing finding Mr and Mrs Steven tied to their beds, and the two Frogston Avenue police constables told how they had challenged the two burglars and arrested one of them. The pathologist Professor Anthony Busuttil testified that the face of Florence Steven had marks from a ligature at the corners of her mouth, indicating that she had been gagged quite hard. Whereas it was unlikely that a healthy person would die from being gagged, this experience could be lethal in an elderly person with heart disease. Robert Steven had died from natural causes in January 1992, and Professor Busuttil had performed the autopsy: there were still scars from the handcuffs on both wrists, and residual nerve damage to the hands. On the fourth day, the trial was dropped due to legal difficulties concerning a late claim of an alibi and incrimination from Michael Cushion.

As the trial resumed in May 1992, a tape recording of Robert Steven describing his ordeal was played in court. A glove mark on a vacuum cleaner in the murder house matched the gloves belonging to David Tustin. Giving evidence in court, Tustin described himself as a self-taught expert on antiques. When Michael Cushion had told him 'We have a place up north that is like a museum and we would like somebody to give us an idea what is worth taking from it', he had willingly offered his services. As Michael Cushion and another burglar known only as 'George' were wrapping up the antiques indicated by Tustin, he became aware that there were two old people in the house, but it had been the other two villains who had tied them up. In cross-examination, Tustin was described as a glib and inventive liar, looking quite gentlemanly with his bald head, neatly trimmed beard, and old-fashioned clothes, but a hardened criminal to the core. His lengthy record of previous convictions for serious crime, going back to 1956, was reviewed in court. And why had he said nothing about the old couple left tied up in the house he had just burgled when arrested by the two constables, instead leaving them behind to suffer torture and death? There was nothing whatsoever to support the presence of a third burglar in the murder house.

In court, Tustin blamed Cushion for everything, whereas the legal counsel for the younger burglar did his best to incriminate Tustin, to give his own client a chance to walk free. A hardened villain, albeit not with a criminal record matching that of Tustin, Cushion did not give evidence in court. The jury found both the accused guilty of murder and Lord Kirkwood sentenced them to life imprisonment for 'a cowardly and callous attack on two very elderly people in their own home', adding ten years each for attempting to murder Robert Steven, and four years each for burgling the house.[24] 'Beasts!' exclaimed the front page of the *Edinburgh Evening News*, illustrated with large colour photographs of Tustin and Cushion coming out of court, adding that after their conviction for the Frogston Horror, the English police wanted to question them for a series of unsolved burglaries and robberies of frail and elderly people. There were a few early bulletins about their life behind bars: in January 1993 they tried an appeal against their sentence, but without success, and in October the same year, Tustin was robbed of a £500 watch by two other prisoners when held at Saughton Prison awaiting transfer to an English jail. The two Frogston murderers may well still be alive today, and quite possibly still 'inside', although they have done nothing newsworthy during their latter time behind bars.

MURDER IN DUMBIEDYKES ROAD, 1993

The Jordanian mystery man Jahya Abbas had come to Scotland in 1977. He worked as a kitchen-boy at various restaurants and hotels, until his behaviour became too erratic for this to be feasible. In 1983, he was run over by a car and left with serious face and leg injuries, ending up getting his hands on a tidy £40 000 compensation from the insurance company. This money allowed him to live in some style without having to do any work: drinking and taking drugs, revelling and beating up prostitutes. In early 1993, when he was 45 years old, this disturbed Jordanian moved into the flat at 22/5 Dumbiedykes Road, where he soon made himself profoundly unpopular. The flat was a foul-smelling den, prostitutes came and went, and Abbas liked to slam the doors hard in the middle of the night. Since he never cleaned his flat or washed the dishes, the stench emanating from his flat was powerful indeed. His battered old silver Jaguar, with which he had once demolished a wall and a lamp-post in Dumbiedykes Road, was towed away by the police due to an accumulation of parking tickets.

On June 16 1993, when Jahya Abbas had forgotten to buy a power card for his electricity meter, the power to his flat was cut off. The bedraggled Jordanian went round to all the neighbouring flats begging for hot water, but since he was well known as the local 'nutter' who liked to scream at people for no reason at all, he had little claim to charity. When he knocked at the door of 22/4 Dumbiedykes Road, he was admitted by the 30-year-old James McGhee and his two drinking companions. All of a sudden, Jahya Abbas started screaming angrily, accusing McGhee of being an amphetamine dealer, and seizing him hard round the throat. In the struggle that followed, McGhee picked up a knife from the bedside cabinet. When the police came to 22/4 Dumbiedykes Road, the body of Jahya Abbas was found in the bathroom with 17 knife wounds.

On trial for murder at the High Court in October 1993, James McGhee pleaded guilty to culpable manslaughter, on grounds of having suffered from severe epilepsy since the age of 11. Since the 'nutter' Jahya Abbas had clearly initiated the violence, this plea was accepted, and Lord Sutherland sentenced McGhee to imprisonment for seven years.[25] A specialist team of cleaners was called in to empty and fumigate the stinking flat of Jahya Abbas, next door to where the disturbed Jordanian had met his death.

THE MURDER OF DEIRDRE KIVLIN, 1995

The 24-year-old Deirdre Kivlin worked as a catering assistant and lived in her parents' home at 17 Greendykes Drive, Craigmillar. She was a talented amateur actress and singer, who had taken part in the Craigmillar Festival. On the evening of Saturday July 8 1995, Deirdre Kivlin went out partying at the Grey Horse pub in Dalkeith Road, and at the Junction Bar in West Preston Street. She had told her mother that she would be moving into a new flat that evening, and not come home. She was last seen by a member of the Junction Bar staff, standing near some phone boxes at the junction of Newington Road and West Preston Street at 1.50 am. She did not return home, and nothing was heard from her during Sunday, so on July 10, her mother reported her missing.

On August 17, residents at 100 South Clerk Street reported that for several days, a foul smell had emanated from the region of the common back green. Suspecting a blocked drain, workmen were called in to investigate, but the reason for the stench proved to be the decomposing body of Deirdre Kivlin, wrapped in a carpet and forcibly thrust into the drain. She was identified from her dental records due to the advanced putrefaction. She had clearly been brutally beaten to death with a brick or similar blunt instrument, but it was impossible to tell whether she had been

SOUTH CLERK STREET   Newington Parish Church.

21. South Clerk Street, a postcard stamped and posted in 1904.

sexually assaulted. She was wearing the same clothes as she had on July 8, when she had been last spotted very near 100 South Clerk Street; this rendered it likely that she had been assaulted and murdered not long after the final observation of her at 1.50 am on July 9.

The police did their best to sift through the evidence, and to reconstruct Deirdre Kivlin's final hours alive. Nobody had anything but good to say about her: her employers at the catering company, the owners of the pubs where she had been a karaoke artist, and the organisers of the Craigmillar Festival. Her mother told the police that Deirdre had told her that she would be moving into a new flat together with a workmate. This turned out to be an untruth, however, since the workmate had lied to Deirdre about the keys to the flat; the police found nothing to link her with the murder, however. Technical evidence, namely bloodstains in the stair of 100 South Clerk Street, spoke in favour of Deirdre Kivlin being struck down in there, before being dragged down to the basement to be raped and battered to death.

The police found some scraps of paper at 100 South Clerk Street, with figures from the National Insurance number of a known criminal, the 26-year-old burglar Scott Ballantyne, who also had a conviction for assault. It turned out that he was currently in prison for house-breaking, rendering it easy for the detectives to lay their hands on him.

A homeless tramp and glue-sniffer, with a lengthy record of convictions for burglary and petty crime, Scott Ballantyne was a pathetic creature, and certainly looked very much unlike a brutal murderer. He firmly denied murdering Deirdre Kivlin and claimed to have been out of Edinburgh at the time of the murder. He freely admitted having been in the habit of sleeping rough in the stair or basement of 100 South Clerk Street. Importantly, his jacket was found to be stained with blood matching that of Deirdre Kivlin. A man had seen a tramp resembling Ballantyne following a woman the night of the murder, but his girlfriend picked out another man in an identification parade. Incarcerated in Saughton Prison, the timid Scott Ballantyne was given a hard time by the prison bullies, who threw hot water at him, called him a beast and a murderer, and threatened to stab him if he did not have the sense to commit suicide.

On trial for murder at the High Court in January 1996, Scott Ballantyne pleaded not guilty. The police witnesses relentlessly detailed the evidence against him, but he was fortunate to be represented in court by a crack defence team, led by the eloquent Mr Edgar Prais QC. They asked why Deirdre Kivlin would accompany such a wreck of a man, a homeless, glue-sniffing vagabond, into the stair of 100 South Clerk Street? Was it not more likely that someone else, a stronger and more brutal criminal, had murdered Deirdre Kivlin at 100 South Clerk Street, and that the feeble Scott Ballantyne had got some of her blood onto his jacket by mistake when he slept rough in the stair or basement? After all, her skull had been completely shattered after the frenzied assault with a brick or similar object, so that if he had been the guilty man, his clothes would have been awash with blood, not just two small stains. After pondering the evidence at hand, the jury returned a verdict of not proven, and Scott Ballantyne walked free.[26] The Edinburgh newspapers, who may well have expected a guilty verdict, retaliated by calling him a loser, a crook and a pathetic glue-sniffer. Scott Ballantyne told an *Edinburgh Evening News* journalist that he would be fleeing the capital, since he was certain that some 'heavies' were planning to kill him in a revenge attack. In late 1998, he again made the news after attempting suicide by lying down in front of an Edinburgh freight train while sniffing at a bag of solvent, although the train passed over him without causing any injuries.[27]

So, who murdered Deirdre Kivlin? It may well have been Scott Ballantyne: after all, Detective Chief Inspector Ian Cowden, who had led the murder investigation, declared that he thought the police had the right man. Ballantyne wrote a number of letters to a friend while in prison, making various whingeing prognostications that he would rot in prison, but these have little evidential value. Still, it must have been admitted that the defence made some good points in court. It seems highly unlikely that Deirdre Kivlin would willingly accompany a tramp into the stair of 100 South Clerk Street, and it can be questioned whether such a feeble creature as Ballantyne would have had the strength to grab hold of her and murder her without a single person hearing a sound. Deirdre Kivlin was a respectable young woman who was not in the habit of sleeping rough, so it seems unlikely that she willingly went into the stair of 100 South Clerk Street. The case is a mysterious one, and unlikely ever to be solved.

22. *Next to William Hill is the entrance to 100 South Clerk Street, where Deirdre Kivlin was murdered in 1995.*

THE MURDER OF LINDA ANDERSON, 1999

In 1995, the 40-year-old former police clerk Mrs Linda Anderson separated from her husband Kenneth, a clerical worker at the George Hotel in Edinburgh. Since she had a serious drinking problem, he took care of their two children. In 1998, Linda Anderson was living with the Musselburgh man Craig Dundas, of Monktonhall Crescent. They decided to go out for a Hogmanay drinking party at the Tollcross flat of the 30-year-old former army paratrooper Duncan Edwards, a native of Orkney. The two drunks Dundas and Edwards had known each other for quite some time: in 1994, Edwards had been charged with attempting to murder his friend in Musselburgh following an argument, but he had escaped with a month in prison for assault.

The three drunks celebrated a jolly Hogmanay at Edwards' flat at 9 Home Street, Tollcross. All of a sudden, a violent quarrel broke out, and Linda Anderson escaped out into the tenement stairwell, pursued by the other two. The two furious drunks kicked and stamped on her, compressed her neck, and struck her on the head with a bludgeon. After Linda Anderson had been found dead at the bottom of the stairs, Edwards and Dundas were both arrested and charged with murdering her. On trial at the High Court of Edinburgh in May 1999, they blamed each other for the murder. In the end, Duncan Edwards was found guilty of murder and sentenced to imprisonment for life, since he was considered the chief attacker; Craig Dundas was cleared of murder but found guilty of assault.[28]

Since both men had clearly been involved in the assault that cost Linda Anderson her life, Edwards and his legal council Mr Ian Hamilton QC tried an appeal in 2001, claiming that the judge had misdirected the jury. This appeal was successful, but in a second trial in September 2001, Edwards was again found guilty of murder; Lady Cosgrove added that he should serve at least 14 years of his life sentence before he could apply for parole. In 2009, the persistent murderer tried yet another appeal, this time claiming that the legal team representing him in the second trial had let him down, but this time, the appeal was turned down and the prospect of a record-breaking third murder trial did not materialize.[29]

MURDER OF THE STOCKBRIDGE BEGGAR, 2002

In 1998, a tramp named John Brankin became a minor Edinburgh celebrity. A bearded, unprepossessing-looking character, he was a familiar sight in the Stockbridge area, begging in the street. The Stockbridge Beggar squatted in St George's Well, a derelict water mill constructed in 1810 in honour of King George III; the well had finally been blocked off in 1969. He battled with the council for many months to get the right to live there. Many people found his obstructionism praiseworthy: well-wishers gave him a bed, a heater, a camping stove and a Christmas tree complete with decorations. Huddled inside the old water mill clutching a bottle of whisky, the Stockbridge Beggar thanked his friends for providing him with some Christmas cheer.

In the end, the Stockbridge Beggar was forced out of St George's Well, which lacked electricity, gas and running water. He was eventually rehoused in a small flat in the high-rise Castleview House, Moredun, sharing it with another drunk named Keith Connor. In 2002, when the Stockbridge Beggar was 39 years old, his flat was a well-known drinking den for the local youngsters. Two tough girls were among the visitors to the flat: the pregnant 17-year-old Shevonne Clarke and the 15-year-old Pamela Reid. One day, Pamela Reid accused the drunk Keith Connor of being a pervert and a paedophile, since he had made a pass at her. The two girls acted with a zeal that would have delighted a hardened feminist: they recruited two tough 14-year-old boys and returned to Castleview House to administer a beating to Keith Connor;

the Stockbridge Beggar, who was also in the flat, was beaten up as well. As the two girls shared a bottle of vodka after this exploit, they agreed that the pervert Keith Connor had not received sufficient punishment for what he had done: they would once more visit the flat, this time armed with a knife. When the two girls came bounding into the flat, the wretched Keith Connor was lying on the bed in a drunken stupor; they beat and slashed him hard, disfiguring him for life. When he screamed for help, the Stockbridge Beggar came lurching into the room, but Shevonne Clarke plunged the knife hard into his chest, killing him. After the murder, the two girls boasted to a neighbour, apparently feeling quite proud over what they had just accomplished.

On trial for murder at the High Court in April 2002, Shevonne Clarke tried to blame Pamela Reid for the murder of the Stockbridge Beggar, but this was not believed since her own jeans had marks of blood from the murder weapon where she had concealed it after the stabbing. A neighbour had heard the two girls plan the murder together, although the pathetic Keith Connor had been the intended victim, not the Stockbridge Beggar. In the end, both girls were found guilty of murder, attempted murder and assault. They were both sentenced to imprisonment for life, Clarke with a minimum sentence of ten and a half years, Reid with a minimum sentence of eight years.[30] In 2005, they tried to get their convictions overturned, but without success. Shevonne Clarke has not made the news since she was incarcerated, but her cohort in crime more than once made the newspaper headlines. 'Is This a Sick Joke!' exclaimed the *Scottish Sun* in October 2008, after it had been divulged that Pamela Reid had got a job as an assistant in a homeless charity shop. According to the same newspaper, she lost this job in February the following year, after having sneaked off to the pub during working hours. She was released in 2010 and reported to be living with her boyfriend in 2011; there is nothing to suggest that she has committed any further serious crime.[31]

MURDER AT THE WAVERLEY INN, 2005

The Waverley Inn is a large modern Edinburgh pub, situated at the corner of Southhouse Avenue and Southhouse Broadway, Gracemount. In early May 2005, a furious brawl broke out at the Waverley Inn, with pool cues and bar stools being used as weapons. Afterwards, the 38-year-old Grant McDonald was found unconscious on the pub floor. He was rushed to hospital but failed to recover from his severe head and face injuries. As the police were studying CCTV footage from the pub, and appealing for witnesses to the brawl to come forward, the murder pub remained shut until June 3, as a mark of respect, and to allow for refurbishment.

The police soon arrested the two 29-year-old Edinburgh thugs Billy Johnston and Charles Woolard, who stood trial for the murder in December 2005. Johnston had been caught on CCTV raining eight hard punches onto the head of Grant McDonald, before Woolard viciously kicked his head. After a trial lasting two days, the jury found both men guilty of murdering Grant McDonald, and punching and kicking his drinking companion Craig Lumsden. Lord Kinclaven sentenced the two thugs to imprisonment for life, with a minimum sentence of 12 years before they could be considered for release.[32] They tried an appeal in 2009, but it was turned down.[33]

MURDER AT THE 'MARMION', 2006

Marmion: A Tale of Flodden Field was published in 1808, at a time when Walter Scott could do nothing wrong. A long, narrative poem with varied meters, the book describes how Lord Marmion, one of the henchmen of Henry VIII of England, lusts for the wealthy woman Clara de Clare. Together with his mistress Constance de

Beverley, a disgraced nun, he forges a letter implicating Sir Ralph de Wilton, Clara's fiancé, in treason. Sir Ralph demands a duel to defend his honour, but Marmion defeats him and he is forced to go into exile. Fearful of Marmion's attentions, Clara retires to a nunnery. Constance, who has been deserted by Marmion, is incarcerated in the Lindisfarne convent for breaking her vows. She takes her revenge by giving the Abbess documents that prove Sir Ralph's innocence. The Earl of Angus restores Sir Ralph, who has returned to Edinburgh disguised as a pilgrim, to the knighthood, but his plans of revenge against Marmion are overturned by the Battle of Flodden, in which Marmion perishes on the battlefield, whereas Sir Ralph distinguishes himself, regaining his honour and his lands, and marrying Clara. In Edinburgh, the 'Marmion' public house was situated on Captain's Road, Gracemount. A large and nondescript modern pub, it had once been called the Captain's Cabin, before being part demolished and restored with a new name and frontage.

The 22-year-old Jamie Bain was a young Edinburgh gangster. He dealt in cocaine and dabbled in all sorts of crime; since he had several henchmen, and good access to loaded firearms, he was a force to be reckoned with in the criminal underworld. Jamie Bain cohabited with Dionne Hendry, who came from a well-known gangster family with links to the traveller community. Some of the Hendrys were decent, hard-working people, but others were criminals; they were all tough and dangerous people, capable of anything when they were seriously annoyed with some person. In April 2006, the short-tempered Jamie Bain, who could behave like a complete madman when he was 'high' on alcohol and cocaine, beat Dionne up severely after a domestic quarrel. The couple already had an ASBO each for their rowdy and loud-mouthed arguments, but this time Jamie had gone too far. After Dionne had told her family about what had happened, a party of Hendry toughs came calling at the Bain family home in Gilmerton Dykes Avenue. Fearful of what the Hendrys would do to him, Jamie had gone underground, however. The Hendry mob instead called on Jamie's father, who lived not far away, telling him what kind of treatment his wife-beating son could look forward to. Old Bain got in touch with Jamie, who was much annoyed to have been treated with such disrespect. As an up-and-coming young gangster, he fancied himself the equal of the Hendrys. With cocaine-fuelled Dutch courage, he alerted his henchmen and made plans for a pre-emptive strike.

On the evening of April 22 2006, the 26-year-old James Hendry was having a few drinks at the Marmion, together with another tough character, his 32-year-old brother-in-law Alex McKinnon, a former Scottish champion bantam-weight boxer. At 10.50 pm, two young men wearing dark hoodies and balaclavas entered the Marmion. One of them seized up a shotgun, with which he gunned down both Hendry and McKinnon, before making a rapid getaway. McKinnon soon died from his injuries, but Hendry lived to fight another day. Many members of the Hendry family were at the Marmion that particular evening. Furious that two of their own had been gunned down in cold blood, they pursued the gunman through the streets, some in cars, others on foot. Near Jamie Bain's house in Gilmerton Dykes Avenue, they found the young gangster trying to hide. They took the shotgun away from him and gave him a brutal beating with the butt, before leaving him for dead.

When the police found Jamie Bain, they at first thought that he had been shot in the face, due to his extensive injuries. But after surgery, the tough young gangster was soon on the mend, albeit badly scarred. Together with his two henchmen Richard Cosgrove, who had accompanied him into the pub, and Bernard Young, who had sourced the sawn-off shotgun and the masks used during the raid, he faced trial for murder and attempted murder at the High Court of Edinburgh in November 2006. There was widespread revulsion that the southern suburbs of Edinburgh had become 'gangster country' just like some of the

outskirts of Glasgow. A number of witnesses described how the
two attackers had burst into the Marmion and gunned down
Hendry and McKinnon. There was solid DNA evidence linking
Bain to the murder weapon, and all three accused to the masks
and balaclavas used in the raid. Bain claimed memory loss as a
result of the beating he had received, and Cosgrove unsuccessfully
pleaded that Bain had forced him to accompany him into the pub.
Since the defence hardly had a leg to stand on, all three gangsters
were found guilty of murder and sentenced to imprisonment for
life; Bain with a minimum sentence of 22 years, Cosgrove with
a minimum of 16 years and Young with a minimum of 17 years.
All three had previous police records: Bain with 15 convictions
for public order and road traffic offences, whereas the other two
ruffians had convictions for vandalism and assault.[34]

Behind bars for a considerable period to come, the three
Marmion gangsters would have plenty of time to ponder their
pointless and cowardly crime. Even if they had succeeded in
'removing' both Hendry and McKinnon, there were still plenty
of angry, vengeful Hendrys alive, ready for a vendetta against the
Marmion gunmen. And surely, when planning an expedition to
shoot down some very dangerous people, it would have made
good sense to have a getaway car on standby outside the pub.
No doubt, the cocaine taken in quantities by the ringleader Jamie
Bain had impaired his judgment and made him think he was
capable of anything. In prison, he has been in constant trouble
for illicitly keeping mobile phones. In 2008, he abandoned an
appeal against his conviction. The same year, Adam Hendry, the
brother of Dionne, beat up Jamie Bain's father, mother and sister,
and was sentenced to nine months behind bars. In 2014, Jamie
and Dionne got married at Shotts Prison. Not long after, her
parked car was the target of a shotgun blast; a warning from the
Hendrys, it was thought. In 2016, Jamie Bain got caught for the
ninth time keeping a mobile phone and a Bluetooth device in his
cell. In early 2019, he was beaten up by two other rough types

and had his expensive Rolex watch stolen.[35] As for James Hendry, who had such a narrow escape at the Marmion back in 2006, he continued his life as a hard man. In 2008, he was annoyed by a drunk urinating in his girlfriend's garden, and struck him a mighty blow, killing him and serving 40 months 'inside' as a consequence. In 2019, the now 39-year-old Hendry himself died suddenly and mysteriously, from disease according to the newspapers.[36]

The Marmion murder pub also went through troubled times. It was closed for several days after the murder, to be searched by the police, but eventually reopened under its old name. Since the local people remembered the murder, it was never a success; in 2008 Punch Taverns put it up for sale, but they failed to find a buyer. In June 2011, the Marmion became a Tesco Express, with the address of 2 Gracemount Drive: a sad fate indeed for Edinburgh's most famous modern murder pub.

MURDERER MURDERS MURDERER IN MILTON STREET, 2013

The Edinburgh thug Craig Mackenzie belonged to a gang of rough youngsters who congregated at the Hawkhill Court estate, situated in Restalrig, north Edinburgh. In March 1993, when he was 20 years old, he and his friends Alexander O'Brien, James Reid and Stuart Tuckey decided to go out for some fun. They met the 25-year-old David Edwards, a brain-damaged drug addict they used to bully, and fed him a mixture of alcohol and drugs, with an added measure of sugar to upset his diabetes. Their intention was to make Edwards entirely oblivious to his surroundings, before taking up to Calton Hill, which they knew to be a pick-up spot for homosexuals, and selling him to the highest bidder. Since the fastidious Edinburgh homosexuals did not go in for such perverted practices, the thugs went home disappointed. They discussed selling the 'daftie' Edwards to some London director of 'snuff movies' for £30 000, but their contacts in the cinematographic world were not sufficient to make such a deal, so they took him home to a flat in Hawkhill Court, where they kicked and stamped him to death just for the fun of it.

After the gang of thugs had realized what they had just accomplished, they took the body away from Hawkhill Court and buried it in a shallow grave next to a disused railway line near Restalrig Road. Fearful that the foxes and badgers would dig up and devour the remains of 'Daft Davie', they later moved the body into the grounds of Seafield Crematorium more than half a mile away, using a wheelbarrow, and reburied it in one of the flower beds there. But a gravedigger discovered the newly dug grave, the police were called in, and the gang were soon tracked down and arrested. They stood trial for murder at the High Court of Edinburgh in July 1993. The case attracted a good deal of newspaper interest, and the young gangsters were likened to Burke and Hare for their callous disregard for human life. In the end, Mackenzie and Reid were found guilty of murder and sentenced to imprisonment for life, and the other gang members were given custodial sentences as well. In prison, Craig Mackenzie seemed to have become a reformed character. He was helped by a prison charity founded by Sir Elton John, and was instrumental in founding a service for informing prisoners about AIDS and other disagreeable diseases. Behind bars, he befriended the triple axe murderer Thomas McCulloch, who had spent four decades in custody. Thanks to his charitable work, Craig Mackenzie became a candidate for early release: in 2005, his original 14-year sentence was cut by two years and he was released shortly after.

Craig Mackenzie kept in touch with several of his former prison buddies, one of them the murderer Andrew Fisher, a rough type who had killed his wife in Dunfermline in 1990 and spent 11 years 'inside'. In 2013, Fisher lived in Musselburgh and worked as a part-time shop assistant. He regularly visited Craig Mackenzie, who worked with various charities for criminals and homeless people, at his flat in Milton Street, Abbeyhill. Since Fisher drank hard and liked to smoke strong marijuana cigarettes, he could behave as a complete lunatic at times. One day in July 2013, he went into Edinburgh to help Craig Mackenzie with his charitable work. Returning home, he looked like if he had been drinking hard, before he got 'stoned' by smoking two of his potent 'joints'. The following day, he telephoned his partner Sandra White and told her that he had murdered Craig Mackenzie, because he suspected that his former prison buddy had been surreptitiously drugging and raping him. And indeed, after a 999 call had been made to the police, the lifeless body of Craig Mackenzie was found inside the flat at 21 Milton Street, with 32 knife wounds to the head, neck and torso. Andrew Fisher pleaded guilty to culpable homicide on the basis of diminished responsibility and was indefinitely detained at the State Mental Hospital, Carstairs, where he hopefully would be restrained from causing any further mayhem.[37]

IV.

WEST EDINBURGH

From central Edinburgh, the immediate western suburbs are Coates and Haymarket, Roseburn and Dalry, Murrayfield and Corstorphine. There are some populous south-western suburbs, Gorgie, Slateford, Longstone and Saughton prominent among them, and several north-western suburbs as well, like Blackhall and Clermiston. The most ancient of the murder houses of West Edinburgh is the top-floor flat at 228 Morrison Road, where Richard Robertson stood accused of killing his little son in 1895. Then we have 'Ormelie', the fine Corstorphine mansion where James Kirkwood narrowly evaded the death penalty for murdering Jean Powell in 1938. The strange tale of Alan Wilson, the paedophile schoolmaster and Edinburgh tour guide who ended up murdered and dismembered at 28 Merchiston Road, is hopefully without any precedent or antecedent. The career of Theresa Riggi, the Monster Mother of Slateford Road, could have inspired a horrid modern 'splatter' film; so could the misdeeds of the brutal Irishman Seamus Dunleavy, of Balgreen Road infamy, who murdered his own mother, dismembered the corpse and buried the remains in a shallow grave on Corstorphine Hill.

Unsolved murder mysteries abound in West Edinburgh, the oldest being the Wester Coates Terrace enigma of 1924: did William Laurie King get away with murdering his own mother? Then we have the Glasgow Road mystery of 1966: who murdered the successful businessman David M'Menigall, and got clean away with it? The Kingsknowe Road North mystery of 1981 may well belatedly have found a solution, since in 1997, the burglar Paul Andrews was linked to the murder of Aileen Printie by DNA evidence described by the police as strong. Then we have the greatest modern mystery of Edinburgh, the murder of Louise Tiffney at 2 Dean Path in 2005: her son Sean Flynn escaped with a 'not proven' verdict at the time, but the remains of the murdered woman have since been found, and Flynn will be facing a retrial later this year ...

MURDER IN MORRISON STREET, 1895

Richard Robertson, aged 35 and born in Galashiels, was an Edinburgh joiner who lived in the top flat at 228 Morrison Street, Haymarket, with his 32-year-old wife Janet and their four children. He was a hard drinker and often cruel to his wife and children while in his cups. The neighbours called the police at regular intervals, to rescue Janet from her violent husband; they also made a report to the Society for the Prevention of Cruelty to Children that the children were neglected and often mistreated. When Inspector James Turnbull came calling in November 1895, Robertson said that he regularly ill-used his wife and that he would do it again. The children were pale and pinched-looking, but they had no marks of recent violence. The youngest son Colin was just a few months old.

1. *Portraits of the two Robertsons, from the Edinburgh Evening News, February 3 1896.*

On November 16 1895, Richard Robertson had been drinking hard. He was lying on the bed, with the little boy Colin next to him. But when

213

Janet Robertson lifted Colin up, he was dead and cold. "Oh, my lamb is dead!" she cried out. "'Tis you who've smothered him", Richard replied drunkenly. Since there were marks of violence on his head, she accused her husband of murdering the child, saying that she would be going to the police. Richard begged her not to, for the sake of the children; he promised that he would stop drinking and be a better husband to her. They would just have to bury Colin somewhere, or throw him into the canal, and then they would get away scot-free. The following morning, when Richard had sobered up, they walked into Princes Street Gardens with Colin wrapped in a cloth and hidden from view. Richard leapt over the railings near the Castle, dug a shallow grave and put Colin into it, with a stone over the body. When he emerged, he looked quite jolly, particularly considering what he had just accomplished, laughing merrily and saying that many a poor wretch would have been proud of such a grave.

Richard Robertson knew that he could keep Janet in check as long as she stayed at home, through disciplining her with his fists, but there was trouble when she wanted to travel to Glasgow to see her mother Mrs Grace Downie. He solemnly warned her against blabbering about the sad fate of little Colin, saying that he had got work in Leith and would become a better man. But as soon as she was away from her husband's influence, the volatile Janet was incapable of keeping her secret, telling her mother that "Richard has murdered the child!" Grace Downie went to the SPCC, and they called in the police, who arrested Richard Robertson in Leith and Janet in Glasgow. Detective Officer Alexander Walker took Janet into Princes Street Gardens, but she was incapable of pointing out where Colin had been buried. It was quite a shallow grave, however, and the detective was able to find it himself.

On trial for murder at the High Court of Edinburgh in February 1896, both Richard and Janet Robertson were legally represented. Grace Downie gave evidence about Richard's drunken habits and violence to his family, and described how

Janet had told her about the murder of little Colin and his interment in Princes Street Gardens. Jessie White of 14 Morrison Street, the former landlady of the prisoners, had seen little Colin and could identify his distinctive night-dress. Several neighbours at 228 Morrison Street had also seen Colin or heard him scream. Inspector James Turnbull of the SPCC had also seen Colin when he came to see the dysfunctional Robertson family at Morrison Street; he had also seen the night-dress, which he could identify. The police witnesses described how Colin's remains had been retrieved, and Sir Henry Duncan Littlejohn declared that the cause of death had been a series of heavy blows to the head, leaving the vault of the cranium entirely shattered. The defence urged that Colin might have fallen upon a fender during a drunken squabble between the prisoners, who after all had no motive to murder the child. The verdict was not proven and the two Robertsons were set at liberty.[1]

Richard Robertson was, in my opinion, a very lucky man. It had been a mistake from the prosecution to try him and Janet together, instead of allowing her to be a witness against her husband, but there must have been some reason for this that is not discernible today; either she gave a poor impression, sharing her husband's drunken habits, or there were concerns that she would prove loyal to her husband and stand by him until the end. The prosecution had proven that Colin existed, that he had died from violence to the head at 228 Morrison Street, and that he had been deposited in Princes Street Gardens, but the motive for the murder remained a crux for the jury. Probably, the drunken Richard had knocked him hard on the head following some hygienic mishap in the bed. Richard Robertson would have done well if he had headed straight for a shop sign saying 'Lottery Tickets' after his fortunate escape at the High Court, but there is reason to believe that he instead chose the shop sign saying 'Whisky', and that this dismal family tyrant continued his old life of drunkenness and violence. Woe unto the mother-in-law who had 'squealed' in court; woe unto poor loyal Janet, the recipient of so much domestic abuse; woe unto the three remaining Robertson children, who had been so cruelly treated. With a violent and drunken father, living in what was little better than a slum tenement, they were at considerable risk of joining little Colin in Heaven very soon; the Good Old Days indeed, in Merry Auld Edinburgh, as expressed by George R. Sims:

She's taken to drink, they tell me. The husband? Oh, they say

He muttered a drunken 'Curse you!' and went off to his wench next day ...

2 *The murder house at 228 Morrison Street today.*

MURDER AND MYSTERY IN
WESTER COATES TERRACE, 1924

James Rae King, the son of the commercial traveller William Laurie King and his wife Mary, became a successful Edinburgh chartered accountant. He was well known in the city and served as Vice-Moderator of the Edinburgh High Constables. James Rae King lived at 33 Polwarth Gardens with his wife Agnes and his two sons William Laurie, born in 1902, and Alexis, born in 1908, but later moved into the large detached house 'Redgorton' at 2 Wester Coates Terrace. It was the wish of James Rae King that his eldest son should carry on his own firm, and William Laurie King became apprenticed to a chartered accountant, although his main interest in life was chemistry. He was allowed to carry on his chemical experiments in an outhouse built in the garden, and to build up a stockpile of chemical supplies, which he stored in the attic. The firm of James Rae King acted as auditors to the motor garage of Liddle & Johnston, and William went there with regularity, secretly befriending the young cashier Edith Ross, to whom he gave a ring and a wristwatch.

On May 30 1924, when William Laurie King was 22 years old, his family sat down at a frugal late-night supper of bread and butter, cheese, jelly and coffee. There had recently been serious discord between William and his father, since he had refused to sit his examination to become a chartered accountant, declaring that after two years as an apprentice accountant, he had made his mind up to study chemistry at Edinburgh University. Although James Rae King was bitterly disappointed by this, he had to give in and allow his eldest son to change his career. William had always been kept very short of money by his father, being allowed just two pounds and ten shillings per month, with some loose change added as pocket money by his mother. Being interested in photography, he had recently tried to purchase two cameras from a shop, but his father had refused to help him out with some money, since he wanted

William to be taught a lesson that such things cost money, surely a disagreeable experience for a young man of 22. Nor had William's relationship with his mother always been the most bonhomous: she refused to accept that he had grown up and treated him like a little boy. Perhaps after hearing rumours about William's unsuitable dalliance with the garage cashier, she had told the family daily help Marion Armstrong that she was going to 'put William abroad'.

Nevertheless, the late supper began without any drama. The schoolboy Alexis King, who had returned home after playing tennis, cut the foul-smelling cheese but did not have any himself, and William cut a slice of bread for each of the four diners. When James Rae King bit into his cheese sandwich, he complained of a burning feeling in his throat, and complained to his wife that it was a funny piece of cheese she had purchased this week. Mrs King found nothing wrong with her sandwich and ate it greedily, before being handed half her husband's ration and eating that as well. William also ate his sandwich and drank his coffee, without any complaints. But fifteen minutes after the meal, when James Rae King sat smoking by the fire, he complained of feeling ill and told his wife he would be going to bed. She said she would also come to bed. After both of them had vomited twice within half an hour, William was asked to call the doctor, but he was out on another case and William did not leave a message. Instead, Mr King asked William to call the chemist Mr Peebles asking for some brandy. This was duly delivered, and the ailing couple had a tot each before going to sleep. Mr King woke up at 12.30 and asked his sons to see how their mother was; they responded that she seemed much improved after drinking the brandy. In the meantime, William managed to get through to Dr William Fraser McDonald, and explained the situation to him. The doctor, who had just returned from a confinement, agreed that there was not necessary for him to come calling straight away, but that William should let him know if the situation got worse. At 2 am, Mr King rose to vomit once more. He then went into his wife's bedroom and found her lying in her bed, quite dead.

3. The murder house at 2 Wester Coates Terrace.

The shaken Mr King made sure that his brother Dr Robert King and the chemist David Peebles were called in. William called Dr McDonald, who also made an appearance. Mrs Peebles, who also came to the murder house, cleared away all the cups, plates and saucers from the supper table and cleaned them, apparently on her own ill-judged initiative. Since the doctors suspected that Mrs King had been poisoned, the police were called in. Detective Inspector David Fleming took away the remaining comestibles from the kitchen and went to the grocer's shop where he took away the remainder of the cheese. He also raided William's private laboratory and took away a total of 152 bottles of chemicals. When examined, the food and cheese was found to contain no arsenic at all, nor was there any bacterial contamination. The post-mortem showed that Mrs King had been murdered with a large dose of arsenic, not less than 3-4 times the fatal dose in a human being. After it had turned out that a bottle marked 'potassium ferricyanide' in William's jacket pocket did in fact contain arsenious oxide, and that he had clandestinely purchased a pound of this chemical using an order form purloined from the Liddle & Johnston motor garage, William was arrested in June 10. When he was searched, there was a stain of arsenious oxide near his trouser pocket.

On trial for matricide at the High Court of Edinburgh on August 26 1924, before Lord Constable, William Laurie King pleaded not guilty. James Rae King and young Alexis described their home life as very harmonious: there was no motive at all for William to wish to harm either of his two parents, nor had there been any opportunity for him to sprinkle the bread or cheese with poison. Giving evidence in his own behalf, William explained that he had bought the arsenic for some experiments he was planning: he wanted to derive a magenta dye from coal tar, using arsenious oxide as a reagent, and also to make a crystal of arsenious oxide and sulphur for his wireless set. The reason that he had bought it via the motor garage was that the amount he needed was too large to be supplied by an ordinary retail chemist. He had not intended to defraud the motor garage but was waiting for the invoice for the arsenic to be returned. The reason that he had not told the police that he had arsenic in his possession was that he was fearful of getting involved in a murder investigation: he had thrown away the majority of the poison and only kept the small amount he had put in the bottle, which he planned to use for his experiments. The prosecution hinted that William had tried to poison his father, but that his mother had become the victim after he had given her half his sandwich. An expert testified that it was not possible to make a crystal for a wireless set in the way William had described. The defence accepted that Mrs King had died from arsenic poisoning but argued that it has all been an accident: either William or some other person had spilt some arsenic, which had then come into contact with the cheese. In his summing-up, Lord Constable had reservations about the moral character of the accused, but he accepted that there was no credible motive for him to murder either of his parents. The jury was out for just 26 minutes before returning a unanimous verdict of not guilty.[2] There were applause in court, and after Lord Constable had discharged the prisoner, William was congratulated by his family and friends.

To propose a solution to the Wester Coates Terrace mystery, a logical analysis of the known facts is imperative. We know that Mrs King died from arsenic poisoning, and that a dose of at least 10 grains had been administered, a much greater amount than could be the result of accidental contamination. The case was definitely one of murder. In contrast, there is no definite proof that either Mr King or William suffered from poisoning of any kind, since their vomit was not kept for analysis, as it should have been. It would appear likely, from his symptoms the day of the poisoning, that Mr King also took a small dose of arsenic, from which he recovered without ill effect. A matter no writer on the case seems to have discussed is the distribution of the poison on the sandwiches. If we propose that only Mr King's sandwich was poisoned, then he would surely have died as well, since his wife had taken a dose of at least three times the fatal level. Even if we presume that both husband and wife had their sandwiches sprinkled with arsenic, his dose would still have been a fatal one. The explanation is likely to be that Mr King's slice of bread was poisoned with a small amount of arsenic, enough to make him sick but not to kill him, and that his wife was later dosed with a much larger amount of arsenic by the murderer, administered in the brandy or some other drink given to the ailing woman.

There is no doubt that before the murder, William Laurie King clandestinely purchased arsenic and kept quiet about it after the deed. There was a spot of arsenious oxide on his trousers. It remains unproven whether he really summoned medical assistance the night of the murder, and strange that he did not insist that the doctor should come calling straight away when he eventually phoned after midnight. Nor can it be disputed that 2 Wester Coates Terrace was a rather queer household. The courtroom loyalty of James Rae King and young Alexis was impressive, but was it due to sincere conviction that William was innocent, or some perverted wish to 'keep up appearances'? Although the house was a capacious one, the two sons had to share a bedroom. As for William himself, it is strange indeed that although he denied being frightened of his father, he spent two full years training for a profession that did not interest him, in order not to disappoint the paterfamilias. He had also got himself a girlfriend, to whom he had given a ring, without informing his parents about her existence. Before the murder, Mrs King had searched William's pockets and extracted the packet of arsenic, with the words 'What trash is this you have been buying, Willie?' When she realized that she was seriously ill, Mrs King had exclaimed 'Oh! Loch Maree! Loch Maree!', referring to a recent fatal case of botulism in a Highland hotel, where the guests had eaten sandwiches filled with diseased wild duck paste. While ill in bed, she complained of seeing 'lights' in William's eyes but not in those of Alexis; when the electric lights were turned off, the phenomenon was still present, a peculiar matter indeed. When William was seen kneeling next to the body of his deceased mother, he expressed himself in the curiously stilted terms 'Why was Mother taken and I not taken? Why did I not take my exam?' Then there was the matter of two books recently purchased by William and kept in his office at the motor garage: 'Death and its Mystery at the Moment of Death' and 'Death and its Mystery after Death'; sinister titles those, and very unlikely to have appealed to his parents had he kept them at home.

William Laurie King gave a very good impression in court: he seemed to feel his predicament very keenly, and to mourn his mother with sincerity; he managed to provide a believable explanation why he had purchased the arsenic, and his youthful good looks and artless mien cannot have failed to impress the jury, on which there were five women. His father, brother and a number of family friends all agreed that there was no discernible motive for William to murder his own mother, and they could not be shaken in court. James Rae King and young Alexis also agreed that there had been no opportunity for William to apply poison to the comestibles for their humble supper, but this is conjecture alone. Importantly, the bottle containing the arsenic had been left in William's jacket pocket, whereas a murderer with a keen sense of self-preservation would of course have got rid of it. Also importantly, although the bottle was marked 'potassium ferricyanide', this was not an attempt to conceal its proper contents, since potassium ferricyanide is dark red crystals whereas arsenious oxide is a white powder. Although I would agree that the evidence to convict William Laurie King of murder was insufficient, I would myself tend to prefer a verdict of not proven in this particular case, one of the most baffling of the unknown and unsolved mysteries of Edinburgh.

In March 1932, the now 32-year-old William Laurie King married the 24-year-old spinster Mary Annie Rutherford. He lived at Grangedell, Penicuik and described himself as a research student. Inquiries at the School of Chemistry, Edinburgh University, and at the Centre for Research Collections, have failed to ascertain whether he finally achieved his PhD. Since no William Laurie King is recorded to have died anywhere in Britain, it is possible that he later moved abroad. The father John Rae King died in 1936, aged 63, from an epithelioma of the ear and cardiac failure according to his death certificate. The brother Alexis King, who became an accountant, also married in 1932, but he died prematurely from a bronchogenic carcinoma in 1963, aged just 55. His son Charles Alexis King, nephew of the suspected murderer, who could have answered some intriguing questions about his family's sinister past, died as recently as 2012.

MURDER AT 'ORMELIE', 1938

James Boyd Kirkwood was born on September 23 1907, son of the dairyman James Kirkwood and his wife Catherine. After a rudimentary school education, he became a professional gardener, maintaining the grounds of various wealthy suburban Edinburgh people. In 1934, when Kirkwood married the 24-year-old domestic servant Mary Downie at the Haymarket registry office, he was working as a gardener at stately Murrayfield House. He later moved on to the Victorian mansion 'Ormelie', at what is today 20 Corstorphine Road, being employed by Sir William Thomson. The indolent Kirkwood seems to have rather liked his situation as gardener at Ormelie, where he was the only outdoor servant, taking care of the house as well as he could when the fun-loving Sir William was away travelling, sometimes for several months on end. In the summer of 1938, James Boyd Kirkwood lodged at 5 Roseburn Street [it still stands] with his wife Mary and their little daughter. He was looking after Ormelie when Sir William was once more away, leading a comfortable life and working only when he felt like it. On Saturday August 6, as Kirkwood sat drinking at a public house in Roseburn Terrace, the barman saw an unknown young woman come up to him. They left together, in the direction of Ormelie.

The following morning, James Boyd Kirkwood walked into the West End police station in Torpichen Street, telling the astonished sergeant on duty at the counter: 'I killed a woman last night in Ormelie. The body is in the ground.' At first, the police thought they were dealing with a lunatic, but Kirkwood was perfectly calm and collected. He was taken into police custody, as a party of detectives went to investigate at Ormelie. Finding the front gate locked shut, they scaled the high wall. The front door of the house was also locked, but the detectives went through the garage into the garden. In a bed of potatoes and other vegetables, there was a freshly dug up area that appeared suspicious. There

4. Ormelie at 20 Corstorphine Road.

were marks on the concrete path as if something had been dragged along it, and a spade was found with fresh soil adherent to its blade. After the detectives had been digging hard for more than an hour, they found the naked corpse of a woman, later identified as the 36-year-old dairymaid Jean Ronald Powell.

Knowing that Kirkwood held the keys to Ormelie, the detectives searched the house, suspecting that the woman had been murdered in there. The found the murder weapon, a bloodstained hammer with several strands of hair adherent to it. There was also a pail containing a brownish liquid and a scrubbing brush. A bundle found in a corridor turned out to be the cover removed from the sofa in the music room, containing all Jean Powell's clothes, including the underwear. In the music room, a clumsy attempt had been made to clean up the extensive bloodstaining, and the carpet had been shifted to one side. On the table was a bottle of sherry and three tumblers, one of which had been broken. The detectives suspected that Jean Powell had been 'picked up' by the murderous James Boyd Kirkwood, and that she had accompanied him to the music room at Ormelie, where they had drunk sherry and smoked cigarettes together. But when the time came for some hanky-panky, something had gone disastrously wrong, and he had attacked her in a furious rage, beating her to death with repeated blows to the head with the heavy hammer. Jean Powell's landlady at 10 Roseburn Place [it still stands] said she had been a native of Edinburgh; although her parents were both dead, she had a brother and sister alive. On the afternoon of the murder, Jean had finished work at 1 pm and returned to her lodgings, before leaving an hour later, saying she had an appointment to keep.

When James Boyd Kirkwood stood trial for murder at the High Court of Edinburgh in early November 1938, a special defence of insanity was lodged, arguing that he had not been responsible for his actions at the time of his crime. He was described as a somewhat stockily built man of medium height with fair, curly hair, wearing a light grey jacket and trousers and a pale fawn shirt without collar or tie. The prisoner's father James Kirkwood Sr, of Reservoir Cottage, Granton, testified that as a youth, his son had suffered from epilepsy, although he had not had a fit for the last ten years. Young Kirkwood had led a sad and troubled life, his father said, with much marital discord: he had suffered from severe headaches, frequently threatened suicide, and once tried to destroy himself by taking arsenic. Another time, he had gone missing for days, before being found in Port Glasgow, Inverclyde, without any idea how he had got there or what he had been doing. The doctor who had treated Kirkwood for epilepsy in Glasgow in the 1920s was in court to give evidence, as was the medical man who had treated him at the Royal Infirmary after he had taken poison in 1935.

There was no doubt, from the medical evidence, that Jean Powell had been murdered inside Ormelie. James Boyd

Kirkwood had confessed to the murder and correctly stated that he had buried the body in the garden. The technical evidence from the scene of the crime spoke in favour that Jean Powell had been lying on the sofa in the music room when the murderer had attacked her. James Kirkwood's shirt had marks of spurts of blood matching the victim's blood group. The scavenger Alexander Watts, who was acquainted with Kirkwood, testified that he had actually been invited in to see Ormelie the afternoon of the murder, without seeing anything untoward – had this been an attempt from the murderer to create an alibi? Yet the following morning, Kirkwood had cravenly 'chickened out' after spending much time and effort to bury the body and clean up the crime scene: he would have plenty of time to regret his ill-advised blabbering to the police, instead of showing some spirit and taking his chances.

As the trial went on, Kirkwood's legal councel were becoming worried that their insanity defence had failed, and that their client would end up at the end of the hangman's noose. They persuaded Kirkwood to plead guilty to culpable homicide, and the Lord Justice Clerk sentenced him to penal servitude for life, pointing out the extreme ferocity of the murder, and the terrible injuries inflicted on the victim.[3] Dismayed at facing a very long prison term, Kirkwood tried an appeal, but it was turned down. It was never satisfactorily explained what Jean Powell, described by her relatives and landlady as a respectable girl, had been doing inside Ormelie in the first place. It must be presumed that she had gone there willingly as the guest of Kirkwood, to drink sherry and smoke cigarettes in the music room. What we do not know for certain are the exact circumstances of the murder: did she object with the lustful Kirkwood tried to have his wicked ways with her? Or did she in fact consent to have casual sex with the gardener inside the large, empty house, only for some potency mishap, treated with derision, to provoke a furious reaction from the creature Kirkwood.

James Boyd Kirkwood was kicked into a prison cell and the keys were thrown away. He sat shivering in there as the Second World War was won, Churchill deposed and Clement Attlee installed as the new prime minister. But by 1952, he was definitely out of prison, since that year he divorced his wife Mary and married Helen Frances McCraw instead. To avoid unwanted notoriety, he called himself James Boyd, and so did the son he had with his second wife. The murderer expired at the Edinburgh City Hospital on May 17 1973, from dehydration and bronchopneumonia secondary to an oesophageal carcinoma according to his death certificate. The murder house Ormelie has survived him: it still stands at 20 Corstorphine Road, although it has been subdivided into flats.

THE MURDER OF MARGARET BEAGLEY, 1950

Margaret Beagley was a 15-year-old Edinburgh girl, the third youngest of a brood of 14 children, living with her parents at 1 Stanhope Place, Haymarket. After leaving school early, she became a shop assistant. At 4.30 in the afternoon of February 12 1950, when her mother Janet asked her to go on an errand to Granton, Margaret obediently took the bus north from Haymarket, but she never returned home. Just after half past nine in the evening, her father went out to look for her, only to find a considerable police presence in the neighbourhood. It turned out that a certain Mrs M'Gee, of 31 Elgin Place, had found Margaret dead in a cul-de-sac off Sutherland Street, and alerted the police. Margaret had been brutally murdered, through repeated heavy blows to the head from an object like a large stone.

Since a number of senior Edinburgh detectives were soon at the crime scene, inquiries were commencing with commendable promptitude. The Beagley family were questioned, Margaret's movements traced, and various local suspects rounded up and interviewed. It turned out that Margaret Beagley, described as a well-built girl who looked older than her years, with auburn hair and a fresh rosy complexion, had been seen going down Elgin Street between 6.30 and 6.50 pm the evening of the murder, in the company of a dark-haired young man. He was described as being around 20 years old, of slim build and 5 ft 9-10 in tall, and wearing a dark suit. Since this observation was quite close to the crime scene, the police suspected that the young man was the killer. A heavy stone, heavily stained with blood, had been found concealed not far from the body. The post-mortem revealed that contrary to first belief, the girl had not been sexually assaulted. The district where she was found was a strange one in those days, as the *Scotsman* newspaper described it: "The part of the City where the crime was committed, although it is in the West End, is little known by citizens in general. It is situated on the south side of West Coates, the main route to the west, and it consists of an intersecting collection of narrow, dim-lit streets and lanes, in which a stranger might easily lose his bearings. The railway lines west of Haymarket Station are immediately to the south of the area."

To begin with, the Margaret Beagley murder investigation seemed to make good headway. Not less than 16 detectives were working on the case, interviewing a large number of local people and trawling through the criminal underworld looking for possible suspects. On Saturday February 4, eight days before the murder, Margaret had been seen at the cross between Roseburn Street and Roseburn Terrace, in the company of a short young man with dark hair. The breakthrough came on March 14, when the 23-year-old unemployed labourer Alexander Short, of no fixed abode, was interviewed in Glasgow after being caught absconding from a boarding-house in Gilmore Place without paying. When he had checked into the boarding-house on

February 19, he had fraudulently described himself as a sailor in the Merchant Navy, saying that his luggage and money was on the way from his ship. The detectives were overjoyed when Short made certain admissions of being involved in the murder of Margaret Beagley: he was arrested, repeatedly questioned about his activities, and formally charged with murder.

On May 30 1950, Alexander Short stood trial at the High Court of Edinburgh, accused of murdering Margaret Beagley, and later obtaining board and lodgings to the value of 30s., without paying or intending to pay. Long queues of people tried to find places in the public galleries, with others waiting hopefully outside. Lord Thomson presided, and the Lord Advocate, Mr John Wheatley, led for the prosecution. Mr R.P. Morison defended Alexander Short. The Gilmore Place boarding house proprietrix described how Short had cheated her, Mrs Janet Beagley gave evidence about Margaret's movements the day of the murder, and a woman living in Elgin Place described hearing a heavy thud the evening of the murder. Another woman, who had been visiting in the neighbourhood, described meeting and speaking to a young couple who had crossed her path in Elgin Place. She later picked out Alexander Short as the man she had seen in a police identification parade. After 20 of the 53 witnesses cited had given evidence, Mr Morison stood up to make a legal submission, outside the presence of the jury. He had seen the medical reports in the case, which indicated that Short was quite feeble minded, with a mental age of eight. After he had been arrested on the fraud charge, the police had clearly entrapped him into making an admission, something that should not have been allowed.

This turn of events came at an inopportune time for the prosecution. Chief Constable William Merrilees could not deny that Short was feeble-minded, although he asserted that Short had been fit to answer questions, and to make a statement. Cross-examined by the peppery Mr Morison, Merrilees had to admit that he had told Short that a number of witnesses had seen a man of his description near the scene of crime on the night of the murder. The Lord Advocate pointed out that Short had never been threatened or frightened by the police and that it was perfectly fair and proper for the police to take statements from a feeble-minded person. Lord Thomson did not agree, however: after due consideration, he found the statement made by Short to the police not admissible as evidence. As a result, the Crown withdrew all charges against Alexander Short, and Lord Thomson directed the jury to return a verdict of Not Guilty.[4] Short left the High Court of Edinburgh as a free man, in the company of his father and brother, being protected from the large mob outside by the uniformed police. He never did anything newsworthy again and may well be identical to the Alexander Short who died at Leith in 1997, at the age of 71.

The murder of blameless young Margaret Beagley was never solved. The police were clearly convinced that Alexander Short was the guilty man, for reasons that were never divulged in court. Their attempt to entrap a half-wit to admit committing a brutal murder does not inspire confidence in the detectives involved, however; we will never know whether there was strong corroborative evidence against Short, or whether the detectives were led astray by wishful thinking while attempting to solve a high-profile murder in the heart of Edinburgh. Hopefully, Alexander Short showed some gratitude to the clever Mr Morison, who had successfully freed him from his persecutors. The area around Stanhope Place has changed very much since 1950: there are no longer any sinister, dimly lit cul-de-sacs off Sutherland Street, haunted by the spectre of the victim of a senseless and brutal murder that still cries out to Heaven for vengeance, although the humble Beagley family house still stands.

MURDER IN WHITSON ROAD, 1963

In 1963, the semi-detached suburban villa at 16 Whitson Road, Balgreen, was home to the 45-year-old unemployed man Mitchell Balloch and his wife Amy. Balloch was mentally ill with extreme anxiety and depression and had twice been an inpatient at Westhouse Asylum. His wife was of a fierce and neurotic disposition, and they often quarrelled angrily.

In the evening of October 22 1963, Mitchell Balloch came calling at his brother's house at 127 Whitson Road, telling him that something had happened to his wife. When the police were called in, they found Amy Balloch lying on the floor, strangled to death. Her husband admitted that they had been quarrelling once again: she had told him that he ought to get himself a job and broken a vase over his head. In a furious rage, he had hit her with a poker, before seizing her by the throat and strangling her to death.

When Mitchell Balloch stood trial at the High Court of Justiciary in December 1963, there was no question that he was the guilty man. Two doctors gave evidence, outlining Balloch's long history of psychiatric disease, and expressing the opinion that he had been insane when committing the murder. He was ordered by Lord Guthrie to be detained at the Carstairs State Mental Hospital, for an indefinite period of time.[5] Balloch was a sick man at the time, from severe rheumatoid arthritis and chronic bronchitis with emphysema. He was out of Carstairs in 1989, when he died aged 71, from a duodenal ulcer eroding into the pancreas.

THE GLASGOW ROAD MYSTERY, 1966

In early 1966, the 52-year-old businessman Mr David M'Menigall lived in the five-roomed bungalow at 98 Glasgow Road, Corstorphine. He was the chairman and managing director of Central Refrigeration Services, which had offices and a showroom in George Street; every weekday morning at 9am, he drove to work in his elegant Jaguar Mark X saloon car. He was fond of dining out and entertaining, and often took his lady friends for a meal at the fashionable New Town restaurants; the wine merchant who supplied his wine and spirits said that he always bought the best. Mr M'Menigall had been married twice, but both marriages had been dissolved. He was close to his son Martin, who worked for the same company and lived at Clerwood Place, Clermiston. Mr M'Menigall was known to have a heart condition, and during the last year, Martin had taken an increasing amount of responsibility for the refrigeration business.

On February 25 1966, Mr M'Menigall's housekeeper came to 98 Glasgow Road to do some cleaning. She was horrified to find him lying dead on the floor of the bungalow, with severe head injuries. The police were swiftly called in, and Detective Chief Superintendent James Beattie, head of the Edinburgh CID, took charge of the murder investigation. Mr M'Menigall had two dogs, a chihuahua and a terrier, but neither of these animals had been heard to make a racket during the night. A pane of glass in the kitchenette window was broken. The Jaguar Mark X was still parked in the drive. The police made extensive searches of the neighbouring gardens, the playing fields and farmland opposite the murder bungalow, and the embankment of the main Edinburgh-Fife railway, but found nothing interesting. A powerfully built, balding man in his late thirties had been seen at Moir & Baxter's garage nearby, and the police issued his description without any positive result. Behind the garage was a caravan site, but once more, extensive police searches turned up nothing valuable.

Mr M'Menigall, the son of a blacksmith, had made a distinguished career in the refrigeration business: his company was flourishing, and had branches in Glasgow, Dundee and Newcastle. He had never spoken of business rivals or old enemies, even to his son Martin. The evening of the murder, he had dined alone at the fashionable L'Aperitif restaurant in Frederick Street, returning home at 9.30 pm. The police were interested to find out that 98 Glasgow Road had been burgled around Christmas 1965, and clothes and bottles of spirits stolen; might this burglar have come around for a second visit, this time murdering the householder when he was detected on the premises? The police also found out that in the beginning of February 1966, a mysterious man, who might possibly have been working for Mr M'Menigall, had made a telephone call from his house, complaining that his car had run out of petrol. On March 2, motorists in Glasgow Road were stopped and questioned by the police, and those who admitted being around the evening of the murder were questioned if they had seen anything suspicious near the murder house, or any hitch-hiker thumbing a lift from a passing car. A Hillman Minx car had been travelling out from Edinburgh the night of the murder, on the road to Stirling, but according to a newspaper report, the police tracked it down and ruled it out of the murder investigation.[6]

On February March 11, Mr M'Menigall was buried at the Corstorphine Hill cemetery, after a service at St Anne's Church. Already by this time, things were looking bleak for the murder investigation, with no technical evidence and no trace of the elusive murderer. In early May, the police issued a drawing and description of a silver-plated car mascot, in the shape of a horse, which had been stolen from the murder house along with a gold signet ring. But the murder of David M'Menigall

5. Mr M'Menigall and the murder house at 98 Glasgow Road.

was never solved: it remains one of Edinburgh's few remaining murder mysteries, and the clues with which to ponder it are disappointingly few. As the years went by, the M'Menigall murder investigation gradually ground to a complete halt. The anonymous letters to the police were just disinformationist rubbish; no mysterious tramp appeared out of nowhere with a vital clue; no hardened criminal confessed, on his deathbed, to have been responsible for the 'Glasgow Road Job'. But in March 2016, the *Daily Record* had a curious feature about the M'Menigall murder, using information 'leaked' by a retired detective who had worked on the case as a young officer. This individual had several bombshells to impart. Firstly, detectives had wanted to trace a mysterious man who had asked a dog walker for directions in Gylemuir Park nearby, around the time of the murder. Secondly, the owner of the black Hillman Minx car, made between 1947 and 1949, and seen nearby at the relevant time, had never been identified. Thirdly, the horse-shaped car mascot stolen by the murderer was likely to have belonged to an old Ford Mustang, and it was also likely to have been the actual murder weapon, used by the murderous desperado to batter the head of David M'Menigall.[7]

In my opinion, the alternative murder hypotheses considered by the police can be discarded: Mr M'Menigall was twice-married and fond of 'chasing the lasses' so unlikely to have had any homosexual tendencies, and no person found anything to indicate that an old enemy or business rival might have committed or ordered the murder. The guilty man was clearly a burglar, perhaps the same man seen at Moir & Baxter's garage the very same night, before making use of his superior local knowledge to escape through the caravan park behind it. It is strange that an opportunist burglar would chose to break into a house with a fit and able-bodied occupant, but perhaps he was a strong and powerful man himself, or else he thought M'Menigall was still out wining and dining in the New Town. It is also a mystery why the burglar turned murderer did not steal M'Menigall's car keys and drive off in the Jaguar Mark X parked in the drive, but perhaps he wisely deduced that this large and characteristic saloon car was too conspicuous to be used as an escape vehicle. Or perhaps the reason was that the burglar was not at all prepared for a confrontation that fateful night: the murder might just have been the result of a nocturnal encounter between a desperate burglar and an irate householder? Aghast at what he had just done, the burglar turned murderer snatched a few valuables before making off into the night, keeping his dreadful secret until the end of his natural life. The abovementioned *Daily Record* article named the burglar who broke into Mr M'Menigall's bungalow at Christmas 1965 as the 18-year-old John Wills, who was caught by the police and found guilty of burglary in March 1966. He would thus have been out and about at the time of the murder, but would he really have been audacious enough to burgle once more the house he was awaiting trial for breaking into? It would have been interesting to know more about what the friends and criminal associates of John Wills were doing at the time of the murder, but we will never know, since Wills himself died from a drug overdose in 1987, aged just 40.

6. The house at 98 Glasgow Road today.

MURDER IN MCLEOD STREET, 1968

In 1965, the 27-year-old Mrs Jean Murray was left alone with two young children when her husband died mysteriously in a gassing incident. She soon took a lover, the Glaswegian salesman James Smith, and they had a son named Stephen. Jean Murray had soon seen enough of James Smith, however, and she refused him access to young Stephen, something that he seemed to greatly resent. Jean Murray lived at 91 Gorgie Road, but when she went to work as a part-time waitress at a Tollcross restaurant, she used to leave young Stephen with her friend Mrs Janet Greenan, of 5 McLeod Street, Dalry.

On Monday March 11 1968, Jean Murray left Stephen with Mrs Greenan, before going to work. When calling to pick up the child, she stayed for tea. She was dismayed to see the scoundrel John Smith come walking in, saying that he had come to see young

Stephen. Although Jean said that he was not allowed to see the child, he picked Stephen up, before lying him down again when he cried. 'I suppose you'll phone the police now', he smirked. 'Well, you know that is to be expected', Jean Murray replied angrily. 'Before you get the chance ...', James Smith hissed, before drawing a knife from his coat and stabbing her hard in the body.

Mrs Greenan, who had seen the entire horrid scene from close range, gave a shriek and ran out through the door, before desperately banging at the doors to the neighbouring flats to get help. When the ambulance and police arrived, Jean Murray was dead, and James Smith was taken into custody and charged with murdering her. He pleaded not guilty at the Edinburgh Sheriff Court, but when he stood his trial at the High Court in May 1968, the evidence against him was rock solid. The key witness Mrs Greenan told her story without contradictions, and Smith's fingerprints had been found on the murder weapon. The defence asked the jury to find the crime to be one of culpable homicide rather than murder, but the prosecution pointed out that the crime was a premeditated and dastardly one, committed by a depraved man who had been rejected by his mistress. The jury was out for just 15 minutes before finding James Smith guilty of murder, and he was sentenced to imprisonment for life.[8]

THE INFAMOUS SALISBURY
CRAGS MURDER, 1972

Helga Konrad, an 18-year-old German girl, led a solitary existence at her parent's farm in the village of Schwerbach, situated in the highlands of West Germany. She took an interest in learning English and typing, and fed the animals at the large farm as well as she could. One day she read an advertisement in the *Rhein-Zeitung* of June 24 1972: 'Young man (21) seeks for missing [sic] opportunity a nice girl with a view to marriage later.' Although there was no photograph of her putative swain, who might after all have been hideously deformed, she decided to take a chance on him. But although Ernst Dumoulin was a good-looking and personable young German, neatly dressed and equipped with a red Fiat sports car, he was a con artist and up to no good; those teratologically inclined would suggest his monstrosity was hidden away on the inside, like Evil in a Mask. The innocent Helga was quite unable to see through him, but the stern Herr Konrad flatly refused when Dumoulin proposed a whirlwind marriage, since he had doubts whether this flashy young man had the means to support his daughter in the manner she was accustomed. Dumoulin returned a few days later to give Helga a ride in his sports car for 15 minutes or so, something Herr Konrad reluctantly agreed to. But the guilty pair had no intention of returning to the farm: Dumoulin kept driving until they were in France, where he sold the car, which he had bought in Germany using a dud cheque, to pay for two single airline tickets to Edinburgh.

On September 19 1972, Ernst Dumoulin and Helga Konrad took a room at Mr Herbert Wood's guesthouse at 9 Torpichen Street near the West End. Mr Wood was used to various dodgy foreigners coming to stay, but the young couple made a good impression and Dumoulin paid him three weeks' rent in advance. Helga told Mr Wood and his wife that her husband planned to become a financial adviser in Edinburgh, with herself acting as his secretary. Dumoulin made no exertions to do any work, however, but he knew that after spending three weeks in Scotland, a foreign couple was allowed to marry there. This plan was executed with success, with the Woods acting as witnesses at a simple ceremony at the registrar's office on Friday October 13, a fateful date indeed, followed by a meal at a restaurant in Shandwick Place. When the newly-weds retired to their room, Mr Wood assumed they had retired for the night, but he was surprised to hear them leave a few hour later.

7. *The former guesthouse at 9 Torpichen Street, once occupied by the murderous Ernst Dumoulin and his unfortunate bride.*

In the early hours of the following day, Mr Wood was woken up by the police bringing back a dishevelled-looking Ernst Dumoulin. It turned out that a seaman had discovered the body of a young woman at the foot of Salisbury Crags. When he got in touch with the police, they were met by a distraught-looking Ernst Dumoulin, who explained that he and Helga had gone for a walk up the Crags to admire the lights of Edinburgh, when she had suddenly slipped and fallen down a precipice. Initially, there was no suspicion that a crime had been committed: the creature Dumoulin was allowed to remain in his hotel room, where he played the theme of the recent blockbuster film 'Love Story' again and again. The next day, after the police had taken Dumoulin away for some routine questioning, Mr Wood took the opportunity to clean his room. He found the receipt for a £412 368 life insurance taken out on Helga the day before she died, and lost no time before taking it to the Edinburgh detectives investigating the mysterious death on Salisbury Crags. They found that the brazen Dumoulin had actually come to the Edinburgh office of Hambro Life Assurance the morning after Helga had died, presenting the insurance policy and hoping to claim the money, but here he had misjudged the mentality of the Caledonian insurance officials, who were wholly adverse to paying large amounts of money to some dodgy foreigner without proper investigation.

The detectives made sure that Herr Konrad was communicated with: when he came to Edinburgh, the sordid background of the marriage became clear, as did Dumoulin's shady past as a con artist. The suspected murderer had gone into a Princes Street bank and applied for a loan of £10 000, falsely claiming that he possessed valuable assets in Germany, whereas the truth was that he was almost entirely penniless, even lacking the means to pay the premium for the life insurance policies he had taken out. On trial for murder at the High Court of Edinburgh in January 1973, before Lord Wheatley, the case for the prosecution seemed a strong one: Herr Konrad and Mr Wood presented their damning testimony without contradictions, describing how the prisoner had successfully spirited Helga away from her home, leaving a trail of debt behind as he absconded to Edinburgh, and married his naïve victim there in a preconceived plan. The medical evidence spoke in favour of Helga being pushed down the precipice. Dumoulin and his defence team claimed that Helga had known about the plan to defraud the insurance company, although the original plan had been for Dumoulin himself to fake a swimming accident at Cramond Island in the Firth of Forth. When they had climbed the Salisbury Crags, Helga had tried to push him over the precipice, but God had saved him from her murderous assault; in the ensuing scuffle, she had herself fallen to her death. Dumoulin made a far from good impression in court, however, and in his summing-up, Lord Wheatley described him as "a ready and conniving liar". The jury returned a majority verdict of Guilty and Lord Wheatley sentenced the prisoner to imprisonment for life.[9]

The cell doors of Saughton Prison closed behind Ernst Dumoulin and the keys were thrown away. Sixteen years later, the keys were retrieved, the cell doors swung open, and the Salisbury Crags murderer given a hard kick in the backside in the direction of his old haunts in Germany. It is strange but true that he remarried there, without conspiring to murder his second wife, and became a Lutheran minister in a small town; his duties are said to have included conducting marriage ceremonies, hopefully happier and longer lasting ones than his own first disastrous lapse into matrimony. In 2006, when the 54-year-old Dumoulin was interviewed by *Bild* magazine, he freely admitted his guilt in murdering Helga for the insurance money, but said that had found God in prison and become a better man. He would be 68 years old if he is still alive today, and I can see no evidence that he has expired; since the thought of a convicted murderer conducting Christian religious ceremonies is a repellent one, this Teutonic Elmer Gantry has hopefully retired from the ministry. Helga Konrad's short life is commemorated by a memorial seat at Salisbury Crags, not with some bloodcurdling curse against her murderer, or the text 'Vengeance is Mine, saith the Lord', but with the simple dates of her birth and death, and the information that she is buried back home in Schwerbach, where she should have stayed with her family, instead of travelling to Edinburgh with a murderous monster in the disguise of a common con artist. It does not take a close student of *God's Revenge against Murder*, by one Mr Reynolds, to make an educated guess about the creature Dumoulin's probable destination in the Afterlife: for him there will be no triumphant passing of Peter's wicket, and no choirboys braying out hymns in German, but rather phantasmagoria resembling some of the paintings of Rubens, with the Fallen Angels descending into Hell accompanied by serpents, dragons and other unclean beasts …

MURDER AND MYSTERY IN
SLATEFORD ROAD, 1973

The 68-year-old Mr Alexander Stewart was a veteran Edinburgh bookmaker. He himself ran a betting shop at 91 Slateford Road, and his 55-year-old wife Gertrude had another shop in Glanville Place, Stockbridge. The Stewarts lived at 7 Orchard Place, Comely Bank, with their adult son and daughter. In February 1973, Mr Stewart was semi-retired due to chest disease, but he still ran the Slateford Road betting shop. But when his wife came to collect him after work on February 28, she found him lying dead on the shop floor. He had been brutally beaten to death with a hammer or similar instrument, and the shop had been robbed by the murderer.

The hunt for the Slateford Road murderer was led by Detective Chief Inspector George Imrie, of the Edinburgh murder squad. It was clear to him that this was a premeditated, planned murder, for the sake of plunder. A systematic search of all cars seen parked near the betting shop was carried out, and since a witness had seen a 'C' registration Ford Cortina parked nearby, more than 15 Cortina owners had been questioned. More than 100 punters frequenting the shop had been tracked down by the police; a total of 70 people who had been in the shop on February 28 had been questioned, but another 28 customers had not been identified. Mrs Stewart had telephoned her husband just before 6 pm, and they had spoken for about 10 minutes. The last betting slip of the day was dated and time stamped 17.51, just after Mr Stewart had ended his phone call. A neighbour at 89 Slateford Road had heard screams from the shop, just after the national news had begun on BBC1 at 6 pm, but had done nothing decisive to investigate. Was the murderer the last customer of the day, and had he made his escape just before Mrs Stewart came to pick her husband up five minutes after 6 pm?

Going through Mr Stewart's accounts with the help of his wife, the detectives could deduce that the murderer had stolen £568.32 from the betting shop. An Edinburgh town councillor, Mr Donald

Swanson, had found the murder weapon, a joiner's hammer with the shaft wrapped in two blood-stained handkerchiefs, on a barbed-wire fence near the betting shop. One of the handkerchiefs had the initial 'L' in the corner, and the other the initial 'K'. On March 16, the detectives were still advertising for more punters from the shop to come forward, and appeals for witnesses were made at football matches in both Edinburgh and Glasgow. The East of Scotland Bookmaker's Association offered a reward of £1000 to any person who gave information that led to the conviction of the killer.

Later in March, Mrs Gertrude Stewart, who was carrying on business as usual in her betting shop, was visited by her regular customer Douglas Rhodes Knowles. When he made a bet, she thought the handwriting very much resembled that on the final betting slip received by her husband, and immediately telephoned the police. Knowles was an inveterate gambler, and the police found more than 100 betting slips with his handwriting at various Edinburgh bookies. A police handwriting expert found that they coincided with the betting slip handed in by the murderer, putting £1 on Hibs to beat Rangers in the Scottish Cup replay at Easter Road. When the detectives raided Knowles's flat, they found £90 in £5 notes hidden underneath the bathroom carpet. Prior to the murder, Knowles had been very hard up, but after the Slateford Road slaying, he had spent money freely. The detectives also found a handkerchief marked 'L', exactly matching the one wrapped around the murder weapon. Soon after the murder, Knowles and his wife had disposed of a raincoat and a pair of shoes. Knowles was promptly arrested, and he was charged with the murder of Alexander Stewart at the Edinburgh Sheriff Court on April 7.

On trial at the High Court in July 1973, Knowles pleaded not guilty, and denied having been anywhere near the Slateford Road betting shop the day of the murder. Various fingerprints had been retrieved from the murder shop, but none of them were from Knowles; nor was there any technical evidence against him, and no eyewitness had seen him at the scene of the murder. A police

8. Slateford Road, a postcard stamped and posted in 1920. Reproduced by permission of Mr G. Burgess, Dunbar.

expert confidently identified the handwriting on Mr Stewart's final betting slip as that of Knowles. Then there was the matter of the handkerchief marked 'L' that exactly matched the one left behind by the murderer; an aunt of Knowles rubbed salt into his wounds when she testified that she had given him similar handkerchiefs about five years earlier. A coat and a pair of shoes belonging to Knowles had been disposed of after the murder, to destroy vital evidence. The jury was out for more than two and a quarter hours before returning a majority verdict of guilty to murder.

Lord Cameron thanked the jury for their attention in a difficult and complex case, and sentenced Knowles to imprisonment for life.[10] Not every member of the legal fraternity was impressed with this harsh verdict, made on handwriting and circumstantial evidence alone, but there was never an appeal and Knowles went to prison as ordered. It would appear that he died in 1978, aged just 57. As for the murder shop at 91 Slateford Road, it is today the Freewhelin' Cycles bicycle shop. It has changed little since the time of the murder of Alexander Stewart.

MURDER AT THE RAVENSWOOD
GUEST HOUSE, 1974

In 1974, the ground and lower ground floors of the tall terraced house at 13 Torpichen Street, two doors away from where the murderous Ernst Dumoulin had hatched his dastardly plot two years earlier, was the Ravenswood Guest House, a downmarket establishment catering to various impoverished types, both foreign and homegrown, who needed a roof over their head. On March 25 1974, the body of the 24-year-old widow Mrs Elizabeth Croal was found inside a cupboard in a ground floor back room at the Ravenswood Guest House. She had been strangled to death, and her murderer had left behind no worthwhile clues. The police found out that Elizabeth Croal had been a widow since her husband Alan had fallen out from an upstairs window in the Dalkeith Road, and died. Her newspaper photograph shows her as a rather dowdy-looking woman, who appeared a good deal older than her chronological age. Her aunt Mrs Elizabeth Whitney said that Elizabeth Croal used to have a boyfriend named James Storrie, but she had jilted him after an affair lasting four years, and instead begun 'walking out' with a most unsatisfactory character, the homeless 27-year-old unemployed labouring man Ian Knowles. He had beaten her up more than once and put her in hospital with a broken jaw.

Since it turned out that Ian Knowles possessed a key to the Ravenswood Guest House, he was taken into custody by the police; at the Central Police Station, the muscular ruffian tried to break free, hitting a police sergeant and a constable, and breaking three panes of glass. He appeared before the Edinburgh Sheriff Court on April 2, to be charged with the murder of Elizabeth Croal. On trial at the High Court in June 1974, Knowles pleaded not guilty. But a schoolboy had seen him and Elizabeth Croal at 4.30, walking towards the Ravenswood Guest House; twenty minutes later, Knowles had been observed leaving the guest house

9. The murder house at 13 Torpichen Street,
where Elizabeth Croal was murdered in 1974.

alone. There was nothing to suggest that any other person than Knowles possessed a key to the murder room, or to the cupboard inside which the body had been found. The defence tried to implicate Elizabeth Croal's old boyfriend James Storrie, but without any success; Knowles had a history of violence against women, and the aunt testified that he had often beaten Elizabeth up. Ian Knowles was found guilty of murder and sentenced to imprisonment for life; an appeal in November 1974, alleging that the trial judge had misdirected the jury, was dismissed.[11]

MURDER AT THE SHISH MAHAL, 1977

Mohammed Akram, a Pakistani immigrant living in Edinburgh, called himself Jack Suhanuek after he had come to Scotland. A steady, industrious young man, he worked as a sales assistant in a wine and spirits shop, earning enough money to be able to marry and father a young son. A keen photographer, he sent a number of photographs of his wife and son to his parents back in Pakistan.

On May 19 1977, when Jack Suhanuek was 24 years old, he went to the Shish Mahal restaurant at 6 Brougham Street, Tollcross, with his friend Mohammed Masood. They had quite a few drinks before deciding to buy some take-away food. Jack Suhanuek, who was somewhat the worse for drink, became seriously annoyed with the restaurant staff, and wanted to start a fight with the waiter Abdul Malik, but Mohammed Masood managed to dissuade him. As Jack Suhanuek came lurching out of the restaurant toilet, he went straight for Malik and punched him two or three times. Malik seized hold of him with a hearty goodwill, and other members of the restaurant staff came running to his aid. In the end, Mohammed Masood managed to extricate his friend from this undignified brawl, as the waiters and kitchen boys were milling about unrestrained, but Suhanuek collapsed on the steps. Much blood was coming from his side, and it was clear that he had been stabbed several times. A nurse came running up to help, but he had no pulse, and died on the scene shortly after.

Detective Chief Inspector Brian Cunningham, who took charge of the murder investigation, made sure that all the restaurant staff were closely interviewed about their observations the evening in question. The kitchen boy Suna Miah said that he had seen Abdul Malik grab hold of Jack Suhanuek and stab him repeatedly with a knife that he used to carry. This looked promising, and Malik was charged with murder at the Edinburgh Sheriff Court. But at his High Court trial in late July 1977, Abdul Malik was well defended by Mr Ranald Sutherland QC.

He pleaded not guilty and lodged a defence of incrimination by naming four other men, three of whom belonged to the restaurant staff, as the killers. One of these men was said to have returned to his native Bangladesh. After Suna Miah had given his evidence incriminating Malik, Mr Sutherland countered by claiming that after the knife had been taken away from Jack Suhanuek, a certain Kotai Miah, who was now out of the country, and then Suna Miah himself, had stabbed him hard with it! The jury was out for 35 minutes before returning a majority verdict of not proven, and Abdul Malik was discharged.[12]

This was probably the correct verdict, due to the divergent witness statements, and the crowd of angry, excitable foreigners milling about inside the restaurant. Abdul Malik probably played some part in the scuffle, but it attracts suspicion that Kotai Miah, who was alleged to have stabbed Jack Suhanuek hard, had fled the country, hardly the action of an innocent man. The murder restaurant at 6 Brougham Street is a restaurant still: for a while, it was the Big Fat Greek Kitchen, where nourishing meals of tzatziki, moussaka and feta cheese salads could be had, and no murderous sub-continental types were lurking about, but today it is the Taxidi Greek café and bistro.

MURDER AT THE CALEDONIAN ROD AND GUN SHOP, 1977

The 50-year-old bachelor Mr Douglas Dinnie was one of Scotland's leading sea anglers, and the winner of many angling trophies. He was treasurer of the Leukaemia Research Fund Angling Club, and did much work to organize various fund-raising events. He lived with his elderly mother at Murieston Crescent and kept the Caledonian Rod and Gun Shop at 268/270 Gorgie Road.

On July 29 1977, Douglas Dinnie was found shot dead in a back room at the Caledonian Rod and Gun Shop. Suspicion soon concentrated on the 18-year-old shop assistant Ross Sutherland, who was known to be a nasty piece of work. Mr Dinnie had intended to dismiss him for his general slovenliness. On trial for murder at the High Court in October 1977, Ross Sutherland pleaded guilty to murdering Douglas Dinnie and stealing £138, seven rifles, five pistols and 3950 rounds of ammunition, and was sentenced to imprisonment for life.[13] The murder shop is today the Chinese Mini Market.

Ross Sutherland had held Mr Dinnie up with a gun to get the keys to the shop, he said, and he had gunned down his boss when he became recalcitrant. The arsenal of weapons stolen had been disposed of to people with connections to the Ulster Defence Army, and they were later used for terrorist purposes. In 1979, Ross Sutherland, serving his life sentence at Dumfries Prison, testified at a terrorist trial at the Glasgow High Court, identifying some of the weapons used by nine suspected terrorists as those he had stolen at the Caledonian Rod and Gun Shop.[14]

EDINBURGH'S MURDER CHURCH, 1977

Alexander 'Sandy' McGraw, an 88-year-old retired foundry worker, spent much of his time at St Andrew's Roman Catholic Church at 77 Belford Road. In between praying devoutly, he did odd jobs, emptied bins, and tidied up the garden. The present incumbent, Father Anthony Kiernan, and several of his predecessors, found him a useful asset to have about the place. On September 12 1977, Alexander McGraw was found collapsed in one of the pews of the church. When Father Kiernan said 'Sandy, what has happened?', the old man gave a groan. His rosary was lying nearby. Since the priest saw a trickle of blood running from the collapsed man's mouth, he thought McGraw might have suffered a stroke or a haemorrhage, but at the Western General Hospital, he was told that the old man had in fact been stabbed hard in the stomach.

After emergency surgery for his deep stab wound, Alexander McGraw seemed to recover briefly, but the following day, he suffered a stroke, and he died three days later. Since the stab wound was the cause of death, the case was now one of murder. The police appealed for observations of Alexander McGraw earlier the day of the murder: a slimly built, elderly man with a bushy white moustache, wearing a tweed bonnet, a brown jacket and navy trousers. It was rightly considered mysterious why this harmless old man had been stabbed to death while quietly praying inside a church. But the police soon had a vital clue. Mr Hugh Young, chief reporter of the *Daily Record*, had an anonymous telephone call from a man who wanted £500 for a story about 'a serious incident' in Edinburgh for which the caller was responsible. The reporter wanted more information to part with any money, but the caller was unwilling to provide any. When he called again, the police were standing by. This time, the caller asked for £2 500 for his story, money he wanted for his mother, he said. When the reporter asked him if he was talking about the murder of the old gentleman inside the church, the caller said "The man is dead, stabbed through the stomach. I felt it go in."

The police managed to track this mysterious telephone call down to a hostel for the mentally ill in Northumberland Street. The police went there and arrested the 26-year-old mental patient Lawson Imrie, who suffered from chronic psychotic illness. He was known to dislike churches and religion, and was suspected of having made two attempts to burn down St Ninian's Roman Catholic Church, in 1972 and 1976, using lighted candles. When challenged about the phone calls to the *Daily Record*, Imrie willingly admitted being the man responsible, since he needed money and wanted to become famous. When he had gone to St

Andrew's Roman Catholic Church the day of the murder, he had seen the pathetic old man in the pew and stabbed him for the purpose of robbery. He added that the murder had just been an unfortunate incident, for he had only intended to wound the old man to get himself into the newspapers. The social workers told the police that Imrie had more than once boasted to them either that he was going to become famous one day, or that he had committed a crime to make the newspaper headlines.

Lawson Imrie was arrested by the police. On December 2, he was brought before the Edinburgh Sheriff Court to be charged with the murder of Alexander McGraw, pleading not guilty to the murder charge, as well as to two charges of wilful fire-raising. When the trial began on December 12, Father Kiernan described how he had found Alexander McGraw collapsed in the church on September 12, when he had taken a boy there for altar boy practice. Hugh Young described his telephone conversations with the murderer, and a tape recording was played in court. Dr Robert McAulay, lecturer at the department of forensic science at Edinburgh University, who had carried out the post-mortem, attributed Alexander McGraw's death to the severe stab wound and hypothermia. Since the old man had otherwise been perfectly healthy, he could have lived for another ten years had he not been unprovokedly attacked in the church. The outcome was that Lawson Imrie was found guilty of culpable manslaughter, the charge being reduced for reasons of diminished responsibility, and he was committed to the State Mental Hospital, Carstairs, without limit of time. In 2003, when Imrie's nephew committed a murder in Edinburgh, he was said still to be incarcerated at Carstairs. Since there is no record of any person with the distinctive name of this Edinburgh Herostratos expiring in Scotland or England, and since it would be a foolhardy decision to free such a desperate character to commit further ecclesiastical atrocities, he may well be there today.[15]

THE MURDER OF AILEEN PRINTIE, 1981

The 31-year-old bank clerkess Miss Aileen Printie lived in the ground floor flat at 4 Kingsknowe Road North, Longstone. She was the daughter of the late John Printie, but her mother Teresa and her brother and two sisters were still alive. At 7.40 am on August 22 1981, Aileen Printie was found murdered in the bedroom of her flat, in a pool of blood; she had severe head injuries after being brutally beaten with a brick. Her body had been covered by the quilt from her bed. Her wallet had been stolen, as had, bizarrely, a plastic ice bucket from the kitchen. Between 9 and 9.30 in the evening before the murder, Aileen's sister Moira had repeatedly tried to phone her, but only to find that the line was engaged. When Moira finally got through, Aileen said nothing about this long and unexplained telephone call, and in spite of a police appeal, whoever was on the phone never came forward.

A few days after the murder, Aileen Printie's wallet was found by a lorry driver in a demolition area behind 4 Kingsknowe Road North; a small sum of money had been stolen, but her driving license and credit cards remained. The missing ice bucket was not found. Since there were no signs of an obvious forced entry to Aileen Printie's flat, the police speculated that the murderer was either some person she had invited into the flat, or a strong man who had managed to overpower her after she had opened the door. Aileen Printie was a respectable young woman, who had always disapproved of casual affairs, and tended to avoid criminal or unbalanced members of the opposite sex. A cheap cuff link, inset with a square synthetic blue stone, was found at the crime scene, and it was found likely that it had been left behind by the murderer. These cuff links had been sold over all of Scotland, 1000 of them in all, at £2 a pair. At 11.45 the night before the murder was discovered, a young man presumed to be in his twenties, and wearing jeans and a leather jacket, was seen walking into Slateford village in the direction of the city, carrying a plastic bag that seemed to contain an ice bucket! Or had the killer perhaps remained in the murder flat until the early morning hours, mixing with the many commuters into central Edinburgh to avoid attracting notice? By late October 1981, it is recorded that the detectives investigating the murder of Aileen Printie had interviewed 4 000 people and taken 1 000 witness statements. Appeals to find the young man in the leather jacket had been unsuccessful, as had house-to-house searches in the local neighbourhood, and a trawl through known burglars and violent criminals. As the years went by, the activity in the hunt for the murderer of Aileen Printie decreased steadily. From time to time, it was debated if the killer had been a person known to her, an intruder who murdered her just for the fun of it, or a burglar who had managed to gain entry into the murder flat.[16]

But in 1997, there was a major breakthrough in the murder investigation: the police managed to analyse samples of DNA from the crime scene, and to compare it with that of suspects who were still alive. In all, ten or so people were tested, and one of them was a match: the 32-year-old father-of-three Paul Andrews, who had been a prolific housebreaker in the Longstone area back in 1981, when he was just 16 years old. He had never known Aileen Printie, but the police suspected that he had entered the flat believing it to be empty, only to be confronted by the householder. Since Andrews had been a strong and sturdy lad, beating a woman to death with a brick was not beyond him. In repeated questionings, the police put pressure on Paul Andrews; he protested his innocence, as did his family. Aileen Printie's mother Teresa was told that the police now had a main suspect, and that they were taking measures to make him face trial. But Andrews drove his car to a quiet area near Edinburgh, doused himself in petrol and set himself alight, being found inside his burnt-out car the following day. He remains the only credible suspect in the hunt for the murderer of Aileen Printie.[17]

10. The murder house at 4 Kingsknowe Road North.

MURDER IN LAURISTON PLACE, 1984

In the early 1980s, the 57-year-old John McEwan lived in the modern flat at 135/1 Lauriston Place with his 54-year-old wife Ann. They had been married for 38 years and had six children alive. On February 1984 they went out drinking beer and whisky at Laurie's Bar, 105 Lauriston Place, and when he got very drunk, she was seen to threaten him with a knife. On the early hours of February 3, John McEwan was found dead at 135/1 Lauriston Place, with a deep knife wound in the left thigh, and his wife Annie was arrested and tried for his murder.

Annie McEwan pleaded not guilty, with a special defence of incrimination, blaming the family friend Marcus Morrison, of the Greyfriars Hotel at 2 Cowgatehead, for the murder, although he denied all involvement in court. Dr Anthony Busuttil, who had carried out the post-mortem, described the 'torrents of blood' that would had resulted from the severing of the femoral artery when John McEwan bled to death. Annie wept piteously in the witness-box, describing how she and her husband had been drinking hard all day. But after a three-day trial, the verdict was that of not proven: no person had seen the stabbing, and the possibility remained that some other person had waylaid John McEwan as he was entering his flat in a very befuddled state. When it was announced that Annie McEwan was discharged, there was clapping and cheering from the public benches.[18]

THE MAD AXEMAN OF CHESSER GARDENS, 1984

The 69-year-old pensioner John Ross lived in the downstairs flat at 7 Chesser Gardens, Gorgie, with his twin sister Mrs Barbara Horne, his 77-year-old elder sister Margaret Ross, and his 46-year-old niece Mrs Sheila Still. He still worked part time as a green-raker at the Dalmahoy Country Club. In his youth, he had spent many years in Australia and New Zealand, but in 1974 he had returned to spend his declining years in his native Edinburgh. As the years went by, John Ross became increasingly obsessed with money, particularly the state of his tax returns. He had some money invested, and an assiduous tax clerk had found errors in his tax return, with regard to bank interest, and he was questioned by the Inland Revenue. The sum involved was just a few pounds, but John Ross thought it a great disgrace to have been exposed as a taxation fraudster. A morose, paranoid loner,

11. The little house at 7 Chesser Gardens, where the Mad Axeman swung his axe to murderous effect in 1984.

he developed a fixed idea that he would be going to prison, thus bringing disgrace upon his family. To his disturbed mind, the only solution would be to murder all the other inhabitants of 7 Chesser Gardens, to spare them the shame of his impending imprisonment.

On March 20 1984, John Ross rose at 5.45 in the morning. He grabbed hold of an axe and a rope and went to his sister Margaret's bedroom. He beat her to death with the axe and tied the rope around her neck. He then attacked his niece Sheila, and there were the grossest scenes as she fought desperately for her life against the axe-wielding maniac, in a veritable bloodbath. As she lay senseless on the floor in a pool of gore, he seized hold of her throat and throttled her. The upstairs neighbours had heard the commotion as the Chesser Gardens axe murderer decimated his family, but they did not call the police; ten minutes later, John

Ross came knocking at their door, to admit the carnage he had wrought, exclaiming 'I have murdered them! Sheila would not die, she was too strong. What will my beloved niece say? I have betrayed them!' The police came to 7 Chesser Gardens and took John Ross with them. It turned out that in spite of her appalling injuries, Sheila was still alive; she was taken to hospital, but her ventilator was switched off on March 29.

On trial for murder at the High Court of Edinburgh, John Ross freely admitted the double axe murder, adding that he had intended to murder his twin sister Barbara as well. The psychiatrists who had examined Ross testified that he had been bordering on insanity at the time he committed the murders, although he was not now in need of psychiatric treatment. The defence counsel made it clear that the Inland Revenue bore no responsibility for the tragedy, since they had accepted Ross's answers to their queries, and written the matter off; it was the prisoner's own delusions about his taxation problems that had led to the misguided 'mercy killings'. After John Ross had been found guilty of murder, Lord Wheatley said that the big problem in this case was the proper disposal. Since the psychiatrists had made it clear that there were no grounds for a hospital order to be made, Ross would have to go to prison for a period of five years.

An *Edinburgh Evening News* reporter managed to get an exclusive interview with the sole remaining inhabitant of 7 Chesser Gardens, the murderer's twin sister Mrs Barbara Horne, described as a quiet and gentle woman. At the time of the murders, she had been lying awake in her bedroom, wondering at the strange noises emanating from the other rooms of the flat. Several times, her brother John had peered at her around the door, but fortunately for her, he had never entered the bedroom. Although he had murdered her entire family, and expressed his intention to murder herself as well, she could still find it in her heart to forgive his terrible deed.[19]

THE MURDER OF ANN BALLANTINE, 1987

Ann Ballantine was born in 1966 and grew up in a flat in Warriston Road with her parents Graham and Isobel Ballantine; she had a younger sister named Grace and a younger brother named Alan. Although she was unemployed and lacked professional training, she moved out of the family home and took a small flat of her own at 20 Yeaman Place, Dalry. In 1986, she worked as an unpaid volunteer at the Canongate Youth Project, looking after disabled youngsters. Money was tight but her parents helped her to get by. A good-looking and vivacious young woman with long black hair, she was a great fan of heavy metal music and used to hang around the Venue Club in Calton Road, consorting with various rough types from the biker fraternity. In late 1986, she had split up with her boyfriend Joe Burden, but remained upbeat about her future, and looking forward to celebrating Christmas with her family.

The last time Isobel Ballantine saw her daughter was on November 17 1986. Ann liked to lead an independent life and had a somewhat bohemian lifestyle, but when she did not come to the family home for Christmas, her parents knew something was wrong. The visited the flat in Yeaman Place and put letters and some money through the letterbox, asking Ann to phone her family even if she was skint. After there had been no response, the Ballantines went to the police, who took their concerns seriously. Picking the lock of the Yeaman Place flat, they found everything in good order, with no signs of a burglary or a struggle. A strange assortment of things turned out to be missing from the flat: a black leather jerkin, a brass petrol lighter with Ann's initials engraved, a photo album and a black shoulder bag. The police did what they could in tracking down Ann's friends, but without finding any trace of her.

On January 21 1987, some workmen spotted the naked body of a young woman floating in the Union Canal, with its hands

12. 20 Yeaman Place.

and feet tied together. Although the body was badly decomposed, it could be identified as that of Ann Ballantine through her dental records, and through a distinct scar on her head. The police technicians found that Ann had been raped and strangled to death; although she had been dead for nearly two months, she had only been in the canal for a few days. This would indicate either that she had been murdered in the flat at 20 Yeaman Place, with the body afterwards being moved to some secure location by the killer, or that she had been murdered somewhere else, presumably in some secure hideout available to the killer, where dead bodies could be stored for weeks on end without risk of discovery. The police searched warehouses, disused garages and derelict buildings, without finding any clue to where Ann's body had been stored. They suspected that the murderer was a man who knew Ann well, and found a suspect who was known to the Ballantine family as a disagreeable person, and whose name was mentioned in Ann's diary; a report was sent to the procurator fiscal, but there was insufficient evidence for a prosecution.

Another hypothesis is that Ann Ballantine was murdered by a serial killer, who took some mementoes of her away from the murder flat. It is not known whether Ann prostituted herself on a part-time basis, which is a pity since this would potentially have brought her into contact with some very unsavoury types. Christopher Halliwell murdered two women in 2003 and 2011, but the police suspected that his tally of victims was a good deal higher than that. Many items of women's clothing were found buried with those of one of his victims, and already in 1985, he had boasted of being a serial killer; yet nothing connects this Wiltshire-based cab driver with Edinburgh. In 2019, the former detective Chris Clark pointed the finger at the 'Beast of Bramley' John Taylor, a parcel delivery driver based in the outskirts of Leeds, currently serving a life sentence for murdering the 16-year-old Leanne Tiernan in 2000, as well as a number of sex attacks. He had nothing to connect him with Edinburgh, although he might have been passing through the Capital while going to Glasgow looking for prostitutes. Taylor, who would have been 30 years old in 1986, had kept the body of his victim in his kitchen freezer for nine months before dumping it. Our old 'friend' Joseph McGinlay, who murdered Betty Cassidy in 1974, was securely locked away in 1986, although he was allowed out of prison in 1997 to murder Mandy Barnett. The murder of Ann Ballantine, one of the greatest mysteries of modern Edinburgh, is unlikely ever to be solved although the police investigation is still actively pursued; having committed the perfect murder, the killer may well still be alive today.[20]

THE MURDER OF CAPTAIN KAYE, 1987

In the 1970s and early 1980s, the brothers Lieutenant-Colonel Alistair Kaye and Captain Ian Kaye, both of them retired army officers, lived in the semi-detached villa at 5 Wester Coates Terrace. Alistair, known widely as 'The Colonel', was a cheery extrovert, but Captain Kaye was a very morose and gloomy man, reclusive and prematurely aged. After Alistair Kaye had died in 1986, his brother lived on in the house. Captain Kaye told their old handyman Alexander McGregor that although there was no longer any need for him to do any work inside the house, he could still manage the garden. In 1987, the Captain was just 67 years old, but he looked much older: nearly six foot tall but quite stooped and cadaverous, and weighing just six and a half stone. He rarely left his house, except for a daily expedition to the local newsagent to purchase the *Times* newspaper, and seldom spoke to the neighbours. His only living relation was a second cousin living in Dunblane, but even he had little contact with the reclusive Captain Kaye.

On April 2 1987, the gardener Alexander McGregor found Captain Kaye lying in a pool of blood in the kitchen of 5 Wester Coates Terrace. The frail recluse had been badly beaten and tortured, and repeatedly stabbed in the head and face. The murderer had forcibly broken his back, before cutting his throat with such force that the head was nearly severed from the body. It was estimated that Captain Kaye had been dead for almost a week. He had recently bought a Fiat Uno motor car, which had been stolen by the murderer and driven to Edinburgh Airport. About fifty detectives and uniformed officers were making house-to-house inquiries, and the police were keen to hear from any person who had seen Captain Kaye after March 25, the last time he had been spotted by a neighbour.

The police searched the murder house thoroughly, looking for clues. On the dining room table was a building society diary, in which an entry for March 25 read 'Keith McG called.' They soon found out that Alexander McGregor the gardener had a 29-year-old son named Keith, who had many convictions for theft, assault and robbery. On May 5, Keith McGregor was arrested by the police, and the following day, he was charged with murder at the Edinburgh Sheriff Court.

When the High Court murder trial began on July 29, Keith McGregor pleaded not guilty, submitting a defence of incrimination: the murder had been committed by a man known as 'Johnny' who he had met while drinking in a pub, and invited to come to Captain Kaye's house. He went on to claim that after the bonhomous Captain had let them both into the house and poured them some lager, Johnny gave him a lot of advice about business. All of a sudden, Johnny had seized hold of the frail old man and pushed him to the ground, before cutting his throat. After warning Keith McGregor that he would be next if he did not keep his mouth shut, Johnny drove him home in the Fiat Uno.

Mrs Carolyn Hateb, who had been cohabiting with Keith McGregor for a year, testified that he had spoken to her about the Wester Coates Terrace murder, admitting being in the murder house but claiming that another man had killed Captain Kaye. A man named Edward Howes, who had been drinking with Keith McGregor in a pub, testified that McGregor had been speaking of having murdered an old man in the kitchen, before giving him a lift home in a nearly new Fiat Uno. Howes had thought he was joking at the time, but the following day, when Keith McGregor gave him a lift into Edinburgh in the Fiat, he was horrified when McGregor had casually told him that the car had belonged to the 'old guy' he had killed. When he asked McGregor to stop, since he did not want to be seen in a car belonging to a murdered person, the self-confessed murderer had driven into the Edinburgh Airport car park and left the Fiat Uno in there. Mrs Kathleen Baillie, a neighbour of Keith McGregor in Westburn Gardens, Wester Hailes, could also testify about his unwise blabbering while in his cups. When invited into McGregor's flat for some drinks, she had been astonished when he had suddenly exclaimed 'It is thick blood that comes out of your neck. He took a long time to die. It was horrible!'

Keith McGregor's counsel submitted guilty pleas for the stealing of the car, and for the theft of the murdered man's bank card, from which a total of £1000 had been stolen, using Captain Kaye's personal code. But McGregor still maintained, even during a harsh cross-examination, that the story of 'Johnny' was the true version of events, although the prosecution pointed out how unlikely it was that the reclusive Captain Kaye would have poured drinks for, and discussed business with, a complete stranger from the street. And what about the torture preceding the murder, to obtain Captain Kaye's personal bank code? The jury found Keith McGregor guilty of a brutal, cruel and premeditated murder, and he was sentenced to imprisonment for life.[21] I saw the murder house in 2003, but it has since been pulled down and replaced with a modern-style building.

THE MURDER OF ANDREW KERR, 1992

The 30-year-old unemployed man Andrew Kerr had formerly been a waiter on board the luxury ocean-liner Queen Elizabeth II. He rented a flat at 37/4 Palmerston Place, Haymarket, from Tam Paton, the former manager of the Bay City Rollers. On Friday March 20 1992, Andrew Kerr went out partying at the Edinburgh gay bars. On the early hours of Sunday March 22, the neighbour Colin Clark discovered his dead body inside the flat. He had been murdered in a frenzied attack and stabbed 17 times in a bloodbath.

Palmerston Place, Edinburgh

13. A postcard showing Palmerston Place.

Detective Chief Inspector George Brown, leading the murder investigation, presumed that Andrew Kerr had been murdered by some person he had invited home to his flat, since there were no signs of a forced entry. Kerr did not have a steady boyfriend, but some associates of his in the Edinburgh gay underworld said that it would have been in character for him to have taken some casual acquaintance back to the flat for sex. Ian Dunn, convener of the Scottish Homosexual Rights Group, suspected that a gang of vicious rent boys were behind the murder, but Chief Inspector Brown told a journalist that there was no evidence for this. The police were busy preparing a personal profile of Andrew Kerr and tracking known associates of his. The major clue was that the evening of the murder, the neighbour Colin Clark had seen a man leaving Andrew Kerr's flat: he had been around 30 years old, with a balding head, a round face and a plump nose.

The 26-year-old hospital porter Graham Kerr, younger brother of the murdered man, told an *Edinburgh Evening News* journalist that Andrew had always been careful with the company he kept. He had often travelled back to Dundee, to visit his mother, brother and sister. Graham Kerr believed that he had been deliberately hunted down and murdered over some long-standing grudge. The Edinburgh Gay Switchboard organization could report that a veritable wave of fear had gripped the city's gay underworld after the murder of Andrew Kerr: fearful of murderous rent boys, they avoided the homosexual prostitution racket, and viewed all strangers as potential murderers.

On March 26 1993, less than a week after the murder of Andrew Kerr, the police got a tip that the guilty party was the 27-year-old unemployed Livingston man Daniel Ward. He willingly confessed to stabbing Andrew Kerr when questioned by the police, and he took detectives to a close in Livingston where he had hidden the murder weapon. The witness Colin Clark picked him out as the man he had seen leaving Kerr's flat. Ward had been speaking to his mother, and to a friend, about stabbing a man and killing him. The impression of a blood-stained bare foot in the murder flat matched that of Ward. On trial for murder at the High Court in July 1992, Daniel Ward pleaded guilty at the advice of his legal counsel. He had been taking anti-depressive drugs before drinking vodka with Andrew Kerr in his flat. Passing sentence, Lord Caplan said "Well, Mr Ward, as a result of taking drugs combined with alcohol, you committed a crime which can be described only as of maniacal savagery. I must sentence you to imprisonment for life."[22]

THE MURDER OF HEWIE NOBLE, 1994

The 57-year-old retired seaman Hewie Noble was openly homosexual: he liked to invite younger men to his house at 81 Broomhall Drive, Corstorphine, for some casual sex. On Christmas Day 1994, Hewie Noble was found murdered in his blood-spattered bedroom, with deep stab wounds to his face, chest and abdomen. He had 11 broken ribs and several broken bones in his face. The hunt for the murderer was not going to be a testing one for the police, since the 24-year-old pharmacy worker Iain Mackie was still in the locked murder house; the police found him sitting in the living-room with his chest smeared with blood.

Mackie said that he had gone to see Hewie Noble for a chat and a drink or two. Noble invited him upstairs to have a look at a pornographic magazine. In the bedroom, he made a grab at the trousers of the younger man, and Mackie picked up a knife from the dressing table to warn him off. He had then suffered a convenient memory lapse, before returning to his senses standing over Noble's mangled body with the knife in his hand. Trapped in the locked murder house, he had then tried to commit suicide, he claimed, and showed the police some superficial injuries to his neck and left wrist.

On trial for murder at the High Court in May 1995, Iain Mackie pleaded not guilty. The evidence against him was overwhelming, however, and after a four-day trial, the jury returned an unanimous verdict of guilty. Lord Milligan sentenced Iain Mackie to imprisonment for life; the young man is said to have shown little reaction as he was led from the dock.[23]

THE MURDER OF MANDY BARNETT, 1996

The 23-year-old Amanda 'Mandy' Barnett was born in London, but in the 1990s, she travelled north and moved into a first-floor flat at 18/2 Murdoch Terrace, Fountainbridge. Described as petite, with short cropped reddish-brown hair, a nose stud and a cockney accent, she was a rave fan who spent much of her spare time partying. She had just got a job as a cloakroom attendant at the Subway night club in the Cowgate. Her six-year-old daughter lived with relatives in Luton. Mandy Barnett had a distinctly dodgy boyfriend, whom we have previously encountered in this book: the murderer John Balsillie, jailed for life after killing old Jessie Moffat back in 1976, He had befriended Mandy Barnett after being let out on parole in 1993, but in 1996 he was back in prison after being caught burgling a house.

In spite of his various demerits, John Balsillie appears to have been genuinely fond of Mandy Barnett, and vice versa. What she saw in him is uncertain: perhaps she thought him exciting as an experienced criminal who had once murdered an old woman in cold blood, but still she visited him in prison as often as she could and waited for his daily telephone call. But when Balsillie called Mandy on April 26 1996, a man answered the phone. Moreover, he could recognize his voice: it was that of the convicted murderer Joseph McGinlay, who had recently been released from prison! After Mandy had failed to appear on her usual visit to the prison, the frantic Balsillie alerted the guards at Saughton Prison that something must be seriously wrong at Mandy Barnett's flat. Nobody answered the door when a constable came knocking, but Balsillie had given the guards his key to the flat, and they passed it on to the police. Entering the flat, they found Mandy Barnett brutally murdered in the bath; she had been stabbed twice in the chest and throttled with a piece of shower hose.

The police had a vital clue in their hunt for the murderer, namely that Balsillie had recognized the voice of the man answering the phone as that of the 40-year-old Joseph McGinlay, a man who had previously showed that he was capable of murdering a woman. In 1974, he had murdered the 16-year-old Betty Cassidy in a Glasgow tenement, but in 1996, he had been transferred to Noranside Open Prison near Forfar, awaiting his release. Since the regime at this prison was far from strict, McGinlay was allowed out on unescorted weekend leave more than once. It also turned out that McGinlay had told his brother-in-law Douglas Traynor about murdering a woman and putting the body in a bath full of hot water. He was arrested and charged with the murder of Mandy Barnett.

On trial for murder at the High Court in March 1997, things were looking far from good for Joseph McGinlay. He pleaded not guilty, blaming the drug dealer who supplied Mandy Barnett with Ecstasy pills for murdering her after she had failed to pay for her drugs. John Balsillie made a good impression in court, and confidently named McGinlay as the man who had answered Mandy's phone on the afternoon of April 26. There were bloody shoeprints in the murder flat, and it turned out that Joseph McGinlay had thrown away a pair of bloodstained shoes after the murder. The man Douglas Traynor told his story of McGinlay's confession without contradictions, although the defence claimed that a member of McGinlay's own family, who wanted him to remain behind bars, had beaten Traynor up with a baseball bat to force him to perjure himself. The defence also suggested that the drug dealer William Hamilton, who had supplied Mandy Barnett with Ecstasy, had committed the murder, but he also made a good impression in court, pouring scorn on the notion that he would kill one of his customers over a drugs debt of just £60.

The jury unanimously found Joseph McGinlay guilty of murder, and Lord MacLean gave him is second life sentence, recommending that he should serve a minimum of 30 years behind bars.[24] A sinister-looking cove, described by some as a Freddie Mercury look-alike, he would remain in prison until 70 years old, having spent his entire adult life behind bars. It was never disclosed how he had managed to get acquainted with Mandy Barnett in the first place, although there was newspaper speculation that she had been prostituting herself. McGinlay would appear still to be alive, and still in prison, today.

THE CALEDONIAN CRESCENT TRAGEDY, 1999

In February 1999, the body of the 33-year-old Edinburgh man Michael O'Toole was found hanging from the Teray Bridge near Largh, Sutherland. He left a lengthy suicide note saying that after murdering his wife Juliet in the ground floor flat at 36 Caledonian Crescent, he had driven 250 miles up to the Highlands, pondering various stratagems to destroy himself, until he had spotted the bridge. When the Edinburgh police was alerted, they found the 34-year-old Juliet O'Toole murdered in her bed, strangled with a dressing-gown cord. The neighbours in Caledonian Crescent described the O'Tooles as a quiet suburban couple who had always seemed to get on well together. Yet there was no doubt that for some motive or other, Michael O'Toole had deliberately murdered his wife, staying in the murder flat for three days afterwards pondering suicide, before making his last drive up to the Teray Bridge.[25]

THE MURDER OF ELAINE COLLIE, 1999

Elaine Collie was born in Londonderry, Northern Ireland, but her family emigrated to New Zealand when she was very young. Returning to Londonderry, she trained as a legal secretary. In 1986, when she was 33 years old, she moved to Edinburgh where she worked as secretary to a government minister and a legal practice until a repetitive strain injury put an end to her career in 1994. After that, she enjoyed her time in Edinburgh, often visiting the Capital's libraries and art galleries, and taking long walks in the parks or along the Water of Leith. She carried a purse full of small change, which she distributed among the beggars infesting Princes Street. A quiet, religious woman, she lived in a small second-floor flat at Muirhouse View, one of Edinburgh's toughest estates.

In early April 1999, the neighbours of Elaine Collie contacted the police, since she had not been seen for several days. She was found dead in the bedroom of her flat, having been tied up, sexually assaulted, tortured and murdered. There were no immediate clues who had carried out such a pointless and brutal murder. Elaine Collie had never committed any crime, and she was a prim spinster who took little interest in wicked men; her friends were mostly elderly and respectable people, wholly devoid of a history of violent crime. On April 1, Elaine Collie had visited Muirhouse Library, before taking a bus to Princes Street to buy a pair of trousers and an Easter egg, the latter a present for her elderly friend Isa Gillespie, who lived in Birnies Court. She had been spotted on CCTV helping another shopper carry some heavy items, and later at 3.45 pm getting out of the lift at Birnies Court after delivering the egg.

Initially, there was police speculation that Elaine Collie might have disturbed an intruder into her flat, or that she had known her killer and willingly let him into the flat. But then it was discovered that the flat next to hers belonged to a notorious criminal, the 41-year-old former security guard John Reid. This individual hailed from Dunbar in East Lothian, where he had worked on the fishing boats for a while. Since he was very fat and never washed or had a bath if he could help it, his pungent body odour became a problem even in these unfastidious surroundings: a Dunbar fishing source told an *Edinburgh Evening News* journalist that "If you were short of a man for the boat he was aye there, but he was dirty. A few guys had him on the fishing boats at the time, but he got thrown off half of them because he was absolutely stinking." In the mid-1970s, Reid was jailed for three months for assaulting a woman in a churchyard. Habitually dishonest, and a notorious car thief, he was hounded out of Dunbar in 1985 after sexually assaulting a 14-year-old girl; fearful of beaten up by various rough nautical types, he would never return to his hometown. Not long after, he was charged with beating up and sexually assaulting a mentally impaired man, although the case never went to trial.

In 1986, 'Jock the Rapist', as he was known in Dunbar, was sentenced to a year in prison for assaulting a 19-year-old woman at the St Andrews bus station in Edinburgh. In all these cases, he had pleaded guilty after lesser charges had been offered to him. In the 1990s, his life of crime continued in Edinburgh: he stole cars, beat people up, and committed petty offences. He liked tinkering with old cars he had bought cheaply, selling them for slightly more than he had paid. In 1999, he was living with a woman in Pilton Drive North, using his own tiny flat in Muirhouse View as a 'giro drop' where he could collect his benefits cheques.

The police found out that soon after the murder of Elaine Collie, the 20-stone Reid had embarked on a drunken drive from Edinburgh to Craigmillar, causing several hit-and-run accidents on his way. He was arrested after being found slumped outside a pub and sentenced to four months in prison for these motoring offences. But his relatively low blood alcohol level led the police detectives to suspect that 'Jock the Rapist' had deliberately got himself arrested as a ruse to take himself out of circulation before the body of Elaine Collie was discovered. They ransacked Reid's possessions, finding a set of keys for Elaine Collie's flat. Another set of keys were made use of to enter Reid's own flat, where the detectives found rope, an electrical cable, a towel, adhesive tape and scissors. A quantity of jewellery was also found, which Elaine Collie's valuation forms and meticulous personal records identified as hers. The final nail into the coffin of 'Jock the Rapist' was hammered in by the police technicians, who found that although the murderer had taken good care to clean Elaine Collie's flat, a single fingerprint remained on her glasses, matching that of John Reid. The cunning murderer had tried to erase every trace of himself from the murder flat and had almost succeeded.

When John Reid appeared at the High Court of Edinburgh in October 1999, many people were appalled at the senseless brutality of the crime: the callous murderer had forced his way into the flat, bludgeoned Elaine Collie on the head, tied her up, sexually assaulted her with a broom handle, tortured her with electric shocks until she gave up the PIN numbers to her bank cards, and finally strangled her to death in cold blood. He stole her bank and building society cash cards, which he made use of to withdraw £100 at Comely Bank and another £250 in George Street, before setting out for his motoring expedition to Craigmillar. The defence did not have a leg to stand on, due to the weight of the evidence against the accused, and he pleaded guilty: an attempt to make the brutal-looking prisoner appear contrite through reading out a letter of apology to the Collie family did not have the desired effect. John Reid was sentenced to imprisonment for life with a minimum sentence of 15 years. Addressing the bald-headed, hulking prisoner in the dock, Lord Cameron said "This was a violent, despicable crime, the barbarity of which must be recognized."[26]

Elaine Collie's brother Fred made sure that her ashes were taken back to Londonderry, where they were interred with those of her parents. He also made sure that a memorial bench dedicated to her was erected in Stockbridge, opposite Ann Street, overlooking the Water of Leith. There was speculation that John Reid might well have committed other murders in the past, in either England or Scotland, but the police retorted that although his half-brother Gordon had died mysteriously in 1993 after his Fenton Barns workshop had exploded, there was nothing to suggest that this was a case of murder. It seemed a mystery how this monster of a man, who made it his business to beat people up and sexually assault various women, would suddenly commit such a brutal and cold-blooded murder, on a harmless woman who had just been in the wrong place at the wrong time, for the sake of gaining £350 and some jewellery. The serial predator Reid had got off lightly a number of times, when attacking vulnerable men and women, being the recipient of a series of decisions to charge him with lesser offences in order to secure convictions. Miss Catherine Mooney, who had shared her Pilton flat with

John Reid, declared herself absolutely horrified by what had happened. This did not prevent the 32-year-old mother of two from appearing in a *Sunday Sport* topless photoshoot, making some spicy revelations about her life with 'Jock the Rapist'.

The murder of Elaine Collie happened when the Internet was still in its infancy, and as a result it is almost totally forgotten today. Her Stockbridge memorial bench is still standing, and on the anniversary of her murder in 2000, her family laid a wreath on her grave in Londonderry. Haunted or not, the murder flat at Muirhouse View still stands today, in a block looking as mean as ever. In 2012, Fred Collie and his journalist son Jason handed over a dossier to the Scottish Prison Service, detailing John Reid's three sexual assaults preceding the murder, hoping that his past as a sexual predator would prevent them from releasing him as early as 2014, when he was eligible for release.[27] Is he perhaps living in the flat next door to yours? No, certainly not! says Mr Jason Collie, nephew of the murdered woman and Associate Digital Editor of the London *Evening Standard*, assuring me that as late as April 2020, John Reid was still safely 'inside' and unable to cause any further mischief, in Edinburgh or elsewhere.

MURDER IN GARDNER'S CRESCENT, 2002

The 30-year-old Alistair Nicole worked as the representative of a medical company and shared the basement flat at 22a Gardner's Crescent, Fountainbridge, with another man named Jamie Fabre. There is nothing to suggest that either of these two had any involvement in drugs trafficking, or organized crime. In the early hours of June 23 2002, two young men armed with knives forced their way into the flat. One of them stabbed Alistair Nicole hard in the side and chest with a large steak knife, murdering him; the other beat and robbed Jamie Fabre.

14. The murder flat at 22a Gardner's Crescent.

Several people had seen the two intruders banging on the door of 22a Gardner's Crescent: a white man in his early twenties, clean shaven and with short black hair, and another, younger man with short ginger hair. The neighbours were appalled that there had been a murder in their quiet, respectable neighbourhood, with a large pool of blood outside the front door of 22a, and a trail of blood for 60 feet in the direction of the Edinburgh International Conference Centre.

The police had no clue why two armed desperadoes would attack and murder a peaceful householder in the middle of the night. They soon had two suspects in custody, however: the 22-year-old drug addict Paul Hampton and the 22-year-old thug Scott Nash. Both men were charged with murder, but it soon became obvious that Nash was the man who had attacked and robbed Jamie Fabre; in court, he pleaded guilty to these offences, and was sentenced to imprisonment for six years. Paul Hampton had a tragic background, since his father had been murdered when he was just five years old. Shortly before the murder of Alistair Nicole, he had been to a wake for his cousin, who had also been murdered. After his uncle had told him that it was because of 'scum like him' that the cousin had been murdered, he had drunk very hard, in addition to the methadone and Valium he took regularly to stave off his craving for drugs.

Paul Hampton suggested to Scott Nash that they should break into a flat, preferably one where drugs were kept on the premises, and rob the inhabitants. He could not explain why they had chosen 22a Gardner's Crescent, where there were no drugs at all. In court, Nash described how Hampton had gone berserk inside the flat, and murdered Alistair Nicole. After Hampton had pleaded guilty to the charge of murder, Lady Smith sentenced him to imprisonment for life, with a minimum sentence of 14 year, for a pointless, unprovoked and appalling murder.[28]

MURDER IN MORRISON STREET, 2003

Mr John Davidson had been a successful businessman, who owned two hairdressing salons and bought and sold property as well. He became an alcoholic in middle age, however, and after a pub he had kept in Kirknewton, West Lothian, had failed, be became a bankrupt. In 2003, when he was 49 years old, he was a homeless tramp, employed as a seller of 'The Big Issue' magazine, and sleeping rough in various squats.

In March 2003, John Davidson met the 18-year-old alcoholic and drug addict Bryan Pearson and brought him to the flat where he was staying for the moment, at 105 Morrison Street. After drinking hard together, these two started fighting: Pearson beat Davidson up severely, with a bottle and with a chair, inflicting 47 head and neck injuries. Pearson made an anonymous 999 call, but when the ambulance arrived, Davidson was dead. The drunken Pearson escaped from the murder flat, but his reprieve would not be a lengthy one. He told six of his friends, and two complete strangers travelling on a bus, that he had just murdered someone, but they did not believe him. He then went to see another friend, with plenty of blood on his clothes, saying 'I have just paggered someone!'

The friend called Jennifer Monaghan, Pearson's mother, asking her to come and talk to her son. Since she knew that Pearson was habitually very untruthful, she thought he was lying, but the following morning she heard about the murder in a radio news bulletin. She went to the Leith police station to give a statement and hand in Pearson's bloodstained clothing, and later brought her son to another police station, for him to give himself up. Having had time to sober up, Pearson made a statement that the murder had been committed by two other drunks, but he was not believed. After all, he had confessed murdering Davidson in front of nine other people, some of them complete strangers, and his clothes were liberally sprinkled with the blood of the murder victim. A bloody footprint in the murder flat matched his shoes. On trial at the High Court in October 2003, Bryan Pearson was found guilty of murder and sentenced to imprisonment for life with a minimum sentence of 12 years.[29]

A SINISTER STORY FROM MERCHISTON AVENUE, 2004

In early 1999, the 46-year-old Alan Wilson seemed to have everything going for him. A short, dapper-looking man with prematurely white hair, he was the principal history master at the fashionable James Gillespie's High School, an influential and well-paid position; said to have been a brilliant, inspirational teacher, he was highly regarded among his colleagues. He had a wife and two children, and appeared to enjoy a happy family life. Alan Wilson was also a director of the still-extant Mercat Tours, a firm specializing in 'ghost walks' and other activities emptying the pockets of the more gullible tourists visiting Edinburgh; furthermore, he was the author of five popular books on local history, including the bestselling *Ghostly Tales and Sinister Stories of Old Edinburgh*. For someone who must surely have undergone a good academic training in history, he was a wholly unreliable and irresponsible author, who seems to have believed everything he had read in a book; he was fond of regurgitating the bogus ghost stories of Elliott O'Donnell and various other dubious yarns about Edinburgh's spectral world, and a great servant of pseudo-history through his career. But History's Muse stood ready to smite Alan Wilson, for the purpose of teaching him a hard lesson for his third-rate historical scholarship, and his fall would be a mighty one.

Later in 1999, one of the schoolboys at James Gillespie's High School came up with a startling accusation: Alan Wilson had invited him home to his flat, given him beer and whisky to drink, and then sexually assaulted him! Several other boys came forward with similar unsavoury tales, and in the end, the disgraced schoolteacher was sentenced to 18 months in prison for eight sexual assaults on three boys between 1994 and 1999. His friends and family shunned him, he was kicked out of the school, cold-shouldered out of the tour company, and hounded out of his clubs. Alan Wilson must have looked forward to his time behind bars with some trepidation, since if there is something that a tough Glaswegian bullyboy hates even more than a paedophile, it surely must be an Edinburgh schoolmaster! But Alan Wilson befriended a hardened criminal named Ian Sutherland, who was serving seven years for a particularly degrading rape of a female prostitute, and this brutal character, who was treated with respect in Saughton Prison, helped to protect the disgraced schoolteacher from the prison bullies and perverts. The fearful Alan Wilson made sure to keep his arse close to the wall in the communal

15. 28 Merchiston Avenue.

shower-rooms, but Sutherland's reputation was such that he never suffered anything worse than a few jibes and jeers.

After his release from prison in 2002, Alan Wilson started work as an independent tour guide, regaling the gaping tourists, who had no idea of the unsavoury background of the dapper-looking Scotsman haranguing them with various tall stories from his old books. When his friend Ian Sutherland was also released from prison, they moved into the ground-floor flat at 28 Merchiston Avenue. Alan Wilson often went out to the gay clubs to chase young men for casual encounters, and the brutal Ian Sutherland invited prostitutes to the flat for some kinky sex; yet the two former prison buddies seemed as good friends as ever. The uneducated bullyboy Sutherland respected Alan Wilson for his superior intellect, and the former schoolteacher took him to concerts and plays to improve his mind. When Sutherland found himself a girlfriend, the sauna worker Tracy Scott, Alan Wilson took them to art galleries and to good restaurants, in a vain attempt to give them some culture. The ever-active paedophile had made sexual advances to his younger friend more than once, but the tough Sutherland, who normally hated homosexuals, threatened to 'put his lights out' if he tried any monkey business. But when Sutherland had enough of Tracy Scott, and kicked her out of the flat, the slimy former schoolteacher thought that his time had finally come.

In early February 2004, Alan Wilson and Ian Sutherland enjoyed a hearty evening meal at their flat, polishing off six bottles of wine between them, enough to put even these two hardened topers into a somewhat frolicsome mood. But when Alan Wilson once more made homosexual advances to his friend, everything changed. The brutal bullyboy Sutherland strangled Alan Wilson to death and put his body in the bathtub. He then contacted Tracy Scott, who agreed to travel south with him for a few days. When Sutherland returned home, he discovered that he had bent his key to the front door. As the locksmith was working away, without any concern, he was unaware that a dead body was putrefying away in the bath just a few feet away; it was very fortunate for him that his bladder was in good working order, so that he did not need to use the toilet before he left! As Tracy sat watching the TV in the living room, Sutherland dismembered Alan Wilson's bloated body, severing all four extremities and cutting off the head as well for good measure. At intervals, he took breaks in this diabolical surgery, to watch a video of his favourite film, 'Natural Born Killers', on the television while enjoying a whisky or two, before returning to the bathroom, knife in hand, to continue butchering the remains of his old friend.

Ian Sutherland hid Alan Wilson's torso underneath the floorboards, putting the other body parts in the flat's small garden. But a neighbour had heard Alan Wilson give a terrible yell when the murderer seized hold of him, and the olfactory senses of other neighbours were made use of to deduce that all was not well at 28 Merchiston Avenue. The police was called in, the dismembered remains of Alan Wilson found, and Sutherland arrested. On trial for murder and dismemberment, Sutherland alleged that Tracy Scott had murdered Alan Wilson as he lay unconscious after heavy drinking, because he was 'always in the way'. But Lord Dawson, presiding, did not believe a word of this, and nor did the jury; Sutherland was sentenced to imprisonment for life, having to serve a minimum of 15 years for the murder, with five more years added for the dismemberment.[30] There have been regular bulletins about his activities behind bars: in 2006, he became a Buddhist, and in 2016, having by then spent 12 years behind bars, he praised the nourishing Christmas food at HMP Glenochil in Stirlingshire, where he was now incarcerated. History's Muse, who selected this unprepossessing figure to permanently end the career of the obnoxious Alan Wilson, is immune to prosecution as being an aethereal creature without definite human form, but this sinister story tells us that pseudo-historians everywhere ought to take heed and mend their ways, to avoid ending up in a sixpartite condition in a dingy little Edinburgh flat.

As for the murder flat, it was still uninhabited and boarded up in November 2004, when 'Edinburgh's House of Horror' was visited by an *Edinburgh Evening News* journalist. There were dirty dishes in the kitchen, filthy underwear scattered everywhere, and Sutherland's collection of nasty video films on top of a chest of drawers; a smell of rotting meat and stale tobacco smoke was very much in evidence, and the place was disgusting in the extreme. On the bookshelf was John Grisham's thriller *A Time to Kill*, and Ambrose Bierce's *The Devil's Dictionary*, the latter very suitable reading for the ghost of Alan Wilson, would it still have been flitting through the premises looking for its lost head and extremities, given his probable destination in the Afterlife. People's memories with regard to murder houses are generally short ones, however, and the flat has long had a tenant today.

THE MURDER OF LOUISE TIFFNEY, 2005

Louise Tiffney was born in 1959, one of several daughters to Rodger and Mary Tiffney. She left home at 17 to move in with a boyfriend, but the relationship ended after a few years. She suffered from anorexia as a child and would be plagued with recurrent bouts of depression throughout her adult life. In the early 1980s, Louise Tiffney cohabited with the Edinburgh cab driver Keith Flynn in a flat in Easter Road. They had the son Sean together, but this fragile, on-off relationship ended after she had suspected that he was seeing another woman on the sly. In 1991, Louise Tiffney started a relationship with the security guard Ian Melville, and she had an abortion after falling pregnant. She next moved in with a man named Brian Robson, and in 1996, they had the daughter Hannah together before the relationship ended. In 2002, Louise Tiffney was living in Flat L at 2 Dean Path, with her two children, inside a historic 1805 watermill that had been converted into flats in 1973. Although troubled by recurrent depression and anxiety, and by severe debt problems, she showed a brave face to the world and looked after her children as well as she could.

Sean Flynn attended St John's RC Primary School, Portobello, and the Holy Rood RC High School. A tall, muscular fellow looking older than his years, he left school at 16 due to a lack of academic interests. In 2001, when he was 17 years old, he purchased a powerful BMW motor car: lacking insurance, he crashed after racing another car on the Livingston to Mid Calder road in West Lothian. Sean himself escaped without major injuries, but the front seat passenger Mario Gagliardini was fortunate to escape with his life, and the rear seat passengers, Sean's cousin Paul Ross and his friend Christopher Magee, were both killed. Knowing that he would face prosecution, and a stiff prison sentence, for causing death by dangerous driving, Sean got a part-time job as a bartender and led a riotous life. He

16. The murder house at 2 Dean Path.

started a relationship with the 43-year-old Yvonne Solo, who was the mother of the boy Mario Gagliardini who had survived the crash. Since Louise Tiffney was of course most displeased with these disastrous developments, her relationship with her son deteriorated markedly. Sean often treated her disrespectfully: he told her to get out of his life; it would be a good idea, he exclaimed, if she stopped breathing altogether.

Louise Tiffney was last seen alive on May 27 2002, leaving her Dean Path flat. On May 28, Sean Flynn phoned her sister Anne, saying that his mother was gone. They searched the Dean Path flat, but when Anne saw that Louise Tiffney's handbag and cigarettes had been left behind, she realized that her chain-smoking sister would not have left home without them. Sean seemed to show little interest in what had happened to his mother. Not long after, he was sentenced to imprisonment for three years and nine months for causing death through dangerous driving. When the police detectives looking for the missing Louise Tiffney visited Sean at the Polmont Young Offender's Institute on July 3, he seemed quite apathetic and had no concerns at all about what had happened to his mother.

After the disappearance of Louise Tiffney had been publicized in the newspapers, and a full-scale police investigation started, there were alleged sightings of her all over Britain, and as far away as Salt Lake City in Utah, but none of them had any substance. Initially suspecting suicide, a force of 80 police constables had been searching the Water of Leith and a number of East Lothian rivers without finding anything interesting. Police helicopters, mountain rescue teams, police dogs and specialist search officers were deployed without any result. The detectives in charge of the case began to suspect that Louise Tiffney's sisters might have been right after all: she had been murdered, and her body taken away from 2 Dean Path in a motor vehicle. Downstairs neighbour Brian Rockall, who lived in Flat G, described hearing the sound of some person running across the floor of the flat above, followed by a loud scream likely to have emanated from a female. A painter's dust sheet had gone missing from the flat; had it been used to wrap up the body of the murdered woman?

The truculent Sean Flynn, who was known to have quarrelled bitterly with his mother in the months preceding her disappearance, became the prime suspect. In May 2002, he had been driving a three-door Nissan Almera belonging to Yvonne Solo; the police got hold of this car and sent it to London to be tested by the forensic experts there. After a rigorous investigation, Mr Anthony Larkin, the lead evidence recovery scientist with the Metropolitan Police, reported back that the boot of the car showed staining with blood matching the DNA recovered from Louise Tiffney's hairbrush and toothbrush, in a pattern consistent with the transportation of a blood-stained body inside the vehicle. An attempt had clearly been made to wash the blood out of the car's carpets. This important breakthrough was followed by another one: the Nissan Almera was spotted by a Meadowbank CCTV camera leaving Edinburgh and driving eastwards at 1.20 am on May 28, and then returning by the same route at 2.31 am, a time when Sean Flynn claimed to have been asleep in bed. The following day, when Sean Flynn claimed to have been in Edinburgh, his mobile telephone was traced to an area east of Tranent in East Lothian. Had this been the murderer returning to see if the grave of his victim was visible by daylight?

Sean Flynn was arrested and charged with the murder of Louise Tiffney. As his trial began in February 2005, there was intense media interest. A teenager murdering his own mother, and almost getting away with it, was news not just in Edinburgh, but anywhere in the world. The case for the prosecution concentrated on the forensic findings from the car, the CCTV spottings of it leaving Edinburgh the night after Louise Tiffney had disappeared, and the tracing of Sean Flynn's phone to the outskirts of Tranent. He had been a strong, beefy lad already back in 2002, and his mother quite a frail, slender woman; he had previously showed malice and ill will against her on several occasions. The strategy of the defence was to point out that there was no rock-solid evidence that Louise Tiffney was really dead. Her troubled life was mercilessly exposed in court: her anorexia, anxiety and depression; a number of failed relationships and three abortions; long-standing debt problems that were spiralling out of control. Keith Flynn was called to testify that Louise Tiffney had been a volatile person who had been difficult to live with, and then one of Louise's sisters admitted that she 'would fly off the handle' and 'do something that was out of normal character'. The eloquent Frances McMenamin, for the defence, described Louise Tiffney as a troubled, extravagant, volatile and very selfish person, and pointed out that in the days prior to her disappearance, she had failed to take her antidepressive medication. Had she committed suicide after all, or perhaps left her family never to return? Many court reporters expected a guilty verdict, but after

Lord McEwen had addressed the jury, they returned a verdict of not proven. There was fury among the Tiffney family members, and old Rodger Tiffney shouted abuse at Sean Flynn.

When interviewed by a journalist after the trial, Sean Flynn was as cool as ever: he thought his mother had walked out after an argument, never coming back due to her mounting debt. The Tiffney family was outraged by the outcome of the trial, the attitude of Sean Flynn, and the way Louise's character had been vilified during the trial. They urged the police to keep up their efforts to find her body, through ambitious digging projects at stately Gosford House in Longniddry, East Lothian, but without success. But in April 2017, the remains of Louise Tiffney were found by a cyclist in the grounds of Gosford House, just as her sisters had predicted. Detailed forensic testing was performed to find a clue as to the identity of the murderer, but without the desired result. As late as April 2018, Scottish Tory leader Ruth Davidson urged the police to renew their efforts to solve Edinburgh's greatest modern murder mystery, and in November the same year, the Lord Advocate, James Wolffe QC, applied to the High Court for authority under the Double Jeopardy laws to set aside the acquittal of Sean Flynn. This individual had lived in Glasgow for a while before being declared a bankrupt in 2009, but was believed to have moved abroad after this experience. In January 2019, the Crown Office applied to have Sean Flynn's acquittal set aside and a fresh prosecution brought, but this was opposed by the defence solicitors.

If the technical evidence is believed, then Sean Flynn is likely to be the murderer of Louise Tiffney. The prosecution treaded lightly regarding the question whether he had planned and premeditated the murder. Planning would explain why the car was kept in readiness for transporting away the corpse, and why a grave of superior quality had been found in rural East Lothian. But what kind of monster would deliberately plan and execute the murder of his own mother, with such exemplary coolness?

It would of course be possible that Flynn, who was a strong and beefy lad, had struck his thin and frail mother a mighty blow after she had annoyed him, before finishing her off with a knife and simply being lucky to find a good hiding-place for the body in the countryside. If the arguments of the prosecution are believed, this 18-year-old adolescent, presumed to be of mediocre intellect, succeeded where many an adult murderer had failed miserably: he coolly did his mother to death, got rid of the body, and did not blabber to anyone, including the experienced detectives who questioned him. If the body of Louise Tiffney had been found in 2005, with clear evidence that she had been murdered, this would have been likely to have turned the scales, but once more he was lucky. As it was, the case was one of 'murder without a body'. Such prosecutions have had success more than once south of the border, the first murderer convicted being the Pole Michail Onufrejczyk in 1954, and one of the latest Mark Bridger, who murdered little April Jones. In Moray, Nat Fraser was convicted of the murder of his wife Arlene in 2003, although her remains were never found; in Edinburgh, David Gilroy was convicted of the murder of Suzanne Pilley in 2012, in spite of successfully disposing of her remains. Sean Flynn was fortunate to be represented by a first-class legal team, who successfully blackened the character of the murder victim Louise Tiffney, to render it possible that she had either committed suicide or simply walked out on her family. The existence of the 'Not Proven' verdict in Scottish jurisdiction was a venomous temptation to the jury; the defence evidence had beguiled them, and they did eat.[31]

The murder house at 2 Dean Path still stands, in good order. Louise Tiffney's old flat has an inhabitant today, as does that of Brian Rockall, a neatly dressed, bald-headed figure who gave evidence at the trial. But in 2009, the 44-year-old Rockall had become a desperate man, an online gambling addict who was using the household money to fund his habit. In July 2009, he beat his elderly mother Valerie, with whom he shared the flat, to death before hanging himself. "It's shocking. I am really scared now. It always seemed such a safe place to live around here" exclaimed a timorous neighbourwoman after the Curse on Dean Path had claimed two more victims.[32] Since 2009, the house has remained murder free, however, although many of the locals know of its notoriety.

There have been interesting late developments in the Tiffney case, namely that in 2019, the debate whether Sean Flynn should face a retrial under double jeopardy laws continued: in November, three Edinburgh judges sat down in a hearing pondering the evidence. Sean Flynn was not present. It would have been interesting to know what he had been up to since the verdict back in 2005, but apart from newspaper rumours that he had gone bankrupt and spent time in Berlin, nothing much transpired.[33] At least he had kept clear of serious crime since his narrow escape in court. In January 2020, the judges decided in favour of a retrial, clearly the trial of the decade for Edinburgh murder enthusiasts.

THE MURDER OF HUGH CAMPBELL, 2006

Hugh Campbell used to work as a civil service messenger, but he retired early in 1989, aged just 53, to run a pub in the Isle of Bute. After developing a serious drinking problem, he had to close the pub down. After his wife Sandra had died in or around 2000, he moved to Edinburgh, where he ended up in a flat at 1 Muirhouse View, the very same block where Elaine Collie had been murdered back in 1999. He had several children, including a daughter who lived in Drylaw, and four young grandchildren, to whom he was devoted. When he was sober, Hugh Campbell was a friendly and cheerful old fellow, who helped elderly and decrepit neighbours with the gardening free of charge. When he was on the drink, he turned his tiny flat into a boozing-den for various undesirable types from the large and rowdy Muirhouse estate.

In June 2006, when Hugh Campbell was 70 years old, his neighbours became worried when they had not seen the old man for some time. They shouted at his door without eliciting any response. When peering through a window, one of the neighbours thought he could see Hugh Campbell lying dead in a pool of blood on the living-room floor, with a green plastic bag or his head. Next to his body was an instrument rather resembling a large hammer. When the police were called in, they swiftly ascertained that Hugh Campbell had been beaten to death after a brutal and sustained attack. They knew that his flat was used as a drinking-den by various rough types, and were vigilantly studying the abundant CCTV footage of people coming to 1 Muirhouse View, in the hope they would find the murderer.

Detective Inspector Gareth Blair, who led the Campbell murder investigation, soon verified that the hard-drinking murder victim had invited various undesirables for a party the evening of the murder. One of the guests, a woman known as 'Maggie', had been overheard by a neighbour talking to Hugh Campbell, but there had been other guests as well. Campbell had last been seen alive at 5 pm on June 12, and had been discovered dead at 7 pm on June 13; there was good evidence that he had been murdered late in the evening of June 12, by one of the two men and two women he had invited to his flat. A number of empty bottles from inside the flat were tested for DNA and fingerprints. The police handed out flyers in Muirhouse Gardens applying for witnesses. A short man aged around 30 had been seen outside the murder flat on June 12, as had a woman of about the same age, with straggly hair and no front teeth. The habitual criminal Michael Brennan was soon in police custody, and remanded after an appearance at the Edinburgh Sheriff's Court on June 16. On trial for murder at the High Court of Edinburgh in January 2007, the drifter Brennan, who had a long history of violent crime, and who had just served a jail sentence for assault, was found guilty of murder and sentenced to imprisonment for life, with a minimum of 16 years in jail.[34]

THE MONSTER MOTHER, 2010

Pasquale Riggi, a successful Colorado petroleum engineer, moved to Europe in the 1990s, first to the Netherlands and then to Lowestoft, England. By this time, he had three children with his wife Theresa, a native of California: the twins Austin and Luke, born in 1992, and the daughter Cecilia, born in 1995. Theresa Riggi rather fancied herself as the perfect 'luxury wife' for a high-flying petroleum executive. She was a gourmet chef, an expert on the artistic arranging of flowers and laying of tables for grand dining parties, and a talented singer and musician.

Fast forward a few years, and we find the Riggi family in Aberdeen, where Pasquale had secured another lucrative position in the petroleum industry. But by this time, all was not well in their marriage. Theresa was becoming increasingly neurotic and unbalanced, and she was obsessive in mothering the children, forcing them to carry electronic tracking devices whenever they were outdoors, and mobile telephones pre-programmed with her number, for use in an emergency. In the end, Pasquale Riggi found her quite impossible to live with, and he wanted a divorce. When they separated, he remained in the family home in Aberdeen, and she moved to Skene, taking the children with her.

Fearful that she would lose the children, the now 47-year-old Theresa Riggi moved to a second-floor flat at 166 Slateford Road, Edinburgh, a nondescript modern building wholly devoid of any architectural merit. On the evening of August 2 2010, she phoned her husband, accusing him of being in collusion with their solicitors to take her children away from her. Being told that he had no choice but to allow the legal process to continue, she hissed 'Say goodbye then!' The transatlantic Medea of Slateford Road had finally snapped: she proceeded to beat and stab all three children to death in a bloodbath. She then disconnected a gas pipe to blow the house up, but fortunately there was only a limited gas explosion. Theresa Riggi climbed up on the balcony of the flat, and dived head first towards the ground, but a brave neighbour managed to break her fall. Suffering from a collapsed lung, some broken bones and several self-inflicted minor stab wounds, she was taken off to hospital as the police and emergency services discovered the triple child murder: the mangled bodies lying next to each other on the floor like if in some bizarre mortuary.

On trial for murdering her children at the High Court in Edinburgh, there was no doubt that Theresa Riggi was guilty. Psychiatrists said that although she had narcissistic, paranoid and hysterical personality disorders, she was fit to plead and stand trial for her atrocious crime. She pleaded guilty to murdering her three children and was sentenced to imprisonment for sixteen years.[35] Pasquale Riggi said that "The horrific manner in which my children died will leave an indelible mark on the rest of my life. As a father, my natural instincts were geared towards safeguarding my children from the dangers of this world. It pains me to the core that I was unable to protect them from the selfish, brutal and murderous act that ended their lives so unfairly."

Theresa Riggi was carted off to Scotland's only all-female prison, Cornton Vale near Stirling. This prison was full to the rafters with tough, uncompromising female criminals, who did not at all approve of the 'Monster Mother', as Theresa Riggi had been dubbed by the Edinburgh press. They did not care for Americans, or multiple child killers, or stuck-up women who fancied themselves better than them. The conceited and histrionic Theresa Riggi still thought of herself as the perfect parent and boasted of her culinary and musical expertise. An incident when she was kicked hard in the backside and sent sprawling downstairs did nothing to perturb the self-confidence of the deluded Monster Mother. But after breakfast on November 19 2011, the tough criminal Angela Hamilton sneaked into the cell of Theresa Riggi and slashed her repeatedly across the face with a razor, disfiguring her for life. After this outrage, Theresa Riggi was moved to the Rampton Secure Hospital in Nottinghamshire, due to the not inconsiderable risk that she would be murdered at Cornton Vale Prison. Here, the Monster Mother eked out a few more years of her miserable existence, before being found dead in her cell in March 2014, from bronchial pneumonia according to official sources, but from suicide according to some people 'in the know'.[36]

THE MURDER OF LEE DUNCAN, 2011

Lee Duncan was a young Edinburgh man, who grew up in Longstone before his family moved to Wester Hailes. He had no academic ambitions and left school at 16, being barely able to read and write. He worked as a hotel dishwasher and porter for a while, but hard graft and honest toil was not to his liking. He began smoking cannabis as a teenager and became a heroin addict in his early 20s. After a spell in Saughton Prison for driving while 'high' on drugs, he tried to get his chaotic life into some order: he enrolled in a methadone programme to fight his addiction to heroin, and got himself a flat at 142/7 Lauriston Place, Tollcross, and a girlfriend named Kirsty Nelson who was the mother of a young child. He took his methadone as prescribed but freely smoked cannabis and crack cocaine, supporting himself as a drug dealer selling cocaine and other narcotics to various undesirable types in the neighbourhood.

In 2010, there were rumours in the Edinburgh underworld that a contract had been put out on the now 30-year-old Lee

Duncan, who was accused of raping a woman, selling defective drugs, and being a police informant. The wretched man soon became a nervous wreck, who seldom dared to leave his flat, always kept his door locked and chained, and had a hammer underneath the bed ready for use if some rough types tried to 'jump' him during night time. His mother and sister, both of them respectable people, did what they could to help the jittery drug dealer, who seemed to be afraid of his own shadow. On February 24 2011, when Lee Duncan and Kirsty Nelson were smoking some crack cocaine in his flat at Lauriston Place, he was worried that he had recently received some threatening text messages, to the effect that he would soon be stabbed to death. The following day, when Kirsty came to the flat, she found the door unlocked and Lee Duncan dead inside, lying in a huge pool of blood. He had been brutally murdered with a claw hammer. She went to see the neighbour Gary Parker, another drug addict who had been one of Lee Duncan's customers, and he came to look at the body, saying 'Yeah, I think he is dead too.'

Due to his chaotic life, and the threats against him from the Edinburgh drugs underworld, the police faced an uphill task trying to catch the Lauriston Place murderer. Four rough-looking teenagers had been seen in the street outside Lee Duncan's flat the day of the murder, but they were never identified. Instead, the police concentrated on the man Gary Parker, who had screamed abuse at Lee Duncan a month before the murder, and who might be the author of the anonymous text messages he received. Specks of Lee Duncan's blood were found on his boots. When in police custody, he was said to have confessed to the murder in front of another criminal. But when finally put on trial in August 2013, Parker denied everything. Like many of the people inhabiting the shabby flats in that part of Lauriston Place, he was a rough character, and certainly capable of murder, but he claimed to have an alibi, entertaining two other men in his flat the day of the murder.

He suspected that the murder of Lee Duncan was committed by gangsters and named two men he thought might be responsible. The bloodstains on his boots might have been caused by him walking past the corpse when told by the ambulance paramedics to open the curtains of the flat, and the man alleging that he had confessed to the murder might just be a liar. Gary Parker was found not guilty of murdering Lee Duncan, and the case had remained unsolved ever since.[37]

THE MURDER OF PHILOMENA DUNLEAVY, 2013

On June 7 2013, the dismembered remains of a woman were found by a cyclist in the Corstorphine Hill nature reserve in Edinburgh. After the head and both legs had been cut off, she had been buried in a shallow grave. The body was painstakingly exhumed by a team of forensic specialists, but since putrefaction had set in, it was difficult to trace her identity. No Edinburgh woman around retirement age had gone missing at the time, and the body contained no identification documents or other worthwhile clues, except that her rings were still in situ, one of them a traditional Irish Claddagh ring. Cosmetic dentistry, carried out in Hungary, led to the suspicion that the murdered woman was an East European migrant worker or beggar. An appeal on the BBC's Crimewatch show drew a blank, but an attempt at facial reconstruction using up-to-date computer software, by Professor Caroline Wilkinson of Dundee University, had the desired effect. Soon after the reconstructed image had been released, a woman phoned from Ireland and declared herself convinced that the murder victim was her relative, the 66-year-old Dublin woman Philomena Dunleavy.

The Dunleavy family were no strangers to tragedy. Philomena had recently left her husband James after suffering a stroke, and her behaviour could be erratic at times. Her son Terence had been murdered aged just 27, after getting involved with a Dublin drugs gang, and one of her daughters had also died mysteriously at an early age. This left her eldest son James, also known as Seamus, who was a labouring man, the youngest son Austin who was completing a football scholarship at a college in the United States, and the remaining daughter Kym who worked as a medical secretary in Dublin. Seamus Dunleavy was a rough character with a string of convictions for petty crime; there had been suspicions that he had joined his brother in Dublin organized crime for a while, but left in a hurry after Terence had been gunned down. The police were interested to find that he was now living in a flat over a shop at 168 Balgreen Road, not far from Corstorphine Hill, and working as a jackhammer operator on the Edinburgh trams project. When the flat was raided, the detectives found Philomena Dunleavy's identity card and some clothes belonging to her, as well as a sum of 870 Euros. In early May, he had thrown out a bed and set fire to it, allegedly because an incontinent friend of his had soiled the mattress. A large suitcase that was known to have been in the flat was no longer there, and a spade with a broken shaft was found on the back green.

The 40-year-old Seamus Dunleavy was arrested and charged with murder. He stoutly denied all involvement in his mother's tragic death, saying that she had turned up in late April to pay him a visit, but that one day she had just walked out and disappeared, leaving some of her possessions behind. This was normal behaviour for her, he asserted, due to her severe stroke and various other health problems. Since there were doubts concerning his sanity, he was sent to the State Mental Hospital, Carstairs, to be psychiatrically assessed while awaiting trial for murder. As the trial begun at the High Court of Edinburgh in January 2014, Seamus Dunleavy's father James and brother Austin were both present in court. The forensic evidence spoke in favour of Philomena Dunleavy being knocked down and throttled by the murderer,

17. Balgreen Road, a postcard stamped and posted in 1935.
Reproduced by permission of Mr G. Burgess, Dunbar.

although she might well still have been alive as he hacked off her legs with a saw and a large knife. Seamus Dunleavy had resented that his mother had left his father and got involved with another man, and a neighbour had overheard them quarrelling angrily about this. The shopkeeper Mohammed Razaq, a man of Pakistani origins who kept the shop underneath the Dunleavy flat at Balgreen Road, claimed to have been a great friend and spiritual advisor to his neighbour, and instrumental in his recent conversion to the Moslem faith. Razaq could verify that Seamus Dunleavy had resented his mother, and that after her disappearance, he had said that he was hearing voices and that he might be a bad man. He had also told a workmate on the tram project that he had done something bad, although he did not specify exactly what. A nut found among the stomach contents of the murdered woman matched some found in the flat at 168 Balgreen Road.

The defence pointed out that all this evidence was entirely circumstantial, and that no witnesses had seen the murder, the transportation of the remains to Corstorphine Hill, or the burial in the shallow grave. Still, the jury found Seamus Dunleavy guilty of culpable homicide, and Lord Jones sentenced him to nine years in an ordinary prison, followed by nine further years of supervision to prevent him from decimating his family any further. In 2018, his sister Kym, who had never quite recovered after her mother's murder, was given a suspended sentence for shoplifting and forging prescriptions for sleeping tables, to which she had become addicted, blaming the tragic murder of her mother for upsetting her mental balance. Seamus himself is still 'inside', but he might be let loose on the public in 2023 if he behaves himself.[38]

18. The murder flat at 168 Balgreen Road, which witnessed the grossest scenes in the Corstorphine murder and dismemberment in 2013.

MURDER IN HUTCHISON ROAD, 2017

Frazer Neil, a sturdy Edinburgh youngster with ambitions to become a male nurse, met the four years younger Hannah Dorans at a first aid volunteer course. They moved into a flat together and became engaged in 2015. Hannah worked as a care assistant but Frazer was long term unemployed and spent his time in idleness. The couple drifted apart and she dumped him in early 2017, something he took very badly. He had always been something of a control freak and liked to send her abusive text messages. When he learnt that she was seeing another man, he lured her to his Slateford flat at 131 Hutchison Road on February 11 2017 and attacked her in a furious rage, strangling her to death with a dressing gown cord.

The following morning, Frazer Neil telephoned the police and admitted killing his former girlfriend. He was also charged with stealing a computer and some medical equipment at a shop. When admitted to bail, he was ordered to stay with his mother, but the burly murder suspect sneaked back to the murder flat dressed all in black and frightened his former neighbours severely. On trial for murder at the High Court of Edinburgh, before Lady Scott, the now 25-year-old Frazer Neil pleaded not guilty. The defence argued that Frazer was a bondage-loving sadist, and that Hannah had died by accident during some perverted sex game gone wrong, but this was not believed. The jury found Frazer Neil guilty of murder and Lady Scott sentenced him to imprisonment for life, with a minimum sentence of 19 years.[39]

V.

NORTH EDINBURGH

The northern suburbs of Edinburgh consist of a number of erstwhile villages, Restalrig and Trinity prominent among them, as well as many newly constructed houses from the 1920s, 1930s and 1950s. The harbour village of Granton has expanded a good deal, with modern houses added to its drab suburban streets. Although the aesthetic value of the North Edinburgh architecture is limited, its criminous merits are not negligible. Trinity boasts two perfectly good double murder houses, at 25 Earl Haig Gardens and 10 Lixmount Avenue. The flat at 13 Ferry Gate Crescent, Drylaw, is the site of one of Edinburgh's worst modern horrors, the murder of little Mikaeel Kular in 2014 ...

MURDER AND SUICIDE IN ALBERT STREET, 1933

John Sullivan had fought in the Boer War as a young man before becoming a soldier in India. He returned to his native Edinburgh in early Edwardian times, became a lithographic stone-dresser, and married his girlfriend Lillie Murray in 1903, when he was 32 years old and she 23. The couple moved into the first flat at 57 Albert Street, near Leith Walk, and soon had two children, the son John and the daughter Margaret. In May 1933, everything seemed normal in the Sullivan household. The now 61-year-old

John Sullivan had suffered from some unspecified illness but was now on the road to recovery. John the younger, an unemployed electrical engineer, was still living with his parents at the age of 27.

On May 12 1933, John the younger had slept long, being awakened by the sound of the one o'clock gun from the Castle. When he went out into the kitchen, he found his parents lying in a huge pool of blood, with their throats terribly cut. When he ran out of the flat to summon assistance, he met his sister Margaret who was coming home to have luncheon with her parents; he told her under no circumstance to go into the house, but to go to see an aunt who lived in central Edinburgh. The police found no evidence that any person had broken into the flat but considered the case as one of murder and suicide. Since the Sullivans had always been popular in the neighbourhood, no person could understand the motive for the tragedy. When Mrs Sullivan had been out shopping in the morning, she had seemed her usual cheery self, speaking to the neighbours on her way back. They had been looking forward to their summer holidays, planning to attend a number of picnics and a motor excursion to Killiecrankie.[1]

WIFE MURDER IN WARDIEBURN PLACE EAST, 1939

Allan Cameron Bennett was born in 1897, the son of humble Scottish parents. He served as a soldier in the Royal Scots for a while, seeing action in the Great War. On August 20 1921, he married Mary Duncan, and they went on to have ten children, all living in a crowded Leith flat. He was known for his angry temper: in 1933, he smashed 54 panes of glass at the Leith office of the Ministry of Pensions, in an attempt to attract attention for an old grievance of his. He was fined £2 for this outrage and would have been sent to prison had it not been for his large family. In 1935, he was convicted for assault, and the following year, he was again fined £2 for beating a man up with a poker in the street. When the Second World War broke out, six of the Bennett children were evacuated, but the two eldest, who were already out in service, and the two youngest toddlers, remained in the family home. At this time, the Bennetts lived in the ground floor flat of a recently constructed three-story Corporation tenement at 10 Wardieburn Place East, Granton.

In November 1939, the old soldier Allan Cameron Bennett was serving as a private in the National Defence Company. But although they had ten children alive, all was not well between him and his wife: he suspected that she was being unfaithful to him, and they sometimes quarrelled angrily in their tiny flat. On November 18, Allan Cameron Bennett seized hold of Mary with a hearty goodwill and cut her throat with a razor. The neighbours heard her screams and called the police. When the constables entered the flat, they found Mary Bennett lying dead on the bedroom floor. The two youngest children were playing in another room, like if nothing had happened. It turned out that Allan Cameron Bennett had run off to give himself up at a police box in Granton. He was taken into police custody and charged with the murder of his wife. When he stood before the Edinburgh Sheriff Court on January 13 1940, he was described as a small and well-built man, clean shaven and with a fresh complexion. The defence entered a special plea of insanity.

Before going on trial on January 23, Allan Cameron Bennett had been examined by the psychiatrists Professor David Kennedy Henderson and Dr William McAlister. Dr McAlister found out that a few days before the murder, Bennett had been examined by a military doctor and declared unfit for further service. McAlister considered Bennett to be in a grossly disordered mental condition, with delusions that he was being poisoned and that his wife was having an affair with another soldier from the same company. The other soldiers had been conspiring against him, he thought, since they were Catholics and he was an Orangeman. Since the medical evidence suggested that Allan Cameron Bennett was insane and unfit to plead, the Lord Justice Clerk ordered him to be detained during the King's pleasure.[2] There is good reason to believe that the Wardieburn Place East wife murderer died at Larbert in 1970, aged 74.

DOUBLE MURDER IN
EARL HAIG GARDENS, 1959

James Bennett was born in 1894 and served in the Royal Artillery during the Great War, losing a leg and part of an arm, and becoming an invalid. His injuries did not prevent him from opening a successful shoe repair shop in Edinburgh, which he managed for many years. In 1922, he moved into the ground floor flat at 25 Earl Haig Gardens, Trinity, a quiet and secluded square owned by the Scottish Veterans' Garden City Association and reserved for disabled ex-servicemen. He married twice and had issue with both wives; one of his daughters got married and left home, but in 1959, his 25-year-old younger daughter Irene was living with him in the flat. She had a job as a typist, but still managed to cook, clean and look after the flat, and help her invalid father with various daily chores. In spite of his maimed condition, the now 65-year-old James Bennett remained hale and hearty: he walked with the help of a wooden leg and a heavy stick. He had sold the shoe shop three years earlier, after inheriting money, and liked to go out drinking beer with his old soldier friends.

On Saturday November 21 1959, James Bennett went out in the afternoon to drink some beer. Mrs Mary Brunton, who lived

1. 25 Earl Haig Gardens, Trinity.

next door at No. 26, could hear him returning home by taxi late in the evening, before hobbling inside. Some time after, there was a heavy thud from next door, and Irene gave a scream. Mrs Brunton thought it might just have been a domestic argument, but still she went out to look through a window, but the house was in darkness and nothing could be heard from its interior. On Monday November 23, Mrs Brunton noticed that the milk, rolls and newspapers were still on the doorstep of No. 25 at 1.15 pm. She looked through the bedroom window and saw James Bennett lying motionless in bed. She went and told her husband, and he called the police. It turned out that James Bennett was lying dead in his bed, with a single bullet from a .22 rifle lodged in his brain.

The body of Irene Bennett was lying on the floor nearby, with multiple bullet wounds to the head and chest regions.

The police soon found out that Irene Bennett had been seeing a man named Alexander Bain Stirling, a 24-year-old car salesman from Loanhead, although she had stopped consorting with him after discovering that he was married already. He had taken this rejection badly and had been pestering her, and she had told a neighbour that she was quite worried what this demented suitor might be capable of. Since Stirling was known to be driving a new red Ford Zephyr, registration TFS 53, the headline of the *Edinburgh Evening Dispatch* was 'Red Car Murder Hunt Steps Up!'. The reporter of course also went to see and photograph the city's most famous recent murder house: "All was quiet in Earl Haig Gardens to-day. Only a solitary constable patrolling outside, and the freshly boarded-up front window of No. 25, gave a clue to yesterday's tragic discovery. Many of the blinds in houses around the square were drawn as a mark of respect for Jimmy Bennett, the man everybody knew and liked."

It turned out that Alexander Main Stirling was an adopted child, who had done his national service in the RAF, and had no previous convictions for serious crime. He lived in Morningside with his wife and two children but worked as a sales assistant at his father's second-hand car firm in Loanhead. A description of him was issued by the police: "About 5ft 10in tall, clean shaven, dark brown hair, chubby face, blue eyes, straight nose and thin lips. They say he may be wearing a sports jacket and flannel trousers, and a bluish grey overcoat of thin material." The hue and cry was up for Alexander Main Stirling all over Britain, but the fugitive had a head start of several days. The police speculated that he might be quite some distance away from Edinburgh, if he had been driving night and day. But on November 24, Police Constable Raymond May was cycling along Southgate Street, Gloucester, when he spotted a red 1959 Ford Zephyr with the 'right' registration number travelling north towards the town centre. He went to the nearest telephone to alert the patrol cars. Soon afterwards, Constables Ronald Savage and Stanley de Gama saw the red Ford Zephyr two miles away on the road from Gloucester to Painswick. They gave chase in their powerful patrol car, and drove in front of the Ford Zephyr, forcing it to stop. They made a dash for the doors, but the tired-looking, bleary-eyed Stirling made no attempt to resist or escape, merely saying 'It's all right, I know what you want me for.' The two patrol constables made sure that Alexander Main Stirling was taken into custody, and that the car, the contents of which included a .22 rifle with a silencer and a plentiful supply of ammunition, was properly searched. Stirling was back in Edinburgh on November 25, where he was formally charged with murder, and appeared in court the following day. He appeared quite despondent after his dramatic attempt to escape had failed.

When Alexander Main Stirling faced trial at the High Court of Edinburgh on March 8 1960, he wished to plead guilty to the capital murders of James and Irene Bennett, but this was not accepted. There was much public interest in the trial, with 50 people queuing up outside the court. Mrs Elizabeth Smith, the sister of Irene Bennett, testified that she had known about Irene's association with Stirling, and that her father had disapproved of it. She identified several of the items taken from the escape car as belonging to her sister. A number of friends and colleagues of Irene Bennett testified that she had told them that she had wanted the affair with Stirling to end, and that she had been annoyed with his impudence. Mr and Mrs Brunton told how the murders had been discovered, Stirling's father explained his background in life, and a miner identified the .22 rifle produced in court as the one he had lent to Alexander Main Stirling, at the latter's request. After the police and forensic specialists had given evidence, Mr Grant the Solicitor-General addressed the jury. He pointed out that the murder weapon had been identified, and that it had been in Stirling's possession at the time of the murders, that property belonging to Irene Bennett had been found in the escape car, and that Stirling's palm prints had been found on the window through which the murder made his entry into the flat. The jury took just 11 minutes to reach a verdict of guilty, and Lord Thomson donned the traditional black tricorne hat when he passed sentence of death onto the prisoner.

Alexander Main Stirling heard the death sentence with the same calm indifference he had displayed throughout the trial. In prison awaiting execution, he refused to see any visitors, and threw away all letters and notes addressed to him. But on March 18, just 12 days before the execution date, he asked for counsel to frame an appeal, claiming that the verdict was contrary to the evidence, and that Lord Thomson had misdirected the jury. The Criminal Appeal Court turned it down, however, and the day of reckoning seemed to loom for the creature Stirling. But still, this cowardly double murderer received a last-minute reprieve, and was spared the gallows with what must have been a very narrow margin.[3] Instead he entered a prison cell, where he would have to stay for many years to come. In August 1970, it was announced that Stirling had been released by royal prerogative since he suffered from an incurable disease. He died from carcinoma of the oesophagus at an Edinburgh nursing home a few weeks later, aged just 35.

DOUBLE MURDER IN
LIXMOUNT AVENUE, 1969

In 1969, the ground floor flat in the terraced house at 10 Lixmount Avenue, Trinity, was home to the 43-year-old commercial traveller Alan Smith, his 40-year-old wife Kathleen and their 11-year-old son Paul. They had lived at Lixmount Avenue since their marriage 15 years earlier. Alan Smith was a former pupil of George Watson's College and had played rugby for the Watsonians. He worked for Lochore & Ferguson Ltd, the Greenock sugar millers, covering the Edinburgh and East Lothian areas. He was a keen family man, devoted to his wife who had been suffering from a nervous complaint for several years, and proud of his son who was a promising pupil at George Watson's College. He was popular and well respected among his friends and neighbours.

On July 24, Alan Smith received a curt letter from his employers, asking him to report for a personal interview bringing all his files, all company property and the company car. He interpreted this as indicating that he would lose his job, something that might put his family in dire straits financially and worry his poor wife intensely. She might suffer a severe mental relapse, and the young Paul would suffer the shame of having an insane mother. The only solution to this problem he could think of was to murder his wife and son, before committing suicide.

Alan Smith put three barbiturate tablets in the evening coffee drunk by his wife and child, but the morning after, they were sleeping peacefully, having suffered no ill effects. He then seized his wife by the throat, throttling her to death, before treating young Paul in the same manner. After putting a phone message on the answering machine of his employers, to the effect that he would not be coming to work since he was lying dead with his family, he slashed his wrists with a knife and collapsed on the floor.

The neighbours in Lixmount Avenue raised the alarm after noticing that the curtains of the downstairs flat at No. 10 were still drawn in mid-afternoon. When the police entered the flat, Kathleen Smith and young Paul were lying dead on the bed, but since Alan Smith was still alive, he was taken to the Edinburgh Royal Infirmary on a stretcher. He made a full recovery and was able to stand trial at the High Court for the murder of his wife and son. His defence counsel, Mr F.W.F. O'Brien QC, made a valiant effort on his client's behalf, pointing out the tragic circumstances of the double killing. The suicide attempt was no sham, but the scars on both wrists were still visible, to remind Alan Smith of the very terrible thing he had done to the family he loved. The bonhomous judge, Lord Johnston, agreed that this was a case where justice itself called out for mercy. After pleading guilty to culpable homicide, Alan Smith was sentenced to imprisonment for just 12 months.[4]

2. The murder house at 10 Lixmount Avenue.

MURDER IN FERRY ROAD DRIVE, 1977

In 1977, the 42-year-old Mrs Marion Stratton was living in the first floor flat at 52 Ferry Road Drive, Pilton, with her boyfriend Norman McKinnon. She had a history of violence when drunk and had two convictions for assault; in 1972, when she lived in London, she was sentenced to nine months' imprisonment for attempted murder. On September 23 1977, Norman McKinnon and Marion Stratton were enjoying an all-night drinking party at 52 Ferry Road Drive. At 5.30 am, she stabbed him to death in a drunken rage, and the police took her into custody and charged her with murder. On trial at the High Court in December 1977, Marion Stratton pleaded guilty to the charge of culpable homicide. Two consultant psychiatrists testified that she suffered from a personality disorder, and that she was bordering on insanity at the time of the murderous attack. Admitting that life had not been kind to her, and that in many ways she had suffered enough, Lord Maxwell sentenced her to six years of imprisonment.[5]

THE ELGIN TERRACE MURDER, 1981

The 60-year-old Margaret Anderson shared a flat at 40/1 Elgin Terrace with her sister, the 52-year-old Mrs Doris Watson. In the weekends, they were sometimes visited by their 20-year-old nephew Michael Scott, a troubled youngster with vicious drinking and glue-sniffing habits. In January 1981, Scott murdered Margaret Anderson, and raped and murdered Doris Watson. He tried to commit suicide after the murders but survived to stand trial. He was found guilty of murder and sentenced to imprisonment for life; he was still in prison in 2002, although there was talk of him being released in the relatively near future.[6]

MURDER IN RESTALRIG ROAD SOUTH, 1986

On September 24 1986, Police Constable James Gordon was ordered to call on the 54-year-old railway worker Stanley Gray, in his first-floor flat at 92 Restalrig Road South, since he had not been seen for several days. Nobody answered the door, although Constable Gordon could hear that the television set was turned on inside the flat. Looking through the letterbox, he could see a heavily bloodstained chair in the lounge. He then pushed hard at the door, and it flew open: the murdered railwayman was lying on the floor in a pool of blood, dead from multiple stab wounds.

The police detectives set up an incident room at the Leith Police Station. They appealed for witnesses having observed anything suspicious near the murder house, and since the attack had been a particularly vicious one, also for any person having discovered bloodstained clothing. Three young men were soon in custody: the 27-year-old John O'Day and his younger cohorts Charles McKay and Alexander Burns. On trial for murder in January 1987, they admitted that after Stanley Gray had beaten up O'Day's mother, with whom he had had an association, they had decided to teach him a hard lesson. They went to 92 Restalrig Road South to confront him, and after an angry altercation, O'Day and Burns had assaulted the much older railwayman, punching him hard. O'Day admitted that he had then seized up a knife and stabbed Gray to death, and he was found guilty of murder and sentenced to imprisonment for life.[7]

MURDER IN LOWER GRANTON ROAD, 1986

The 54-year-old bachelor Geoffrey Pratley worked as a loader in the Edinburgh cleansing department and lived in a first-floor flat at 12 Lower Granton Road. A loner with few friends, he sometimes went out to visit the Leith pubs, but otherwise had no extravagant habits. On November 17 1986, Geoffrey Pratley's dead body was found in his flat, by his younger friend James Stewart. He had been murdered in a brutal and sustained attack with a carving knife: there was an 11-inch gash in his throat and 16 stab wounds to his body.

The police set up an incident caravan in Lower Granton Road and appealed for witnesses to come forward. Police dogs searched the area near the murder house, hoping to find the murder weapon. And indeed, two days after the finding of the body, a carving knife with a blade matching Geoffrey Pratley's injuries was found on the foreshore at Granton. A few days later, the 30-year-old petty criminal Alexander Fitzpatrick gave himself up to the police, confessing that he had committed the Lower Granton Road murder, after Geoffrey Pratley had made homosexual advances to him.

And indeed, Alexander Fitzpatrick's fingerprints were found on beer cans and other objects in the murder flat. Standing trial at the High Court in March 1987, he pleaded not guilty of murder. He confessed that he had stabbed Geoffrey Pratley to death but claimed that he had been acting in self-defence. He had been drinking beer in Pratley's flat, when the householder had suddenly burst into the room stark naked, carrying a knife. Disgusted at Pratley's homosexual advances, Fitzpatrick had attacked and stabbed him, injuring his own hand in the process. He then drank excessively, before returning to the flat in Greenock where he was staying at the time. When he came home, Fitzpatrick had been so distraught that the other people living in the flat had called the police, fearing that he would destroy himself. A flatfooted constable arrived in due course, but he did not take Fitzpatrick's confession seriously, since there was no current knife assault on the police record. Weeping profusely, Fitzpatrick exclaimed 'I will probably get life for this. Have you got a car to take me away?'

But the slow-witted constable misunderstood the drunken Fitzpatrick's story about a man who wanted to 'touch him up'; clearly, there had just been an altercation between two silly 'poofters', and he left the flat in disgust after telling Fitzpatrick to sober up.

But Alexander Fitzpatrick did not make the most of this fortunate and unexpected reprieve. Although he had half a dozen convictions for petty crime, he had never been involved in violence before, and the thought of having killed a man filled him with disgust. Returning to Edinburgh, he told his step-sister and her family that he had stabbed Geoffrey Pratley, who was a family friend. She cleaned and dressed a wound to his hand and washed the blood off his shoes. When Fitzpatrick was in court on trial for murder, all these people gave evidence, including the silly Greenock police constable, who was sternly admonished for his thoughtless actions. There was also solid technical evidence against Fitzpatrick: his fingerprints on the beer cans in the murder flat, and bloodstains matching Pratley's blood on his clothes. The jury found Alexander Fitzpatrick guilty of murder, and he was sentenced to imprisonment for life.[8]

THAT WEE MAN IS DEID, 1987

On Monday June 29 1987, there was a jolly drinking party in the flat at 2 Wardieburn Place North. One of the guests was the 65-year-old pensioner John Jamieson, who was badly crippled from arthritis in his hands and knees; another the 20-year-old hoodlum Thomas Waldie. They were all swigging away merrily, until the householder of the flat, 68-year-old Mrs Mary Raeburn, thought they had had enough. Thomas Waldie asked to spend the night in the flat, but since she knew that he had strong thieving tendencies, she told him there was no room. Instead,

John Jamieson offered Waldie a roof over his head for the night in his own flat at 59 Granton Crescent, and the two mismatched drinking companions lurched off into the night together.

The following morning, Mary Raeburn was disgusted to find Thomas Waldie sprawled inside her living-room. He had made use of his burglary skills to pick the lock and let himself into the flat. She gave him an angry talking-to and sent him packing from the flat. She then noticed that her video player was missing. Having a very good idea who might have stolen it, she called the police. At about the same time, a young man named Christopher Mullen saw Thomas Waldie, whom he knew as a thief, come walking along carrying the video player. Although Waldie objected that he had bought the machine, Mullen told him to come into his flat for the matter to be resolved. Too hung-over to resist, Waldie lurched after him with the video player. All of a sudden, he said that he had chibbed [knifed] an old man twice, adding 'If you do not believe me, here are the keys to his house.'

The public-spirited Christopher Mullen made sure that the police came and picked up Waldie and the video player. When Mary Raeburn came to identify it as her own machine, she could hear Waldie shouting 'I have killed that wee man! That wee man is deid! That wee man is deid!' from the back seat of the police car. And indeed, the wretched John Jamieson was found stabbed to death at 59 Granton Crescent. His wallet, keys and pension book had been stolen. At the police station, Thomas Waldie made a statement: 'I stabbed a man named Johnny tonight. He tried to touch me up, so I stabbed him in the chest and neck. He is definitely dead. I suppose it is 20 years.'

On trial for murder at the High Court, Thomas Waldie pleaded not guilty on grounds of self-defence. But a number of witnesses testified that Jamieson had been 'alright' and definitely not a homosexual. Moreover, he had been a cripple, and hardly capable of sexually assaulting a strong and fit young man. Since John Jamieson had a very high alcohol level in his blood, more than four times the legal limit for driving, he must have been most grossly drunk. He had been holding a knife in his hand when found murdered, but the medical evidence strongly indicated that it had been placed there after death, by the murderer. The Crown suggested that robbery had been the motive for the murder, and the jury agreed, finding Thomas Waldie guilty of murder. Lord Morison sentenced him to imprisonment for life.[9]

GRANTON CRESCENT AGAIN, 1989

William Potter lived at Wyndford Avenue, Uphall, West Lothian, with his much younger wife Arlene and their little daughter Lucy. Arlene's brother Ronald Colbron came to stay with them for a while, but William Potter soon resented his in-laws, and accused them for trying to break up his marriage. And eventually, there was an estrangement between William and Arlene: she left him and took Lucy with her, and went to live in a council flat at 35 Granton Crescent. In 1989, when William Potter was 56 years old, he was becoming obsessed with his broken-down marriage. Still claiming to love his departed wife and daughter, he greatly resented it when Arlene refused him access to Lucy in June 1989. On July 12, they had an angry quarrel in the landing outside her flat, which ended with him stabbing her hard seven times, killing her.

On trial for murder at the High Court, William Potter broke down and cried in the witness box as he described his difficult situation in life. Since there was no doubt that he had stabbed Arlene to death in a fit of rage, many were surprised when the jury found him guilty only of culpable manslaughter, since they believed there was a degree of diminished responsibility. Lord Caplan said he had to respect the verdict of the jury, but the fact remained that Potter had taken the life of an innocent woman and deprived their child of her mother. He was sentenced to imprisonment for nine years.[10] The brother-in-law Ronald Colbron spoke out in a newspaper, claiming that the reason Arlene had kept young Lucy from her father was a recommendation from the police, since there was suspicion, reported to the social services, that he had been molesting the little girl. He and his family resented that this had never come out in court, leading to the murderous William Potter getting off lightly for his crime.

THE MURDER OF JEAN BRUCE, 1989

Alexander Donaldson, a graduate of Heriot-Watt, joined the police as a young man and was promoted to acting sergeant. In 1937, the 22-year-old Donaldson married the 21-year-old typist Jane Esther Bruce. Good-looking and personable, she was determined to have a theatrical career, and after the birth of their eldest son Erroll in 1939, she took her first steps on the theatrical ladder. Since she did not want to be a stay-at-home wife, she persuaded her henpecked husband to leave the police force. Under her stage name Jean Bruce, Jane Donaldson advanced from being a stage actress to landing some TV roles, appearing in 'Dr Finlay's Casebook' and 'Z Cars'. In 1948, the entire family travelled to New Zealand and Australia, in search of theatrical success. Returning to Britain, they moved on to Orkney, Ross and Cromarty, St Andrews and South Shields. Alexander Donaldson worked as a land assessor for local authorities, but he was never able to stay in a job long because of the need to move on to advance his wife's acting career.

In 1962, Alexander Donaldson and Jean Bruce were back in Edinburgh. Having finally had enough of his strong-minded and demanding wife, Donaldson divorced her in 1963, moving to Musselburgh and marrying another woman. Left alone with four children, Jean Bruce continued her TV career, acting in various dramas and commercials. In 1980, Alexander Donaldson divorced his second wife and remarried Jean Bruce. The marriage was something of a love-hate relationship, since Jean Bruce could not forgive Donaldson for leaving her for another woman. She bullied him mercilessly and taunted him with affairs she had enjoyed with other men. Outwardly, she remained the successful TV actress, good-looking and dignified even in her seventies.

In the 1980s, Alexander Donaldson and Jean Bruce shared a flat at 39 South Trinity Road with their sons Erroll and David. Donaldson had recently seemed very depressed and despondent about the incessant rows with his termagant wife. One day when David Donaldson returned home, he found Jean Bruce dead on the hall floor, with terrible wounds to her head and neck. A blood-stained axe was found in the hall cupboard. After murdering his wife, Donaldson had taken a bus to Broxburn, wandering aimlessly around West Lothian. The police found him at Waverley Station in the evening, and he was taken into custody.

On trial for murder at the High Court in March 1990, the 75-year-old Alexander Donaldson pleaded guilty to culpable homicide. After Jean Bruce had shouted abuse at him, he had grabbed hold of her and thrown her to the floor, but then he could remember nothing more about the murder, he said. Psychiatrists who had examined him said that he had been suffering from depression at the time of the murder, although he was no longer suffering from this illness and no longer needed psychiatric treatment. With extraordinary clemency, Lord Maclean deferred sentence on Donaldson for one year, telling him that "I find this a very sad and tragic case and it would be particularly so for you, having been married for so long, and twice to the lady you have killed." In view of Donaldson's age and the surrounding circumstances of the case, including his mental state at the time that led to the original murder charge being reduced, he could see no point in imposing a prison sentence.[11]

MURDER IN COMELY BANK ROW, 1993

The 26-year-old Fiona Stewart worked as a training officer for the Scottish Life Assurance Company at their head office in St Andrew Square. She had separated from her husband, the Musselburgh man Colin Stewart, and was now cohabiting with the 45-year-old George Fleming in the first-floor flat at 13 Comely Bank Row.

On August 10 1993, there was an anonymous call to the police that a woman was dead at 13 Comely Bank Row. It turned out that Fiona Stewart had been murdered, and her boyfriend George Fleming was the main suspect. On August 11, he was charged with the murder at the Edinburgh Sheriff Court. On August 22, he committed suicide by leaping from a top-floor balcony at Saughton Prison, one of several prisoners awaiting trial who destroyed themselves inside the prison in recent years.[12]

TRAGEDY IN RESTALRIG ROAD, 2002

Geraldine Bray was a single mother of four who lived in the ground floor flat at 116 Restalrig Road. On February 6 2002 she went to play bingo, leaving the children to be looked after by her unemployed half-brother Mark Clark. Later in the evening, Clark made a frantic 999 call, saying that the 3-year-old Chloe Bray had fallen over, hit her head and stopped breathing. In the background, the ambulance controller could hear the terrible noise of the child gasping and choking. When the ambulance arrived, little Chloe was dead.

At autopsy, it soon became clear that Chloe Bray had been brutally beaten to death. She had 53 separate injuries, including three burns from a cigarette lighter. The only adult in the flat at the time of her death, Mark Clark, was taken into police custody. He protested his innocence, saying that it had all been a tragic accident, but was not believed. It turned out that he was a very improper person to be looking after small children: a cannabis-smoking, work-shy loner with learning disabilities. He had been kicked out of school for his vicious tendencies: beating up smaller children, and once throwing a chair at a teacher. He jumped bail shortly before going on trial for the murder in February 2003 but was recaptured by the police.

On trial to the High Court, Mark Clark pleaded not guilty, blaming Chloe's mother and stepfather for the murder. But after a recording of the 999 call had been played in court, and the forensic findings from the autopsy had been detailed, he changed his plea to guilty of culpable homicide, probably at the advice of his legal counsel. He was sentenced to imprisonment for 15 years.[13] There was widespread revulsion in the newspaper press for this brutal murder of a defenceless little girl, by a killer who showed no remorse and left court with a smirk on his face; with some right, he was referred to as 'evil' and as a 'monster'. It also turned out that he was the nephew of none other than Lawson Imrie, the insane Edinburgh church murderer who had been sent to Carstairs back in 1977.

THE MURDER OF MIKAEEL KULAR, 2014

Rosdeep Adekoya, a young woman of Asian origins, lived in a flat at 13 Ferry Gait Crescent, in the Drylaw suburb of Edinburgh. A sluttish woman who liked drinking and partying, and consorting with dubious 'gentleman friends', she had given birth to five children fathered by various dodgy blokes; these children were often left to look after themselves during her wild nights out. On January 16 2014, Rosdeep Adekoya claimed that her three-year-old son Mikaeel Kular had gone missing from his bed in the flat at Ferry Gait Crescent. There was initial speculation that he might have strolled out into the night on his own, but he was a small boy and the front door a heavy one. His father, the chef Zahid Saeed, faced some searching questions what he had been up to when Mikaeel went missing, but he was clearly an innocent man, and had never shown much interest in his little boy. Volunteers were recruited from all over Edinburgh to help look for little Mikaeel, and civilian dogs joined the police dogs trying to sniff him out. But on January 18, Mikaeel's dead body was found in Kirkcaldy, quite near the house of Rosdeep Adekoya's sister.

It turned out that after Mikaeel had misbehaved after a visit to a restaurant, Rosdeep Adekoya had given him a severe beating, ferocious enough to murder him from internal injuries. This unnatural mother then wrapped the body in a duvet, put it in a suitcase and hid it near her sister's house, where she hoped the police would not be looking. Her story about the little boy's disappearance was a deliberate lie, but after some hostile questioning from the police, she eventually broke down and told them where she had hidden the remains of the little boy. In August 2014, she pleaded guilty to culpable homicide and was sentenced to imprisonment for 11 years.[14] There was outrage in Edinburgh at this very lenient sentence, for a murder as cruel and inexcusable as any other in this book. It is not known whether this unnatural mother was treated with respect while behind bars, or perhaps whether she came across some tough Glaswegian termagant who did not like Asians, or child killers, or sluttish women who neglected their children. There was further outrage in December 2018, when there were newspaper photographs of the now 38-year-old Rosdeep Adekoya enjoying day release from Cornton Vale prison, going into Stirling and visiting the library, although she had not even served five years of her original sentence. Rumours said that she would be released already in early 2019, a low price indeed for the life of a blameless little boy, but according to the *Scottish Sun*, she was still 'inside' in June 2019.[15]

VI.

LEITH AND PORTOBELLO

1. Stead's Place in 1960.

In olden times, Edinburgh's seaside suburb of Leith had an evil reputation: among its ramshackle taverns and lodging-houses, drunken seamen fought each other with bludgeons or knives, committing murder more than once. In our days, Leith has undergone a gentrification, however: the Victorian slums have been cleared, taking their murder houses with them. Stead's Place off Leith Walk, where William Bennison poisoned his wife in 1850, still stood as late as 1960, in a derelict row of houses opposite the Leith West railway goods yard, but today there is no trace of the house of horrors once occupied by the murderous 'Holy Willie'. The earliest extant Leith murder house only dates back to 1928. Two Duke Street pubs have been visited by the spectre of murder: the Duke's Head at No. 31 in 1970, and

Minto's Bar at No. 21 in 1998; neither pub is still operational today, the former having become a fast food outlet and the latter part of the 'Lioness of Leith' restaurant. In contrast to Leith, Portobello has always been a quiet and affluent suburb, home to the better class of people. A shopkeeper was murdered at 78 Portobello High Street in 1945, as a result of xenophobic violence from a pair of drunken thugs; not far away stands one of the Capital's true houses of horror, 10 East Brighton Crescent, where three people perished in a bloodbath in 1969 …

THE OUTLAW ALLAN WALES, 1928

Allan Wales was born in 1906, the son of the Leith chemical worker Alexander Wales and his wife Mary. From an early age, he showed strong criminal tendencies. Short in stature but strong and sturdy, he bullied younger boys and stole their money. His first conviction for theft came when he was just 10 years old. In 1922, he was convicted of stealing trousers from a shop window, and a vase from a motor car; since this was the fourth time he had been caught stealing, he was sentenced to three years in the Borstal Institution.

Lacking intellectual ambitions, Allan Wales had left school at 14, but Borstal discipline appears to have done him some degree of good. On his release, he worked as an apprentice plumber for a while, before becoming a coal miner. On December 2 1926, the now 20-year-old Allan married the 18-year-old domestic servant Isabella Hain, daughter of the mason Andrew Hain and his wife Florence, resident at 17 Pirniefield Place, Leith. This humble dwelling was a basement flat situated underneath the main house at No. 15, and consisting of a kitchen, a living room and a small bedroom. Their son Alexander was born on October 2 1927, but already by that time, Isabella had discovered the hard way that her husband was a nasty piece of work. He beat and flogged her with regularity, even when she was pregnant with their child; when the mother-in-law tried to intervene, he beat her up as well and was fined £2 for assault.

In early 1928, Allan Wales lost his job as a dock labourer. Since being unemployed did not agree with him, endless domestic disputes were the result, sometimes ending in violence. When poor Isabella went back to the family home at 17 Pirniefield Place and showed Mrs Hain her bruises, she was invited to move back in with her parents and siblings to escape her wife-beating cad of a husband. Allan thought this a great affront and made efforts to persuade Isabella to move back into his lodgings at 254 Leith Walk, but the two women had seen enough of him and did not budge. Encouraged by Mrs Hain, Isabella sent Allan her wedding ring and their child, with a message that she was striking out for herself: she was looking for a job and no longer had any need for him in her life. Exactly what the angry, short-tempered Allan Wales thought of this proto-feminist initiative we will soon find out.

On June 5 1928, Allan Wales and his mother came to 17 Pirniefield Place to plead with Isabella to return to her husband, but she refused to come with them. Later in the day, Allan returned on his own, in a furious temper. He screamed abuse at Isabella and Mrs Hain and threatened to murder them. When Isabella tried to escape from the flat out into the area, he pursued her. Brandishing a large cobbler's knife he had brought with him, he stabbed her repeatedly in the throat region, exclaiming 'You were asking for it, and you have got it!' Mrs Hain, who had followed them out into the area, stood aghast when she saw her daughter collapse, the blood spurting from her deep stab wounds. Her sense of self-preservation led her to suspect who was next on the death list of the demented murderer, however, and she bounded up the steps with alacrity to take refuge in the house of a neighbour, screaming 'He's done it! He's done it! He's killed her!' as she ran for her life. Dazed at what he had just accomplished, the outlaw Allan Wales remained near the murder scene. After an outcry had been made,

2. The entrance to the basement flat at 17 Pirniefield Place.

quite a crowd was congregating outside 17 Pirniefield Place. Two men who saw Allan's blood-stained hands and cuffs pointed him out to Detective Sergeant Alexander Drummond, who took him into custody, secured the murder weapon, and made sure that the prisoner was sent to the Central Police Office in the High Street.

On trial for murder at the High Court of Edinburgh on July 23 1928, before Lord Alexander, things were not looking good for Allan Wales as the witnesses for the prosecution produced some very damning testimony. Mrs Florence Hain gave a blow-by-blow account of the murder of her daughter, and her own escape from the scene. Since a number of other witnesses, mostly neighbours in Pirniefield Place, had heard the outcries of the two women, and seen Allan attacking Isabella, there was no doubt that he was the guilty man. The defence called Allan's parents as witnesses:

they testified that their son had been very fond of his wife, and distraught when she had left him. The day of the murder, he had asked for a sharp knife to cut the heel of his boot. Dr W.M. McAlister, director-superintendent of the Morningside Royal Hospital, had examined Allan Wales together with his colleague Dr Dodds Fairbairn. The Binet-Simon intelligence test had indicated that although the prisoner's chronological age was 22, he had a mental age of just 10 years. Challenged by Lord Alexander, the doctor had to admit that the prisoner's mediocre intellect did not imply that he had not known what he was doing when he stabbed his wife to death. In his summing-up, Lord Alexander declared himself unable to find any extenuating circumstances in favour of the prisoner. The Binet-Simon intelligence test was, in his opinion, a dangerous tool when it came to the determination of criminal responsibility. After this hostile summing-up, the jury was out for 35 minutes before returning a majority verdict of guilty, and Lord Alexander sentenced Allan Wales to death.

As the convict Allan Wales was awaiting execution in Saughton Prison, a petition was prepared on his behalf by his parents and defence counsel, pointing out his defective intellect, and the jury's unanimous recommendation to mercy on account of his age. Since the murderer's parents were respectable people, 3013 individuals signed the petition when it was exhibited in various Leith shops and factories. Alexander Wales Sr wrote an accompanying letter as the petition was sent to Sir John Gilmour, the Secretary of State for Scotland, pointing out that his son was handicapped with a backward intellect, and provoked into a fit of frenzy by the heartless conduct of his wife. But Sir John Gilmour found no reason to reprieve Allan Wales, since his crime had been a dastardly and premeditated one. The Pirniefield Place murderer was executed at Saughton Prison on August 13 1928, as the first prisoner ever to be hung at that prison; he is said to have walked steadily from his cell to the scaffold, and to have conducted himself with becoming calmness until the end.[1]

ICE CREAM WAR IN PORTOBELLO, 1945

During the Second World War, there was of course a healthy hatred for all Germans throughout Britain. When Mussolini entered the war in 1940, this hatred spread to encompass the country's not inconsiderable Italian population: shops, restaurants and businesses run by Italians were attacked, in Scotland as well as in mainland England. In 1945, the ice cream shop at 78 High Street, Portobello, was owned by the 82-year-old Italian immigrant Giuseppe Demarco. Due to his venerable age and long residence in the local community, he was generally well liked in Portobello and not held responsible for Mussolini's dubious military ruses, although the dachshund-kicking ultra-patriots would of course not go near a shop owned by one of the country's enemies, a detested 'Ice Creamer' who lived as a parasite on the honest Scots.

In spite of his age, Mr Demarco was hale and hearty, and well capable of looking after his shop, assisted by his wife Maria Assunta. On June 5 1945, the hot weather meant that the Demarco shop enjoyed a roaring trade: since the local children all wanted ice cream, the takings were nearly £100. The two local never-do-wells Robert Robertson and Timothy John Donoghue made themselves obnoxious in the shop, shouting xenophobic threats against the hated Italian, but Mr Demarco managed to evict them from the premises. Robertson and Donoghue retired to a pub nearby, where they drunk beer and whisky until quite inebriated. They decided to return to the ice cream shop, in order to teach the bloody Italian a proper lesson this time.

As Robertson entered the shop, Mr Demarco recognized him as the thug who had insulted him previously, and the sturdy old man seized hold of the intruder with a hearty goodwill, landing some well-aimed blows to his face. Mrs Demarco pushed the drunken coward Donoghue out of the shop, so that he fell down

3. Portobello High Street, a postcard stamped and posted in 1905.

and hurt his nose. He meekly joined the crowd standing shouting outside the shop, making no attempt to help his friend. When the witness Mrs Jane Farquhar came to 78 High Street, she saw Donoghue skulking in the crowd outside. Robertson was on the floor after taking a number of hits from Mr Demarco, but he maintained his hold onto the shopkeeper's shirt. Demarco asked Mrs Farquhar to get help, when Robertson suddenly bounded up to his feet and grabbed a lemonade bottle, but she snatched it away from him, exclaiming 'Don't hit him with a bottle!' But the ruffian Robertson seized hold of another lemonade bottle and hit Mr Demarco a glancing blow to the temple. As the elderly shopkeeper collapsed, Robertson kicked him hard as he lay on the floor. The ruffian then proceeded to rob the shop, stealing a bag containing £9 and change, and another bag containing £94. The furious Mrs Demarco screamed and raved, but the coward Donoghue, who had belatedly joined his friend inside the shop, prevented her from running out into the shop, and Robertson broke another lemonade bottle over her head, knocking her out

4. The Demarco murder shop is 'Anna Thai' today.

cold. The two ruffians then tried to run away, but the police had belatedly made an appearance, and they were both promptly apprehended.

Giuseppe Demarco never regained consciousness after this cowardly assault, and he died not long after. Mrs Demarco, who was herself in Leith Hospital for concussion, discharged herself to be able to attend her husband's funeral. The ruffians Robertson and Donoghue were both charged with murder. When their trial began at the High Court of Justiciary in Edinburgh on August 28, Mrs Demarco described how Robertson had struck her husband down, and how Donoghue had held her back until Robertson had knocked her out with the bottle. Filippo Demarco, son of the deceased, testified as to his father's calm and peaceful nature. Various witnesses had seen part of the fight inside the ice cream shop, but only Mrs Farquhar had seen Robertson strike Mr Demarco down. The medical evidence said that Mr Demarco had been quite frail, with established heart disease. In the end, Donoghue was found not guilty and discharged, but Robertson, whose counsel had vainly tried a plea of self-defence, was sentenced to seven years of penal servitude; an appeal in October 1945 was unsuccessful, and it was a good day for Edinburgh's Italian population when the ruffian Robertson ended up in jail.[2] The former ice cream shop at 78 High Street, Portobello, was the 'Butternut Squash' breakfast restaurant for a while, but it is now the 'Anna Thai' ethnic restaurant.

WIFE MURDER IN ALBANY STREET, 1945

In July 1945, the 35-year-old Scots Guardsman William Miller Goodall was home on two weeks' leave from the military, which he spent in the small flat he shared with his wife Elizabeth at 7 Albany Street, Leith. In the late evening of July 30, the former soldier William Meldrum, who lived in the top flat at 7 Albany Street, saw Elizabeth Goodall coming into the stair after him. She looked apprehensively through the glass panel over her flat's front door, to see if anybody was home. Seven or eight minutes later, there was the sound of several gunshots, and when William Meldrum went out into the stair, he saw Mrs Goodall at the ground floor level, in a dying condition.

The following day, William Miller Goodall was charged with murdering his wife at the Edinburgh Burgh Court. He had gunned her down with an automatic pistol. In court, he was wearing civilian attire, and had a cloth cap sticking out of his pocket. When he faced trial at the High Court on October 30, he pleaded not guilty on grounds of insanity. After four doctors had testified as to his mental condition, Lord Mackay ordered him to be detained in the State Mental Hospital until His Majesty's pleasure be known.[3]

THE MOST DANGEROUS MAN IN EDINBURGH, 1970

As Edinburgh murderers come, Donald Forbes must surely be one of the worst of the lot. In 1958, the 23-year-old Forbes robbed the fish factory at 39 Lower Granton Road [it no longer stands], brutally beating the 67-year-old night watchman Allan Fisher to death with a rusty iron bolt. He then went out on a drinking spree with the money he had stolen from the factory but was soon in police custody. Forbes was found guilty of murder and was sentenced to death, but there were public protests when he wanted to marry his pregnant girlfriend, and he was reprieved to face imprisonment for life.

Remarkably for a murderer of such callous brutality, Donald Forbes served just twelve years in prison before being released. In the summer of 1970, having spent six months out of prison, he went to have a drink or two at the Duke's Head public house at 31 Duke Street, Leith. Here he got involved in a quarrel with

DUKE STREET, LEITH.

5. Duke Street, Leith, a postcard stamped and posted in 1916.
Reproduced by permission of Mr G. Burgess, Dunbar.

6. The former murder pub at 31 Duke Street.

the 27-year-old former soldier Charlie Gilroy and his brother Robert. Without any further ado, Forbes pulled up a knife and stabbed both brothers hard, murdering Charlie and injuring Robert severely. He stood laughing at his two victims, finished his pint and calmly left the pub. He was caught by the police drinking in another pub nearby.

Found guilty of murder for a second time, and again sentenced to imprisonment for life, Donald Forbes faced further turbulent times. In 1971, he escaped from the maximum-security wing of Peterhead Prison, stealing a car and making his way back to Edinburgh, where he was recaptured near the site of his first murder. This time, this formidable Edinburgh desperado was sent to the special prison unit at Barlinnie in Glasgow, where they had the resources to keep him under proper restraint. In due course, he was transferred to an open prison, and in spite of protests from the Gilroy family, who felt certain that he was a dangerous psychopath who should never walk free, he was finally released in 1998, having spent 28 years behind bars. In 2003, Forbes was again arrested for wholesale drug smuggling, and put back into prison; he died at the Inverclyde Royal Hospital in 2008, having spent nearly his entire adult life behind bars. It would not have been a great loss if he had really been hanged back in 1958, and Charlie Gilroy's life would have been saved.[4]

TRIPLE MURDER IN
EAST BRIGHTON CRESCENT, 1972

In early 1972, the 45-year-old driving instructor David Anderson was living in the semi-detached Georgian villa at 10 East Brighton Crescent, Portobello, with his 43-year-old wife Dorothy. They had two children: 16-year-old Elaine, who was a pupil at James Gillespie's High School for Girls, and 13-year-old Robert, who attended the Royal High School. Mrs Anderson's mother, the 86-year-old Mrs Sarah Mitchell Smith, was also living in the large and comfortable house. Mr Anderson had been a bus driver for many years, before setting up his own business as a driving instructor. He was a gloomy, introverted character, with few close friends, and a non-smoking teetotaller. The family was very religious, and regularly attended the Dublin Street Baptist Church. The main sorrow in their lives was that their second son Martin had died from Hodgkin's Disease aged just 12.

David Anderson was constantly worrying about the future. The family had used to live in a humble Corporation house at Redhall Place, Longstone, and now when he was responsible for paying the rent for a larger and more salubrious house, and had two children at expensive schools, money was a constant concern. The driving instruction business was not bringing in as much money as he had hoped, and he was fearful of poverty. A bout of severe influenza rendered him even more depressed and despondent. He considered committing suicide, but then he would leave his family destitute. In the end, he decided to wipe out his entire family, to spare them the consequences of his financial ruin.

On January 7, the 19-year-old Kenneth Carvel wanted to see his girlfriend Elaine Anderson, for a meeting in their Scripture group. But the telephone was constantly engaged, and when he came knocking at 10 East Brighton Crescent, there was no response, although both Mr Anderson's Morris 1300 and Elaine's scooter were parked on the drive. Young Carvel called his father, who shared his concern for the Anderson family; after speaking to the neighbours, he called the police. After breaking into the house, the police patrol met with the grossest scenes. In their upstairs bedrooms, Elaine and Robert lay murdered with repeated blows from a heavy hammer, as did old Mrs Smith. Dorothy Anderson had severe head injuries, but was still alive, and her husband was also injured from a suicide attempt. Detectives immediately sealed off the murder house, and an ambulance was summoned to take the injured people to the Edinburgh Royal Infirmary.

Triple murders in Edinburgh are fortunately of rare occurrence. In the *Edinburgh Evening News*, the murderous cataclysm in East Brighton Crescent was largely featured, with interviews with various people who had known members of the Anderson family, and illustrations from the tragic family's album of holiday snapshots from happier days. The murder house at 10 East Brighton Crescent was named, shamed and photographed in all its gory notoriety. Old bus driver colleagues of David Anderson spoke of his abstemious and reclusive tendencies; family friends from Redhall Place described Mrs Anderson as a devoted mother

7. 10 East Brighton Crescent.

and her husband as very reserved; the current neighbours at East Brighton Crescent had never properly got to know the tragic family, who had lived there just six months. The minister at the Dublin Street Baptist Church praised the family's religious devotion, and Elaine's zeal in the Scripture group. The Carvel family, whose public-spiritedness had advanced the discovery of the tragedy, were also interviewed.

Several days after the triple murder, Dorothy Anderson was still said to be in a critical condition, with severe head injuries. Her murderous husband had recovered from his own injuries by January 11, when he appeared before the Edinburgh Sheriff's Court, to be charged with murdering his children and his mother-in-law. On trial at the High Court in early April,

David Anderson's solicitor entered a plea of not guilty, with a special defence of 'insanity at the time'. And indeed, a consultant psychiatrist who had interviewed the East Brighton Crescent triple murderer felt that he had a history of recurrent depression throughout his life. His father and sister had both committed suicide and he had himself attempted suicide at the age of 12. The 'insanity defence' thus had the desired effect, and David Anderson was retained at the Carstairs State Mental Hospital for an indefinite period of time.[5]

As for the murder house, it was put up for sale shortly after the murders. Since it was priced quite favourably, many people went to see it, but since the murders had been such frontpage news, they soon found out about the notoriety of the place. Two friends of mine thought this nice Georgian villa would be ideal for their family, but the horror of the triple murder put them off and they never made an offer for it. Today, although many locals still remember the cataclysm back in 1972, Portobello's most celebrated murder house looks tidy and in good repair.

MURDER IN SANDPORT STREET, 1991

Having spent 22 years as a soldier in the Royal Artillery, Alexander Colquhoun left the army in the 1980s and got a job as a handyman with the BBC in Edinburgh. He was a habitué at the Blue Oyster Club, a gay disco in Rose Street Lane North, and on Christmas Eve 1991, the 51-year-old Colquhoun was partying there as usual. He was seen consorting with two dodgy-looking youths, and there was suspicion that in the wee hours of Christmas Day, he had taken them home with him to his flat at 37 Sandport Street, Leith.

On December 28 1991, Alexander Colquhoun was found stabbed to death in his flat. The burglar alarm had been going off for days, but the other residents had ignored it. It was presumed that he had been murdered early on Christmas Day. The police appealed for witnesses from the Blue Oyster Club, and the cab driver who had taken Colquhoun and his two young acquaintances from Rose Street Lane North to Sandport Street. The appealed to the city's gay community to help solve the murder of one of their own. And indeed, John Hall, a former part-time worker at the Blue Oyster Club, came forward to say that on Christmas Eve, he had seen Alexander Colquhoun with two young men named Cameron Downie and Raymond Warrender. These two were arrested on New Year's Day and charged with murdering Alexander Colquhoun at the Edinburgh Sheriff Court on January 3.

On trial at the High Court in June 1992, the two youths pleaded not guilty. The 18-year-old Downie entered a special plea that he had stabbed Alexander Colquhoun to save himself and Warrender from an attack. They had been drinking with Colquhoun at the Blue Oyster Club, and willingly went back to his flat with him. They had watched a video of three men having sexual intercourse, but Downie had fallen asleep. He had woken up when he heard the 20-year-old Warrender scream 'Cammy, Cammy, the bastard is on top of me! Help me get him off! I can't get him off!', grabbed a knife and run into the bedroom. Seeing Colquhoun lying naked on top of Warrender, he had stabbed him hard in the back, and then again in the chest. According to Professor Anthony Busuttil, there were no defensive injuries, suggesting that Colquhoun had been taken unaware by his killer. The prosecution alleged that the self-defence story was made up: how could the naked, unarmed Colquhoun, who had already been stabbed hard in the back, be a danger to any person? With a majority verdict, the jury found Cameron Downie guilty of murder, and he was sentenced to imprisonment for life.[6]

MURDER IN IONA STREET, 1992

The 82-year-old Mrs Rose McCrudden lived in a flat at 68 Iona Street, Leith, where she had been staying for the last 40 years. In 1992, the flat below hers was inhabited by the burglar John Waldie, who thought it might be a good idea to break into the old woman's flat when she was out, to see that valuables she possessed. But Mrs McCrudden returned home unexpectedly and caught the burglar red-handed. When he assaulted her and grabbed her round the neck, she collapsed from the shock. He tried to revive her by giving her the kiss of life, although his bungling efforts may well have had the effect to suffocate her instead.

John Waldie was initially charged with murder, but the jury accepted his guilty plea to culpable manslaughter, and the bonhomous Lord Caplan sentenced him to imprisonment for seven years. Not without reason, Mrs Margaret McQueen, daughter of Rose McCrudden, found this a very lenient sentence when she spoke out in a newspaper interview, since if the burglar had not come rummaging round her flat, Mrs McCrudden would still have been alive. She sincerely hoped that the other prisoners would give the cowardly burglar a well-deserved beating, and that he would rot in jail.

But John Waldie served only four years of his prison sentence, before emerging from jail as angry and mean-spirited as ever. In late 1997, when he lived in a small flat in a high-rise building in Leith, he went out drinking with his friend Terry Kivlin. When they went home to the flat with a supply of booze and fast food, he at first made Kivlin welcome, before bounding out of the kitchen brandishing a home-made club. Ronnie Smith, another man staying in the flat, saw him hitting Kivlin on the head with it. The terrified Kivlin leapt headlong from a window of the seventh-floor flat, landing hard on the unyielding tarmac below and dying instantly. John Waldie denied culpable homicide, but the jury found him guilty and he was sentenced to five more years in prison.

Only then were they informed that he had in fact killed before. Rose McCrudden's daughter Margaret McQueen rightly branded Waldie 'evil and callous' and told a journalist she was dismayed that he had been let out of prison so very early, to take another life.[7]

MURDER OF THE CAT MAN OF FERRY ROAD, 1996

The 47-year-old Gilbert O'Donnell was a well-known Leith character. Known as something of a 'queer', he dyed his hair jet black and pencilled his eyebrows. Registered disabled due to blindness in one eye, he spent much of his time reading and listening to music. A great friend of animals, he devoted much time to feeding the birds, and putting out saucers of milk for the local cats on the back green of 35 Ferry Road, Leith, where he lived in a small flat. The neighbours, who did not at all care for the hordes of cats invading their property, called O'Donnell 'The Cat Man of Ferry Road'.

On March 4 1996, Gilbert O'Donnell was found murdered inside his flat. He had been brutally beaten to death: fifteen ribs were broken, a lung punctured, the rib cage collapsed, and the liver badly crushed. The neighbours had heard noises in his flat at about 1 am on March 2, indicating that Gilbert O'Donnell had been murdered that night. His sister Maureen told an *Edinburgh Evening News* journalist that Gilbert had been a harmless character, an eccentric without any enemies. He occasionally enjoyed a pint at the Junction Bridge Bar in Great Junction Street but was not a heavy drinker. Feeding the cats and birds was his great passion in life.

The police soon had a suspect in custody. Already on March 5, the 30-year-old former submariner John King appeared at the Edinburgh Sheriff Court, to be charged with murder. Unusually, it took a full year before King stood trial for the murder at the High Court of Edinburgh. He pleaded not guilty on grounds

8. Ferry Road, Leith, a postcard stamped and posted in 1927.

of self-defence, claiming that Gilbert O'Donnell had attacked him with a hammer. Professor Anthony Busuttil compared the injuries inflicted to the murdered man to those suffered in a severe road traffic accident: it was impossible that Gilbert O'Donnell could have walked up or down stairs after suffering such a brutal beating. The most curious matter that came to light during the trial, however, was that a woman had seen Gilbert O'Donnell come walking upstairs later in the day when he was supposed to have been murdered: he had been very pale and white and had not looked at her or said 'Hello'. Remarkably, a woman had seen O'Donnell feeding the pigeons at the Leith Library the very same day, and a shop assistant claimed that he had been in her Leith shop the day after he was supposed to have been beaten to death.

Defending John King, Robert Henderson QC asked whether there had in fact been two separate beatings, one inflicted by his client and resulting in relatively minor injuries, and another administered by the real murderer, resulting in his death. But

338

the jury found John King guilty of murder, and the former submariner was sentenced to imprisonment for life. The motive for the murder, presumably homosexual advances gone wrong, was not speculated about in the newspapers. The purported post-mortem sightings of the Cat Man of Ferry Road remain a mystery still, unless you are a believer in the spectral world.[8]

9. The entrance to the Cat Man's former abode at 35 Ferry Road.

MURDER IN MINTOS BAR, 1998

Mintos Bar at 21 Duke Street, Leith, was situated not far away from Donald Forbes's notorious murder pub, the Duke's Head at No. 31. It was a quiet establishment catering mainly to older drinkers. On the evening of August 6 1998, a crowd of people were emptying their pints on the premises. One of them was a young man with a prominent scar across the right side of his face, who seemed very agitated like if he had taken drugs and was on a 'bad trip'. He believed that the other drinkers were laughing at him and taunting him as a paedophile, and grabbed hold of one of them to ask what was happening. Another pub customer gave him four Valium tablets to calm him down.

The 41-year-old father of four John Young went to Mintos Bar on August 6 with his common-law wife Ally, to celebrate the birthday of a friend. He was severely disabled with sciatica, and unable to work. When he went to the bar to get some peanuts for his wife, the scar-faced man kicked the pub doors open and bounded into the premises, brandishing a large knife. He seized hold of John Young and aimed to stab him in the chest, but Ally leapt over the table and managed to push her husband away from the desperado, so that the knife hit him in the side instead. Paramedics fought to resuscitate him for two hours, but since a major blood vessel had been injured, Young died at the Edinburgh Royal Infirmary a few hours later.

The scar-faced desperado had been seen by several pub customers when he rapidly made himself scarce after his murderous assault. He was identified as the 25-year-old Peter Christensen, arrested by the police, and charged with murder on August 10. On trial at the High Court in December 1998, he struggled with police in the dock after being found guilty of murder by a majority verdict and sentenced to imprisonment for life.[9] In October 2002, when Christensen was in Shotts Prison, his name again hit the newspaper headlines, demanding compensation after his two children had been crushed to death by an Edinburgh dumper truck.

10. Duke Street's other former murder pub at No. 21.

MURDER IN PRINCE REGENT STREET, 1998

The 16-year-old Leith boy William Martin left school early and had a troubled life. At a hostel for homeless people, he had fallen in with an undesirable crowd, among them the 25-year-old street beggar Craig Martin (no relation) and the 19-year-old thug David Fulton. His family helped young Martin to get at flat in a shabby tenement block at 10 Prince Regent Street, Leith, where he lived with his 18-year-old girlfriend Angela Brogan. William Martin was very thin and agile, and he liked to show off his Houdini-like skills as an escape artist, making use of his double-jointed tendencies to get out of ropes and knots. He knew judo and karate, and was supposed to be able to look after himself. In June 1998, William Martin's life looked better than it had for a long time. He was moving out of the shabby old flat in Prince Regent Street into a more salubrious one in Leith Street, and looked forward to attending a catering college to train as a chef.

11. A postcard showing Prince Regent Street, Leith.

To celebrate his great expectations in life, William Martin invited his former hostel buddies Craig Martin and David Fulton back to 10 Prince Regent Street. But unbeknownst to him, both these thugs resented him strongly. William Martin had once informed the manager that Craig Martin used to smuggle in alcohol and drugs, causing him to be evicted from the hostel. David Fulton envied William Martin's recent good prospects in life, and he hoped that if young Martin met with some kind of accident, he could move in with Angela Brogan, who secretly preferred him to her present boyfriend, or so at least he believed. Angela was also in the flat when the two thugs came calling, but when she overheard them talking about murdering William, she thought they were just joking.

As the four friends were larking about in the flat at 10 Prince Regent Street, David Fulton wanted to tie William Martin's hands behind his back. Knowing that he could easily escape the ropes, foolish young Martin allowed this to be done. But his two false friends then seized hold of him with a hearty goodwill, as Angela

Brogan looked on aghast. David Fulton held young Martin in a powerful leglock, before standing on the neck of the helpless youth. The two thugs then pulled a plastic bag over the head of the still living William Martin, before hitting and kicking him hard. Having hidden the motionless body of their victim in a cupboard, the two murderers stole his income support book and some cash, before inviting Angela Brogan out for a meal of chips and gravy.

But the following day, the volatile Angela Brogan had yet another change of heart. She went to the social workers and told them all about what had happened at 10 Prince Regent Street. The police were immediately called in, but it turned out that the body of William Martin had already been discovered, by the landlord of the flat coming to evict him. Craig Martin and David Fulton were arrested and charged with murder. On trial at the High Court in September 1998, the two thugs blamed each other. When Angela Brogan told her story of them planning and executing the murder together, the defence accused her of changing her story. Still, she made a reasonably good impression in court, at least compared with the two accused. The cause of death was that the voicebox had been crushed, blocking the windpipe. There was strong technical evidence against the two accused: their fingerprints were found on the plastic bag, and traces of William Martin's saliva was found on the leg of Craig Martin's tracksuit trousers.

Giving evidence in court, David Fulton admitted tying up William Martin, before Craig Martin had attacked him and strangled him to death. But both thugs were found guilty of murder and sentenced to imprisonment for life.[10] The impassive Craig Martin had probably expected this verdict, but David Fulton, a former pupil at the Bathgate Academy who had no previous record of serious crime, screamed 'There's no justice! It's a kangaroo court!' His mother, who was present in court, collapsed and wept, screaming 'He's done nothing wrong!'

Interviewed by an *Edinburgh Evening News* journalist, William Martin's divorced parents declared themselves pleased with the verdict. The most important question, namely why none of them had provided the young lad with a bed when he needed it, instead of leaving him to sleep in a hostel populated with various undesirable types, was never asked. In 2006, when David Fulton applied for a minimum tariff to his life sentence, William Martin's father, the Prestonpans man Thomas Martin, declared himself to be most displeased.

VII.

CONCLUDING REMARKS

How ancient is the concept of a 'murder house'? The feeling of some degree of reluctance to move into a house, inside which the previous occupant has been brutally murdered, is likely to be quite deep-rooted, among superstitious people at least. Yet I have looked into a number of celebrated eighteenth-century murders, in Edinburgh and elsewhere, without finding any evidence to suggest that the houses involved were given any particular attention by the rather primitive newspaper press of the time. The fact that Rizzio had been murdered inside Holyrood Palace was considered mostly as a curiosity, with the tell-tale bloodstain that could not be washed out being actively shown to the tourists. The house of Mary Blandy, who was executed for murdering her father in 1752, still stands today in Henley-on-Thames. In 1929, when this venerable murder house was admired by the crime writer A. Salusbury McNalty, it was occupied by a doctor, but today it is the Blandy House dental surgery.[1] The concept of a murder house would change in late Georgian and early Victorian times, however. Firstly, the growth of literacy, and the rapid development of the popular newspaper press, meant that news about the recent murders would spread with rapidity. Secondly, some Edinburgh houses were numbered already in the 1760s, and this practice became widespread in late Georgian times; the house-numbers were of course an essential tool for the crowds of mainly lower-class people who wanted to gawp at the murder house. As we know, the Milne murder house at 31 Frederick Street was admired by a veritable throng of people, and the Chantrelle murder house at 81A George Street also became quite notorious.

There was widespread renumbering of the New Town houses in the 1810s, but since then they have kept their numbers and I have found no instance of any Edinburgh murder house being renumbered in Victorian or modern times.[2] Throughout Victorian and Edwardian times, the vast majority of newspapers, Edinburgh and provincial alike, saw it as a public service to publish the full addresses of murder houses, including its number. After the Great War, the newspaper attitude to murder houses would change, however. It was no longer considered obvious that their full addresses should be published, and from the 1920s onwards, this happened less frequently, although that valuable newspaper, the *Edinburgh Evening News*, kept naming and shaming notorious murder houses well into modern times. Today, the full address of a murder house is seldom openly divulged in the newspapers, although media photographs of the crime scene can occasionally be revealing.

There are three main tools for the Edinburgh murder house detective. Firstly, there are online lists of murder trials at the website of National Records of Scotland; these can be made use of to construct a database of Edinburgh murders where the entire [up to 1919] or partial [1920s and 1930s] murder trial files can be inspected at the Register House. Secondly, the Edinburgh Room at the Central Library has a series of murder ledgers, full of press cuttings about murder cases from the 1930s until the late 2000s. These ledgers have proven invaluable for the present book. Thirdly, there are today some very good online newspaper databases, namely the *Scotsman* newspaper on the ProQuest service, the British Library Newspapers and the British Newspaper Archive. The *Edinburgh Evening News* is partially covered by the two latter resources, and online archives of modern issues of various other Scottish newspapers can be searched and accessed via their websites.

Having previously lived in London, and published three books about the murder houses of the English capital, it was curious to note some differences with regard to the attitude to notorious murder houses in the two capitals north and south of the border. In Victorian London, it was of frequent occurrence that notorious murder houses acquired a reputation for being haunted. In particular, the Bloomsbury 'Murder Neighbourhood' in central London was notorious for its wealth of haunted murder houses. No. 12 Great Coram Street, where the prostitute Harriet Buswell was murdered by an unknown assailant on Christmas Eve 1872, was reported to be haunted: all the tenants moved out, and the house was put up for sale. A lady evangelist bought it for a knockdown price and reopened it as Miss Stride's Home for Destitute Girls and Fallen Women. The haunting continued for several decades: the second-floor back room, where the murder had been committed, was always kept locked, due to the eerie, unworldly sounds emanating from it at night. Burton Crescent, situated just at the epicentre of the Murder Neighbourhood, is today known as Cartwright Gardens. The reason the street name was changed in 1908 were the unsolved murders of two women: old Mrs Samuels at No. 4 in 1878 and the prostitute Annie Yates at No. 12 in 1884. Both murder houses were reputed to be haunted, although the ghosts lacked the persistence of the spectre of Harriet Buswell. Another notorious murder house in these parts was not far away: No. 4 Euston Square, where the elderly spinster Matilda Hacker was found murdered in the coal cellar in 1879. Although the servant girl Hannah Dobbs stood trial for the murder, she was acquitted, and Miss Hacker's murder remains unavenged. The murder house acquired a very sinister reputation: it was reported to be haunted, and strange groans and screams were heard in Miss Hacker's old room. The bloodstain on the floorboards in the murder room could not be removed by any amount of scrubbing, and no dog would pass this room of horrors without snarling and whining, and giving indications of intense terror. Still, the haunted murder house stood for several decades, before becoming a victim of the reconstruction of Euston Station in the 1960s.

The Priory in Balham, where Charles Bravo was murdered in 1876, and 2 Ivor Street, Camden Town, where Mary Eleanor Pearcy murdered her rival Phoebe Hogg in 1892, also became quite notorious for their unquiet spectral inhabitants; both are reputed to have been subjected to exorcism rituals in modern times, to get rid of the persistent ghosts. One of the most notorious haunted murder houses of modern London was the grocer's shop at 36 Leinster Terrace, where the manager Mr Edward Creed was murdered by an unknown intruder in 1926. The paranormal expert Elliott O'Donnell declared the shop to be haunted by Creed's ghost, after staying there overnight and experiencing many unexplained and uncanny phenomena. More steady and balanced people than this jittery ghost-hunter also felt the ghost's presence, and as a result, the shop became quite notorious locally. It is said to have stood until the 1960s, although becoming increasingly derelict. In the end, the murder shop was demolished, along with No. 35 next door, and a small restaurant, hopefully without any resident ghost, was constructed on the site. Although Edinburgh has a multitude of ghostly legends, many of them inventions for the perusal of the more gullible tourists visiting the Capital, there is nothing like these notorious haunted murder houses of London, however. No spectre frolicked in the Frederick Street shop where Alexander Milne murdered John Paterson; no spirit haunted the Chantrelle house in George Street; no spectral little babies cried in the slum abodes left empty by Jessie King, the Stockbridge Baby-Farmer. The only Edinburgh murder story featuring a possible ghost is the remarkable story of the 'Cat Man of Ferry Road' who was wantonly murdered in his flat in this busy thoroughfare as late as 1996; several independent witnesses saw him outside his flat, feeding the birds and visiting a shop, the day after he had been beaten to death.

There are several other instances of grisly murders resulting in London streets being renamed: Miniver Place, Bermondsey, where the Mannings had murdered Mr O'Connor at No. 3 in 1849, became part of Weston Street because the houses would not let; Stanley Street, Pimlico, where Frederick Treadaway had murdered Mr Collins at No. 99, became Alderney Street a few years after the murder; the name of the southern part of Euston Square as changed to Endsleigh Gardens in 1880 as a result of the unsolved murder of Miss Hacker. In contrast, I find nothing to suggest that any Edinburgh murder has resulted in the change of the street name, or the renumbering of the houses. There have been few instances of notorious modern murder houses being demolished as the result of the bestial crimes being committed within their walls, like Myra Hindley's house at 16 Wardle Brook Avenue, Greater Manchester, the Wests' house of horrors at 25 Cromwell Road, Gloucester, or Ian Huntley's house at 5 College Close, Soham. From Caledonian soil we have the school gym in Dunblane, where the demented Thomas Hamilton opened fire on the children in 1996, and the murder house at 47 Tay Street, Tayport, demolished at the orders of Fife Council in 2006 after the sex offender Colyn Evans had strangled young Karen Dewar within its walls. In London, the only murder house demolished under mysterious circumstances if the abovementioned grocer's shop at 36 Leinster Terrace; the Crippen murder house at 29 Hilldrop Crescent stood for decades after the crime, only to fall victim to wartime structural damage, and Christie's house at 10 Rillington Place stood for years after the murders, being used as a lodging house for a largely West Indian clientele, before being demolished as part of a slum clearance. In Edinburgh, there is nothing to suggest that any murder house was ever demolished as a result of the crime committed within its walls.

London's most sanguineous cataclysm of murder was the Tooting Horror of 1895, in which the unemployed plasterer Frank Taylor murdered his wife and six of his seven children in a bloodbath, before committing suicide. The murder house at what is today 159 Fountain Road, Tooting, has barely changed at all since the tragedy.[3] Edinburgh has been spared such extensive mass carnage, although the city can boast not less than four triple murder houses. Firstly we have the Juta family home at 21 Falcon Avenue, where the South African student William Juta gunned down his wife, son and mother-in-law in 1915, before committing suicide. Then there is the triple murder flat at 120 Rose Street South Lane, where Joseph Wilmot murdered his family in 1917. The murder flat at 2A Oxgangs Green, where Marie M'Ginty murdered her three children in 1962, is unknown even to the locals. In contrast, the house at 10 East Brighton Crescent, Portobello, where David Anderson murdered his mother-in-law and his two children in 1969, has remained something of a Portobello house of horrors. The Capital's healthy population of double murder houses ranges from the flat at 57 Tron Square, where George Alexander Robertson murdered his ex-wife and his son in a bloodbath, to the peaceful little house at 25 Earl Haig Gardens, Trinity, where Alexander Main Stirling gunned down his former girlfriend and her invalid father in 1959.

Four of the inhabitants of the Murder Houses of Edinburgh have paid for their crimes in the scaffold. First we have Eugène Chantrelle in 1878, then Allan Wales in 1928; John Lynch, the Marshall's Court child murderer, was hanged in April 1954, and George Alexander Robertson, the Tron Square desperado, in June the same year. In 78 of the 124 murders in this book, the culprit was convicted and given a prison sentence of variable severity. The amazing career of the desperado Donald Forbes, who narrowly escaped the hangman's noose for a brutal murder in 1958, only to murder again in a Leith pub after being released from prison twelve years later, is well known, but few people know about the obscure miscreant Alastair William Thompson, who murdered his grandmother in 1968, and then dispatched a Dundee homosexual in 1992 after spending sixteen years behind bars. In eleven instances, the murderer has committed suicide rather than facing justice for his crime. In sixteen instances, the murderer was certified insane and sent to Carstairs or some similar mental hospital. I hope that the Milton Street murder of 2013, in which a convicted murderer, who had spent eleven years in prison for murdering his wife, murdered another convicted murderer in a bloodbath, and was sent to Carstairs indefinitely as a result, is without equivalent in Scotland. In eight instances, there was a more or less convincing case of murder, for which some personage stood trial but was freed. The dismal family tyrant Richard Robertson was extremely lucky to be acquitted for murdering his son back in 1895, helped by the wife he had so often abused. The infanticidal Marion Stone was also very fortunate to be freed after standing trial for murdering her newborn daughter in 1920. Alexander Donaldson, who had brutally murdered his wife Jean Bruce in 1990, and who pleaded guilty to culpable homicide, was fortunate to escape without a prison sentence; a low estimation indeed of the value of the life of the murdered woman.

The unsolved murder mysteries of Edinburgh have been a particular interest of mine for some considerable period of time. A curious early mystery of the Royal Mile concerns the bank porter William Begbie, who was robbed and murdered in Tweeddale Court in 1806; the finger has been pointed at the criminal James Mackoull, who fitted the description of the murderer, although rock solid evidence of his guilt is lacking.[4] The earliest unsolved Edinburgh murder where the murder house remains is the Wester Coates Terrace mystery of 1924, where William Laurie King stood accused of murdering his mother. As a result of some fairly indifferent policework, the gravity of the case not being fully realized until it was too late, the main suspect walked out of court a free man. The full legal documents in this extraordinary case will prove interesting reading when they become available in a few years; moreover, professional genealogical expertise may discover more about the clandestine later activities of the mystery man William Laurie King. The murder house at 98 Glasgow Road, where David M'Menigall was brutally one to death in 1966, is daily passed by thousands of cars and pedestrians in this very busy road, very few of whom have any idea of the secret history of this humble bungalow. The most likely solution to the mystery is that M'Menigall surprised a burglar and was beaten to death as a consequence. The unsolved murder of Aileen Printie at 4 Kingsknowe Road North in 1981 is likely to have a similar explanation: the wretched woman disturbed a powerful intruder, who beat her to death in cold blood, before making his escape and keeping his guilty secret for many years. The case against the young burglar Paul Andrews for committing this murder, based on DNA evidence, is a strong one according to the police, although Andrews destroyed himself in 1997 before facing a court of justice.

The unsolved murder of the 20-year-old Ann Ballantyne, of 20 Yeaman Place, whose badly decomposed body was found floating in the Union Canal in early 1986, is another of the modern mysteries of Edinburgh. The murderer is likely to have been a cool customer, who kept the body in some safe location for weeks, before dumping it in the canal a few days before it was found. Since no person seemed likely to have a motive for murdering this harmless young woman, there has been speculation that she fell victim to a serial killer, although nothing significant has been concluded. The murder of Deirdre Kivlin at 100 South Clerk Street is one that should have been solved. The police thought they had a moderately solid case against the glue-sniffing vagabond Scott Ballantyne, but although I agree that he was an unsavoury character, I doubt whether he possessed the toughness to beat a woman to death in cold blood, or the moral courage to keep his guilty secret for many years. Many would say that the unsolved murder of Louise Tiffney in 2002 is Edinburgh's greatest modern mystery; as we know, the murder charge against her son Sean Flynn was considered 'not proven' at his trial in 2005, due to the exhortations of a first-rate defence team. Now when the remains of Louise Tiffney have been found, ruling out that she destroyed herself or disappeared voluntarily, as the defence suggested, this very same individual is awaiting a second trial, which is eagerly looked forward to by the Edinburgh murder enthusiasts.

Irrespective of its location, a murder house goes through three phases: notoriety, rehabilitation and oblivion. A small minority of murder houses, mainly cheap and unattractive buildings that have witnessed the grossest and most horrible murders, and faced considerable newspaper vilification, never emerge from the 'notoriety' stage, and as a consequence they are demolished. In contrast, all the valuable London and Edinburgh murder houses have been successfully rehabilitated, and most of them have had their secret history conveniently forgotten about, to the benefit of both the night's sleep of their occupants and the property price when the murder house is eventually put up for sale. Edinburgh seems to have escaped the unwholesome London fascination with murder houses in Victorian times, with no alleged hauntings taking place, and no instances of changing the names of murder streets: although there were still Edinburgh people keen to admire the latest murder house, the excesses from south of the border were avoided and Caledonian common sense made use of to assess the situation. The increased mobility in modern society has resulted in a decrease in local knowledge and sense of belonging; although some old Edinburgh people still know their neighbourhoods well, the study of local murder houses is restricted to a few amateur historians with a taste for the macabre. The gradual decline of the Christian religion, and the even stronger decline in various superstitious beliefs, like hauntings and curses, has robbed the murder houses of a good deal of their former notoriety: to a financially astute modern atheist, a building where a grisly murder has been committed is not a house of horrors, just a good buying opportunity. Still, as this book shows, when you walk the streets of the Scottish capital, evidence of its criminous past is everywhere; part of the secret history of the great city is reflected, in a glass darkly, by the Murder Houses of Edinburgh.

NOTES

INTRODUCTION

1. A mainstay of the literature on Caledonian crime is the works of William Roughead, an Edinburgh Writer to the Signet, containing a multitude of murder trials, some of them from Edinburgh; see also R. Whittington-Egan, *William Roughead's Chronicles of Murder* (Moffat 1991). Anon, *The Scots Black Calendar* (Blanefield 1985) is a reprint of a thorough work first published in 1938. Modern contributions include the books by J. Hamilton, *Scottish Murders* (Lanark 2001), R. Halliday & C. Terry, *Scotland's Killers* (Ayr 2005), M. Whittington-Egan, *Classic Scottish Murder Stories* (Glasgow 2007), M. Baggoley, *Scottish Murders* (Stroud 2013) and M. Archibald, *Bloody Scotland* (Edinburgh 2014). A.F. Young, *The Encyclopaedia of Scottish Executions* (Orpington 1998) is a particularly valuable resource. The literature on Edinburgh murders is less impressive. R. Macdonald, *Famous Edinburgh Crimes* (London 1953) is a brief and sketchy account; K. Winton, *Murder in Edinburgh* (Edinburgh 1985) mainly deals with early cases; A Massie, *Ill Met by Gaslight* (London 1987) is a brief account of five classic murders; A. Knight, *Close & Deadly* (Edinburgh 2002) is an excellent account of some interesting 20th century murders, with good murder house detection skills demonstrated throughout; D. Brandon & A. Brooke, *Edinburgh Murders and Misdemeanours* (Stroud 2010) is a sketchy modern concoction intended for the tourists. A. Sharp, *A Grim Almanac of Edinburgh & the Lothians* (Stroud

2009) contains details about some murders not available elsewhere, and M. Fife, *The Story of Calton Jail* (Stroud 2016) is another interesting account.

In this book, the four main Edinburgh newspapers have been abbreviated: Scotsman=SC, Edinburgh Evening News=EEN, Edinburgh Evening Dispatch=EED, Edinburgh Evening News and Dispatch=EEND. National Records of Scotland has been referred to as NRS throughout.

CHAPTER I

1. With regard to Edinburgh history and topography, four key works have been D. Wilson, *Memorials of Edinburgh* (2 Vols, Edinburgh 1891), J. Grant, *Old and New Edinburgh* (6 Vols, London n.d.), *The City of Edinburgh* (Edinburgh 1951), complied by the Royal Commission on the Ancient Monuments of Scotland, and S. Harris, *The Place Names of Edinburgh* (Edinburgh 2002).

2. J. Bondeson, *Murder Houses of London* (Stroud 2014), 96-7, *Murder Houses of South London* (Leicester 2015), 294-6 and *Ripperologist* 163 [2019], 34-41.

3. NRS RH 15/23/16 and SRO 1/33; A.F. Steuart, *Seigneur Davie* (London 1922), W.A. Gatherer, *The Tyrannous Reign of Mary Stewart* (Edinburgh 1958), 94-101, D. Tweedie, *David Rizzio & Mary Queen of Scots* (Stroud 2006), 123-52, R. Stedall, *Mary Queen of Scots' Downfall* (Barnsley 2017); also A. Fraser (*History Today* 16(4) [1966], 243-50), R.K. Marshall in the Oxford *DNB* and J. Bondeson (*Ripperologist* 164 [2019], 59-69).

4. There are many books about the misdeeds of Burke and Hare, including those by J. Barzun (Ed.), *Burke and Hare* (Metuchen NJ 1974), H. Douglas, *Burke & Hare* (London 1974), O.D. Edwards, *Burke & Hare* (Edinburgh 1980), B.

Bailey, *Burke and Hare* (Edinburgh 2002) and L. Rosner, *The Anatomy Murders* (Philadelphia PA 2010).

5. A. Evans (*International Journal of Epidemiology* 39 [2010], 1190-2).
6. *Weekly Scotsman* June 19 1902, *EEN* Aug 23 1902, *Dundee Evening Telegraph* Aug 30 1902.
7. The two main sources about Dr Knox are I. Rae, *Knox the Anatomist* (Edinburgh 1964) and A.W. Bates, *The Anatomy of Robert Knox* (Brighton 2010).
8. J. Gillon, *Secret Edinburgh* (Stroud 2015), 43-4.
9. *SC* April 26 and 27, June 4 and 25 1878.
10. NRS JC 26/1892/30 and AD 14/92/73; *SC* Oct 20 1892, *Dundee Courier* Oct 17 and 18 1892.
11. NRS JC 26/1905/106 and AD 15/05/34; *EEN* June 12 and Aug 30 1905, *SC* Aug 31 1905.
12. NRS AD 15/12/4 and JC 26/1912/108; *SC* Jan 6 and 17 1912, *Dundee Courier* Jan 17 1912.
13. NRS AD 15/19/29 and HH 15/26 and 16/159; *EEN* Oct 27 1919, *SC* Oct 28 1919.
14. *EED* March 1 1954, *EEN* March 1, June 1 and 23 1954, *SC* March 1 and 2, June 2 and 3 1954, Aug 6 2014; A. Knight, *Close & Deadly* (Edinburgh 2002), 126-33.
15. *EEN* Nov 3 1999.
16. *EEN* May 26 and 27, Sept 9 1977, *SC* Sept 21 and 22 1977; A. Knight, *Close & Deadly* (Edinburgh 2002), 134-7.
17. *EEN* May 30, Sept 12, 13 and 14 1977, *SC* Sept 14 1977.
18. *EEN* July 24, 25 and 30, Aug 10 1984, *SC* Aug 1, 2, 3, 4, 8, 9, 10 and 28 1984.

CHAPTER II

1. NRS JC 26/1863/314 and AD 14/63/283; *SC* Feb 10 1863, *Caledonian Mercury* Jan 8, 10 and 11 1863, *Standard* Jan 9

1863, *Dundee Courier* Feb 28 1863; the articles by H. Cowan (*Edinburgh Medical Journal* 8 [1863], 837-55) and D. Yellowlees (*British Journal of Psychiatry* 9 [1863], 119-25 and *Edinburgh Medical Journal* 8 [1863], 912-21).

2. A.D. Smith, *Trial of Eugène Marie Chantrelle* (Edinburgh 1906), W. Roughead (*Juridical Review* 45 [1933], 95-132) and *Rogues Walk Here* (Edinburgh 1934), 131-64, R. Whittington-Egan, *William Roughead's Chronicles of Murder* (Moffat 1991), 177-81, M Whittington-Egan, *Classic Scottish Murder Stories* (Glasgow 2007), 130-42; *Middlesburgh Daily Gazette* June 1 1878, *Dundee Courier* Jan 7 and June 21 1878, *Master Detective* March 1992, 2-10, *EEN* Sept 10 1955 and June 17 2011, *Sunday Times* May 18 2014.

3. NRS JC 26/1880/277 and AD 14/80/48; *SC* Dec 31 1879, *Newcastle Courant* March 12 1880, *Aberdeen Weekly Journal* March 13 1880.

4. NRS JC 26/1881/293 and AD 14/81/104; *EEN* March 15 1881, *SC* March 15 and 16, June 14 1881.

5. *Illustrated Police News* March 2 1889, *EEN* March 11 1889, *Dundee Courier* March 12 1889; W. Roughead, *In Queer Street* (Edinburgh 1932), 75-99, A. Massie, *Ill Met by Gaslight* (London 1987), 127-43, *True Detective* January 1998, 16-21, M. Whittington-Egan, *Classic Scottish Murder Stories* (Glasgow 2007), 198-208.

6. NRS AD 14/90/79; *Dundee Courier* Oct 13 and Nov 25 1890, *SC* Nov 25 and 29 1890.

7. *SC* July 18, 19 and 26 1894, *Dundee Courier* July 18, 20 and 26 1894.

8. *SC* Feb 20 1899, *Illustrated Police News* Feb 25 1899, *Aberdeen Weekly Journal* Feb 18 and 22 1899.

9. NRS JC 26/1902/109 and AD 15/02/27; *EEN* Aug 18 and 19, Nov 3 1902.

10. NRS JC 26/1917/66 and AD 15/17/44; *SC* May 31 and Aug 7 1917, *Daily Mirror* Aug 7 1917.

11. NRS JC 26/1919/93, *SC* Sept 10 and 11 1919, *Dundee Evening Telegraph* Aug 29, Sept 9 and 10 1919, *Aberdeen Press and Journal* Sept 11 1919.

12. NRS JC 26/1920/111, *EEN* July 9 and 19 1920, *SC* July 20 1920.

13. There have been four books about the Merrett/Chesney case: W. Roughead (Ed.), *Trial of John Donald Merrett* (Notable British Trials, Edinburgh 1929), H. McLeave, *Chesney, the Fabulous Murderer* (London n.d.), T. Tullett, *Portrait of a Bad Man* (London 1956) and J. Oates, *Chesney, the Middle Class Murderer* (London 2016); see also *SC* Feb 2, 3 and 5 1927, *Glasgow Herald* March 16 1993, *Daily Mirror* May 30 2018 and the article by N. Duvall (*Social History of Medicine* 30 [2016], 367-88).

14. NRS JC 26/1927/45, *SC* Aug 13, Oct 22 and Nov 1 1927, *Dundee Courier* Nov 1 1927.

15. *EEN* Nov 21, Dec 1 1953.

16. *EED* Dec 12 1953, *EEN* March 23, 24 and 25 and April 7 1954, *SC* Dec 12 and 14 1953, March 15, 24 and 26 1954, Jan 12 2010, *Daily Record* Oct 19 2007; A. Knight, *Close & Deadly* (Edinburgh 2002), 89-95.

17. *EEN* March 7 and 10, June 17 1964, *SC* March 10, June 17 and 18 1964.

18. *EEND* April 25 1967, *SC* April 26 and 27 1967.

19. *EEND* Jan 27, 28 and 30 1967, *SC* Jan 27, Feb 1 and March 4 1967.

20. *Aberdeen Press and Journal* Dec 17 1968.

21. *EEN* June 19, 21 and 22, Sept 24 1968, *SC* June 20 and 21, Sept 25 1968.

22. *EEN* June 3 1971, Jan 21, Feb 29 1972, *SC* Jan 22, March 1, 2 and 3 1972.

23. *EEN* Oct 6 and 13, Dec 30 1977, Jan 16 1978, *SC* Oct 5 1977.

24. *EEN* April 5, 6, 13 and 15, July 27 and 19 1982, *SC* July 29 1982; A. Knight, *Close & Deadly* (Edinburgh 2002), 84-6.

25. *Daily Mirror* Oct 27 1983 and March 22 1985

26. *EEN* May 9, 13 and 15, Aug 22 1987, Feb 10, June 21 and 22 1988, *SC* June 23 and 25 1988; A. Knight, *Close & Deadly* (Edinburgh 2002), 96-9.

27. *EEN* May 26 and 30, Sept 14 and 15 1988.

28. *EEN* Oct 11 1993, Jan 31 and Feb 1 1994, *SC* Oct 13 1993, Feb 1 1994.

29. *EEN* June 22 1998 and Oct 28 1998, *SC* June 23 and 24, Oct 29 1998.

30. *EEN* March 3, 4 and 5, Aug 14 and 15 1998, *SC* March 4 1998.

31. *BBC News* March 15 2012, March 8 and 12 2018, *Herald* May 29 2012, *Daily Express* June 4 2017.

32. *Scottish Sun* June 16 2019.

33. *Scottish Sun* Dec 6 2016, *BBC News* Dec 7 2016 and July 24 and 27 2017, *EEN* Dec 6 2016, *SC* Aug 24 2017.

CHAPTER III

1. NRS JC 26/1865/30 and AD 14/65/284; *Dundee Courier* Oct 6 and 7 1865, *Glasgow Herald* Oct 7 1865, *Caledonian Mercury* Nov 28 1865, *SC* Feb 1 2011; J. Lamb, *Dalrymple Crescent* (Edinburgh 2011), 13-6.

2. NRS AD 14/90/82 and JC 26/1890/33; *EEN* Dec 4 1890, *Aberdeen Journal* Dec 16 1890.

3. *EEN* July 6 and 7 1899, *Daily Mail* July 7 1899, *Dundee Courier* July 7 1899, *Standard* July 7 1899, *Yorkshire Herald* July 7 1899, *Illustrated Police News* July 15 1899.

4. NRS JC 26/1902/104, AD 15/02/21 and HH 17/14; *EEN* Sept 17 1902, *SC* Sept 6 and 18 1902.

5. NRS JC 26/1902/105, AD 15/02/24 and HH 16/94; *SC* June 25 and 26, Sept 18 and 19 1902; there is an excellent Wikipedia page on Colonel Macadam and the tragic events of 1902.

6. *SC* July 16 and 17 1908, *Dundee Courier* July 16 1908, *Dundee Evening Telegraph* July 16 1908, *Manchester Guardian* July 16 1908.

7. *Greenock Telegraph* March 23 1909, *Dundee Courier* March 25 1909, *Northern Times* April 1 1909, *Motherwell Times* May 14 1909, *SC* April 12 2011.

8. E. McKay, *A Discarded Brat* (Inverness 1981).

9. *Dundee Evening Telegraph* Sept 20 and 22 1915, *Daily Record* Sept 20 1915, *Dundee People's Journal* Sept 25 1915, *Daily Mirror* Sept 21 1915, *Illustrated Police News* Sept 23 1915.

10. NRS JC 26/1920/118; *EEN* Sept 27 1920, *SC* Sept 28 1920.

11. *EEN* Aug 23 1920, *Dundee Evening Telegraph* Aug 23 1920, *Sheffield Daily Telegraph* Aug 23 1920, *Motherwell Times* Aug 27 1920.

12. NRS JC 26/1935/45, *EEN* Feb 4 1935, *EED* Feb 5 1935, *SC* Feb 5, 6 and 26, March 26 1935.

13. *EEN* June 27, Aug 17 and 27 1956.

14. *EEN* Nov 27 and 28 1957.

15. *EEN* Sept 26, Dec 5 1961.

16. *EEN* Dec 6 1962, Jan 22 1963.

17. *EEN* June 25, 26 and 28, July 5 and 27, Oct 5 1968, *SC* June 26 1968; D. Leslie, *Carstairs: Hospital for Horrors* (Edinburgh 2015), 75-77.

18. *EEN* Jan 29, April 26, May 7, 8 and 9 1968, *SC* Jan 29, April 27, May 8, 9 and 10 1968.

19. A. McGregor, *The Law Killers* (Edinburgh 2013), 122-33.

20. *SC* Dec 6 and 7 1976, March 8, 9 and 10 1977.

21. *EEN* Oct 20 1978, *SC* Aug 1 1978.

22. *EEN* April 12 and June 21 1983.

23. *EEN* Nov 7 1984, *SC* Nov 8 1984.

24. *EEN* Oct 4 1991, March 10, 11 and 12, May 7, 8,12, 13, 14, 20 and 21, June 6 1992, Jan 9 and Oct 12 1993, April 11 1997, *SC* Oct 4, 7 and 12 1991, March 14, May 12, 13, 16 and 21 1992.

25. *EEN* June 17, Oct 4 and 5 1993, *SC* Oct 5 1993.

26. *EEN* Feb 8, 21, 23, 26, 27 and 18 1996, *Herald* Feb 15, 16 and 28 1996.

27. *EEN* Oct 1 1998.

28. *EEN* May 18 1999, *Herald* Sept 18 2001.

29. *EEN* Aug 10 2009, *SC* Aug 5 2009, *BBC News* Aug 4 2009.

30. *EEN* April 11 and May 1 2002, *SC* April 11 and 30, May 1 2002.

31. *Scottish Sun* Oct 24 2008 and Feb 4 2009, *Daily Record* Oct 23 2011.

32. *EEN* May 10, 13 and 20, Dec 5 and 24 2004, *SC* Dec 5 2005.

33. *SC* Feb 25 and April 22 2009.

34. *SC* May 30 2011, *Daily Mail* Oct 27 2014.

35. *Scottish Sun* May 17 2016, *Daily Record* Jan 23 2019.

36. *EEN* Dec 12 2019, *Scottish Sun* Dec 14 2019.

37. *EEN* July 12 and 16 1993 and Dec 27 2013, *SC* July 8, 9 and 16 1993, *Herald* July 1 1993, *Daily Record* July 13 2013, *BBC News* Dec 27 2013.

CHAPTER IV

1. NRS AD 14/96/80; *EEN* Jan 23 and Feb 3 1896, *Manchester Courier* Feb 8 1896.

2. NRS JC 26/1924/69 and AD 15/24/22; *EEN* Aug 28 1924, *SC* June 11, 12 and 13, Aug 28 and 29 1924, *Sunday Post* June 15 1924; W. Roughead, *The Seamy Side* (Edinburgh 1938), 3-37, M. Whittington-Egan, *Classic Scottish Murder Stories* (Glasgow 2007), 35-46.

3. NRS JC 26/1938/71, *EEN* Aug 8 1938 and Jan 23 1939, *SC* Aug 9, Oct 31 and Nov 9 1938; G. Forbes in *Scottish Memories*, March 2005, R. McKay: *Killers, Crooks and Cons* (Edinburgh 2007), 114-7.

4. *SC* Feb 13, 14, 15 and 21, March 15, May 31 1950, *Dundee Evening Telegraph* May 30 1950, *Dundee Courier* May 31 1950.

5. *EEN* Oct 23 1963, *SC* Dec 28 1963, *Times* Dec 28 1963.

6. *EEND* Feb 25 and 26, March 3, 11 and 14, May 5 1966, *SC* Feb 25 1966.

7. *Daily Record* March 4 2016.

8. *EEN* March 12 and May 28 1968, *SC* May 13 and 18 1968.

9. It is peculiar that although the official legal report of his trial refers to the Salisbury Crags murderer as Ernst Dumoulin, many newspapers have called him Ernest. The main sources about him are *Daily Mail* Jan 25 and Feb 6 1973, *SC* May 3 2006, Feb 26 2009 and May 29 2011, *Daily Record* July 1 2012, *Edinburgh Reporter* Oct 22 2012; F.W.F. O'Brien (*Medico-Legal Journal* Dec 1 1976), A. Knight, *Close & Deadly* (Edinburgh 2002), 7-22, A.W. Taylor (*Master Detective* Nov 2016, 2-7). The question whether Scotland has ever had any convicted murderer becoming a clergyman can be answered in the positive, since the Rev. James Nelson murdered his mother in 1969 and was appointed a minister in 1986, see his obituary in the *Daily Telegraph*, Aug 4 2005.

10. *EEN* March 1,2,9,12,14,15 and 22, April 7, July 17, 18, 19, 20, 23, 24 and 25 1973, March 7 1978, *SC* March 16, July 18, 19, 20, 21 and 24 1973.

11. *EEN* March 26, 27 and 28, April 2, June 14, 24 and 26 and Nov 28 1974.

12. *EEN* May 20 and July 15 1977, *SC* July 26 and 28 1977.

13. *SC* July 30, Aug 1 and 6 1977, *Aberdeen Evening Express* Oct 24 1977.

14. *Aberdeen Press and Journal* May 30 1979.

15. *EEN* Sept 13, 16 and 23, Dec 2, 12, 13 and 14 1977, *SC* Dec 3 and 13 1977; D. Leslie, *Carstairs, Hospital for Horrors* (Edinburgh 2015), 206-9.

16. *EEN* Aug 28 and 29, Sept 11 and Oct 22 1981, *SC* Aug 31 and Sept 3 1981.

17. *EEN* May 19, Aug 8 and Nov 14 1997, *SC* Aug 4 1997, *Daily Mail* May 9 1997, *Daily Record* May 19 and Nov 10 1997, *Sunday Herald* Aug 4 1997.

18. *EEN* May 14, 15, 16 and 17 1984.

19. *EEN* June 26 1984.

20. *EEN* July 3 2017 and Jan 18 2019, *SC* March 10 2009, *Daily Record* Dec 5 2007.

21. *EEN* April 3, 4 and 7, July 30 1987, *SC* April 6, July 31, August 1, 4, 5, 6, 7 and 8 1987.

22. *EEN* March 23, 24 and 25 1992, *SC* March 23, 24, 25 and 27 1992, *Herald* July 7 1992.

23. *EEN* May 3 and 5 1995, *SC* May 5 1995.

24. *EEN* April 29 and 30, May 1 and 3 1996, March 18, 19, 22, 25, 26 and 27 1997, *SC* March 28 1997.

25. *EEN* Feb 27 and March 2 1999.

26. *EEN* April 7, 9 and 12, May 20, Oct 12, 13 and 19, Dec 16 1999, April 13, May 19, Dec 9 2000; *SC* April 9 1999, April 1 2000.

27. *Daily Record* Sept 20 2012.

28. *EEN* June 24 and 26, Aug 4, Dec 6 2002.

29. *EEN* March 19 and 20, Oct 18, Nov 7 2003.

30. *EEN* Nov 14 2004, *SC* Feb 11 2004, *Observer* Feb 15 2004, *Daily Record* Oct 15 2007, *Herald* Sept 23 2014.

31. *EEN* Feb 11, 14-18, 21, 23 and 28, March 8, 17, 18, 21, 24, 25 and 31 2005, March 11 2009, April 2, July 8 and Nov 28 2018, *SC* Feb 11, 12, 15, 18, 19 and 22-26, March 1, 2, 15-17 and 21 2005, *BBC News* April 7 2017 and Jan 11 2019, *Scottish Sun* April 1 2018.

32. On Brian Rockall, see *SC* July 22, 23 and 24 2009.

33. On the retrial, see *BBC News* Nov 26 2019 and Jan 9 2020 and *Scottish Sun* Jan 18 2020.

34. *EEN* June 14, 15, 16 and 20, July 11 2006, *SC* June 15 2006 and Jan 17 2007, *BBC News* July 12 2006.

35. *Daily Mail* March 8 and April 28 2011.

36. *Daily Mail* March 10 2014, *Daily Record* March 23 2014, *Herald* March 15 2014.
37. *EEN* Aug 8, 13 and 29 2013, July 7 2018, *BBC News* Feb 28 and June 7 2011, June 18 2012.
38. *SC* 9, 11, 15, 16 and 17 2014, *Irish Mirror* July 10 2013 and Jan 8 2014, *BBC News* Jan 14 and 17 2014, *Daily Mirror* Jan 17 2014, *Daily Express* Jan 17 2014, *Irish Independent* Nov 16 2018.
39. *EEN* Nov 29 2018, *BBC News* Nov 29 2018, *Scottish Sun* Nov 30 2018.

CHAPTER V

1. *SC* May 13 1933, *Dundee Courier* May 13 1933, *Belfast Telegraph* May 13 1933.
2. NRS JC 26/1940/25, *SC* July 28 1933, Sept 9 1936, Nov 20 1939 and Jan 15 1940, *Sunday Post* Nov 19 1939, *Dundee Courier* Jan 24 1940, *Aberdeen Press and Journal* Jan 24 1940.
3. *EED* Nov 24 1959, March 9, 19 and 25 1960, *EEN* Nov 24 and 25 1959, March 8 1960, *SC* Nov 25 1959, March 9 and 10 1960, Jan 13 2010, *True Detective* March 1998, 23-27.
4. *EEN* July 26, Aug 1, Sept 9 and 12 1969, *SC* July 26 and 28 1969.
5. *EEN* Sept 24 and Dec 6 1977.
6. *EEN* March 19 2002.
7. *EEN* Sept 25 1986, Jan 19 and 20 1987, *SC* Sept 30 1986.
8. *EEN* Nov 18 1986, March 4, 5 and 7 1987, *SC* Nov 19 1986.
9. *EEN* July 2, Oct 20, 21, 22 and 23 1987.
10. *EEN* Oct 31 and Nov 3 1989, *SC* Nov 2 1989.
11. *EEN* March 24 1990, *Herald* March 24 1990.
12. *EEN* Aug 11 1993, *SC* Aug 12, 23 and 24 1993.
13. *EEN* Feb 12 2002, Feb 11 and 14, March 6 and 20 2003, *SC* Feb 12 2002, Feb 14 and March 21 2003.

14. *BBC News* Aug 25 2014 and April 21 2015, *Guardian* Aug 25 2014.
15. *Scottish Sun* Dec 8 and 16 2018, June 8 2019.

CHAPTER VI

1. NRS JC 26/1928/19 and HH 16/189; *SC* June 6, July 24 and 31, Aug 1, 11 and 13 1928, *Daily Record* April 24 2006.
2. *EED* Aug 18, 25, 29 and 30 1945, *EEN* Aug 28, 29, 30 and 31 1945, *SC* Aug 30, Oct 12 and 17 1945, April 13 2011.
3. *EED* July 31 1945, *EEN* July 31, Aug 11, Oct 20 1945, *SC* Aug 1 1945, *Dundee Evening Telegraph* Oct 30 1945, *Dundee Courier* Oct 31 1945.
4. *EEN* Nov 5 and Dec 8 1998, *SC* Nov 5 and 6 1998, April 14 1998 and Jan 13 2010
5. *EEN* Jan 8 and 10, April 7 and 19 1972, *SC* Jan 8, 11 and 12 1972.
6. *EEN* Dec 30 1991, June 3, 4 and 6 1992, *SC* Dec 30 and 31 1991, Jan 1, 2 and 4, June 9 1992.
7. *EEN* Oct 22 1992, April 24 and May 12 1998.
8. *EEN* March 4, 5 and 7 1996, March 6 1997, *Herald* March 8 1997.
9. *EEN* Aug 7 1998, *Herald* Dec 15 1998, *SC* Oct 14 2002.
10. *EEN* June 11 and 12, Sept 30, Oct 3, 8, 9 and 12 1998 and April 15 2006, *SC* Oct 10 1998.

CHAPTER VII

1. J. Bondeson, *Murder Houses of South London* (Leicester 2015), 294-6 and *Ripperologist* 163 [2019], 34-41.